louis
marshall,
defender of
jewish
rights

Morton Rosenstock is librarian
and associate professor of social
studies at Bronx Community
College of the City University
of New York. He received his
M.A. and Ph.D. degrees from
Columbia University. His articles and reviews have been published in *American Jewish Historical Quarterly, Historia Judaica,
Jewish Frontier, Jewish Social
Studies,* and *Library Journal.*

If the Jew
did not exist,
the anti-Semite
would invent him.

—Jean-Paul Sartre,
ANTI-SEMITE and JEW

Wayne State University Press Detroit 1965

louis marshall, defender of jewish rights

by *Morton Rosenstock*

Bronx Community College,
City University of New York

Published simultaneously in Canada by Ambassador Books, Limited,
Toronto, Ontario, Canada

Library of Congress Catalog Card Number 65-19608

Grateful acknowledgement is made to the Morris and Emma
Schaver Publication Fund for Jewish Studies for financial
assistance in publishing this volume.

contents

preface

The first quarter of this century saw the United States emerging as an industrialized, urbanized nation with a major role in world affairs. This transformation coincided with a final period of mass immigration that substantially affected the ethnic and religious composition of America. Among the newcomers was a great wave of East European Jews who had been preceded by a much smaller number of German and Central European Jews. During the era of adjustment to the New World, the older, wealthier, and more Americanized Jews generally assumed leadership of the Jews as a whole.

For many years, the foremost spokesman of the American-Jewish elite was Louis Marshall, a highly successful lawyer with a brilliant mind, deep sense of responsibility, and a dominant personality. Identified with upper-class Jews of Germanic origin, Marshall nevertheless functioned as a leader of all American Jews, especially in the eyes of non-Jews. Although Jewish integration into American life was never fundamentally threatened by organized political and ideological anti-Semitism, Jews were concerned with such anti-Jewish feeling as did exist. Marshall, among his other

7

duties, was inevitably called upon to deal with delicate problems arising from the relationship of the Jewish minority
with the non-Jewish majority.

This book is neither a history of modern American anti-
Semitism nor a full biography of Marshall's many-faceted
career, although it contains elements of both. It is, rather, an
attempt to understand, through the focus of Louis Marshall,
the nature of intergroup problems affecting the status of the
Jews in early twentieth century America and of the response
to these issues by their leaders. How Marshall, exemplifying
American-Jewish leadership during a crucial period, dealt
with problems raised by the impact of mass immigration,
Jewish adjustment to American life, and the defense of
Jewish rights; what his conception of American democracy
and the position of Jews in this country was; what his attitude
was towards various anti-Jewish manifestations and how
successful he was in combatting them; what his sources of
power and his methods of leadership were; what his career
as American-Jewish spokesman reveals of American life and
the role of minority groups within it—these concerns are
the heart of this work.

For their constructive criticism and sympathetic interest, I
especially thank Professor Richard Hofstadter and Professor
Robert Cross. I am indebted for advice to Professor Salo
Baron, Dr. Lloyd Gartner, Mr. Charles Reznikoff, and Professor Theodore Saloutos. Mr. James Marshall kindly con-
sented to the use of his father's personal papers, and Dr. John
Slawson granted access to the archives of the American Jew-
ish Committee. Dr. Jacob Marcus, Director, and Dr. Stanley
Chyet, Assistant Director, of the American Jewish Archives,
Cincinnati, Ohio, were consistently cooperative and helpful,
as were Mr. Harry Alderman and Miss Iva Cohen of the
American Jewish Committee Library, New York. I acknowl-
edge, also, the assistance of the staff of the Jewish Division,
New York Public Library, and of Mr. Henry E. Edmunds,
Ford Motor Company. Last, but far from least, I am deeply

grateful to my wife, Charlotte, for her unfailing patience and understanding.

M.R.

Chapter one

the
position
of
american
jewry

The Jewish community in the United States, relatively insignificant in the early nineteenth century, developed into one of the nation's most important ethnic-religious groups by the time of World War I. Jewish population statistics, approximate though they are, reveal a pattern of continuous, and frequently explosive, growth:

TABLE 1   Jewish Population in the United States [1]

Year	Number of Jews	% of Total Population	% of Jews in World
1820	5,000	0.05	0.16
1850	50,000	0.21	1.06
1880	275,000	0.55	3.44
1900	1,100,000	1.45	10.00
1925	3,800,000	3.25	27.14

The establishment of synagogues proceeded at a rate exceeding even that of the population:

TABLE 2 Jewish Congregations in the United States

Year	Number of Congregations
1850	37
1870	189
1890	533
1916	1,901
1926	3,118

Similar evidence of the rapid and successful organization of a thriving community can be found in the remarkable flowering of Jewish educational, philanthropic and social institutions, especially after 1880.

The Jewish community of the early twentieth century was the result, in the main, of two great waves of immigration. From 1840 to 1880, the source of Jewish immigration was primarily Central European, or German and from 1881 to 1925 it was Eastern European, or Russo-Polish. During these eighty-five years, over 2,500,000 Jews immigrated to the United States, the overwhelming majority of East European origin:

TABLE 3 Jewish Immigration to the United States

Year	Number of Jews Entering U.S.
1840–1880	200,000
1881–1900	675,000
1901–1914	1,346,000
1915–1920	76,450
1921–1925	280,283

This massive movement was directly related to the development of modern capitalism and the progress of the Industrial Revolution in Central and Eastern Europe. Residency limitations, discriminatory taxation, and anti-Semitism did much to spur the early nineteenth century migration of German Jews, but it was basically a change in the German economy, in conjunction with a rising Jewish birth rate and the undermining of the old ghetto communities which caused large groups of German Jews to uproot themselves and seek a new life in America.

The early immigrants from Germany arrived without wealth or commercial connections, but achieved economic success within a generation. Coming in a period when American society was expanding rapidly westward, the German Jews were swept up by this movement and followed on the heels of native and immigrant farmers as distributors of commodities. Practically all of them began with peddling, then advanced into retail trade, real estate, or banking. A sign of their affluence was seen in an 1890 survey of 10,000 Jewish families, predominantly German in origin, which revealed that almost 4,000 had one servant, 2,000 had two, and 1,000 had three or more. By the end of the nineteenth century, the German-Jewish immigrants, displaying great talent for organization and large-scale enterprise, had secured a firm economic foundation. The Americanization of the group was almost completed and the younger generation had begun to enter the learned professions in increasing numbers. Leading German-Jewish families, such as the Strauses, Schiffs, Morgenthaus, Guggenheims, and Sulzbergers, had achieved considerable prominence in public, as well as in business, life.

Jewish emigration from Germany slowed to a trickle after the Civil War as full emancipation was achieved and as Jews were economically integrated into the prosperous Second Reich. The disappearance of this source of Jewish immigration, however, was more than compensated for by the tremendous upsurge of Jewish emigration from Russia, Austria-Hungary and Rumania. As with the earlier immigrants, persecution, particularly in Czarist Russia, was a motivating factor, but poverty, induced by a rising birth rate and the shattering of the old economic structure, was the primary impetus. In the three decades from 1881 to 1910, over 1,500,000 East European Jews arrived in the United States:

TABLE 4   *Jewish Immigration, 1881 to 1910*

Country of Origin	Number of Jewish Immigrants
Russia	1,119,059
Austria-Hungary	281,150
Rumania	67,057
All others	95,534
Total:	1,562,800

This Jewish immigration was a significant part of the general, so-called new immigration of Southern and Eastern Europeans. From 1881 to 1890, Jews constituted 3.7 per cent of all immigrants; from 1901 to 1910, they were 11.1 per cent. In absolute numbers, Jewish immigrants during this period were exceeded only by Italians. In relation to the European population base, however, Jews had the highest proportion of immigrants, and statistics showed that Jews sought a haven in the United States five times as intensively as the non-Jewish population of Europe. In fact, the expulsive forces were so strong that, contrary to the usual pattern, Jewish immigration did not decline as rapidly or as far as did general immigration during depression periods in the United States.

East European Jewish immigration differed in other respects from the new immigration of which it was a part. For one thing, Jews came as family units, indicating their intention of permanently settling. Whereas only 30.5 per cent of all immigrants from 1899 to 1910 were women, 43.4 per cent of the Jewish immigrants were women. Proof of the Jewish desire for a permanent refuge was seen in the fact that Jews had a re-emigration rate four times smaller than that of the average of all other groups. Occupationally, the structure of the Jewish immigration was remarkable. The great majority of all immigrants were unskilled laborers and agricultural workers. These groups were minor among Jews, 67.1 per cent of whom were classified as skilled laborers.

Arriving in an era when the westward movement was over, the frontier closed, and America becoming ever more urban and industrial, the Eastern Jews tended to congregate in the Atlantic coastal cities, principally New York. The Jewish population of New York City, estimated at 60,000 in 1880 (or 3 per cent of the total), soared to 1,500,000 in 1917 (or 30 per cent of the total), over half of whom were concentrated densely on the Lower East Side. By 1925, the eight largest Jewish communities contained two-thirds of the Jewish population of the United States:

TABLE 5   *Jews in U.S. Cities*

City	Number of Jews, 1900	Number of Jews, 1925
New York	500,000	1,600,000
Chicago		270,000
Philadelphia	75,000	250,000
Boston	40,000	70,000
Cleveland	20,000	70,000
Baltimore	25,000	55,000
Pittsburgh	10,000	50,000
Newark	15,000	50,000

The overwhelming influx of Russian and Polish Jews had a considerable impact on the earlier German-Jewish community. German Jews had traditionally looked with revulsion upon the "Ost-Juden" as filthy, backward and unenlightened, and their arrival in great numbers during the last decades of the nineteenth century created embarrassment. Fearful that their own status might be jeopardized, the Americanized Jews were at first hesitant in exerting themselves fully to aid the newcomers. The United Jewish Charities of Rochester, New York, addressing a report in 1889 to a commission of English Jews, wrote that "the Jews have earned an enviable reputation in the United States, but this has been undermined by the influx of thousands who are not yet ripe for the enjoyment of liberty and equal rights." [2]

Nevertheless, the native Jews and their wealthy leaders did provide substantial assistance and guidance. In the long run, no nationality group in the United States did so much for their immigrant brethren as the American-Jewish community. Separated though they were by economic differences and independent cultural and institutional life, the German Jews displayed a sense of responsibility and the East Europeans grudgingly respected their superior accomplishments. The gulf between the two groups existed well into the 1920's, but it began to narrow as common philanthropic activities, overseas relief work, anti-Semitism, the Americanization of the newcomers, and intermarriage brought the communities together.

During the first two decades of the twentieth century, the overriding concern of the poverty-stricken new immigrants was not so much their relationship with the older Jewish community as it was with the desperate struggle for existence, and later, for economic advancement. It shortly became clear that "the deproletarianization of the Jewish immigrant began almost as soon as he became proletarianized." [3] Although their progress was not as spectacular as the earlier German immigrants, striking evidence of upward mobility in terms of occupations, education, and wealth was soon apparent, especially with the coming of age of the second generation.

The economic success of the American Jewish community was accompanied by the almost complete absence of official or governmental discrimination on the continental European model. The Jews of America were free, freer than Jews had ever been since their dispersion from Palestine. For over two centuries after the arrival of Jews in New Amsterdam, anti-

Semitism—systematic propagation of anti-Jewish feeling for political or discriminatory purposes—did not exist. General U. S. Grant's expulsion of Jews from his military district in 1862 was an isolated incident and the order was speedily rescinded. Until the latter part of the nineteenth century, whatever anti-Jewish feeling was present in the United States was derived primarily from the remnants of older European religious prejudice and was never a serious threat to the Jews.

The absence of anti-Semitism for so long was due, in great measure, to the relative invisibility of the early Jewish community. It was also, in part, because America was still in a period of great expansion and its social system had not yet became stabilized. The availability of other ethnic targets, such as the Irish Catholics, and the existence of all-absorbing issues, such as slavery, provided additional social safety-valves.[4]

But as America entered the Gilded Age of the post-Civil War era, anti-Jewish feeling gradually emerged as a noticeable element in the psychology of certain American groups. The refusal of accommodations to Joseph Seligman, the New York banker, at the Grand Union Hotel in Saratoga Springs in the summer of 1877 drew widespread adverse comment in the public press, but it symbolized a growing tendency towards the exclusion of Jews from areas involving leisure-time facilities. In the 1880's and thereafter, advertisements of summer hotels such as "we prefer not to entertain Hebrews or persons suffering from pulmonary trouble," were common. Important social clubs, like the Union League Club in New York, barred Jews from membership. Private schools began to be closed to Jewish children; even quasi-public institutions, such as the Metropolitan Museum of Art, the New York Public Library, and the New York Zoological Society, did not admit Jews to their boards of directors.[5]

John Higham has written that the Jews "lost in reputation as they gained in social and enonomic status. Alone among European immigrant groups, the Jews during this period met a distrust that spread along with their increasing assimilation."[6] This was partly the result of the involvement of wealthy Jews in the social competition of the Gilded Age. Jewish *nouveaux riches,* lacking the social graces, as well as the proper symbols of upper-class status (old family, right church, college education), appeared as crass parvenus. Jews themselves condemned the offenses against good taste sometimes displayed by their coreligionists:

> Secure in the conviction that they possess the great desideratum, they become self-assertive. . . . I have not a single word of defense for the vulgar exhibitions of the Jewish people in public places. These upstarts bring the blush of shame to the face of every decent Jew. . . .[7]

Yet, the Jewish upward thrust would not have met with such severe resistance if the nation had not been undergoing profound social changes. The older, socially elite groups were faced, in the late nineteenth century, with a growing struggle for place and power as their security was threatened by industrialism and the rise of new non-Jewish groups into the middle and upper classes. During this transition, the maintenance of class and status distinctions assumed great importance and the Jews—traditionally pariahs and scapegoats in Europe—furnished an effective object for the raising of invidious barriers in the United States.

During the highly nationalistic 1890's, American nativism was intense and widespread. An ideological anti-Semitism with political undertones began to appear in addition to the earlier social discrimination. The older German Jewish immigrants were acquiring the polish and gentility which may or may not have answered their critics, but the arrival of masses of new immigrants, including large numbers of East European Jews, created a tense situation. In the popular mind, nativistic feeling against immigration was now directed at the newer Jewish group and, implicitly, at all Jews.

Two influential segments of the American population, Eastern patrician intellectuals and Western agrarian radicals —while poles apart in basic orientation—shared a nationalistic jingoism and an anti-middle class attitude which converged on the Jews. Both Henry Adams and Ignatius Donnelly saw the Jew, conniving and grasping, as the symbol and

cause of their discontent.[8] The dominant anti-Jewish stereotype which emerged during the 1890's included elements of
earlier evangelical attitudes (especially strong during the
Silver Crusade): the attribution of distinctive, unpleasant
physical traits; a pervasive concern with money (Shylock); the
wielding of power through control of gold and banks (Rothschild); the existence of an invisible, financial oligarchy
ruling the world; anti-nationalism; and an identification with
trade and the hated, feared city (Babylon). Underlying this
image there remained the ancient, persistent sense of mystery
which shrouded the Jews. With the rise of racialist anti-
Semitism, popularized by Houston Stewart Chamberlain and
soon imported to the United States, the stereotype was almost
complete and remained effective, with additions, well into
the twentieth century.[9]

As second and third generation Jews began to compete
for the choicer middle class positions during the Progressive
era, intensified competition reached down into wider levels
of American society. Despite the relative social and economic
tranquility of this period, the vast Jewish immigration and
rapid mobility lent credence to the anti-Jewish stereotype
and sharpened anti-Semitic feelings. The eminent President of Stanford University, David Starr Jordan, declaiming
against the "unseen empire of finance," managed to list only
one gentile out of fifteen international bankers allegedly responsible for many of the world's ills. A popular journalist,
writing in the muckraking *McClure's,* exposed the "Jewish
Invasion of America" by pointing to the Jewish domination
of the clothing, real estate, entertainment, department store,
and whiskey businesses, in addition to finance.[10]

The peak periods of American anti-Semitism—1880 to
1900, the post-World War I years, and the 1930's—coincided
with those of the European, but never reached the intensity
or achieved the impact of Europe's anti-Semitism. The
American traditions of religious liberty and democracy were
never totally abandoned, even by those elements most suscep-
tible to anti-Semitic propaganda. American Jews reacted,

however, with considerable concern as signs of prejudice and exclusion mounted. "Gauged by European standards, we have no Jewish question in the United States. . . . And still our equivalence is not established. We realize, smouldering under an apparently calm surface, a general antagonism to our race." [11]

The average new East European Jewish immigrant, absorbed in the pressing task of finding economic security, was not acutely conscious of anti-Semitism, but many of the older, more Americanized Jews, precisely because of their rapid rise from persecution to equality, were perhaps "almost as sensitive to the finer disabilities under which they labor as were their forebears to ancient and mediaeval torture." [12] This group took the lead in the struggle for the defense of Jewish rights in the early decades of this century, and Louis Marshall, more prominently than any other individual, spoke for them.

Chapter two

louis marshall: spokesman for the jews

American Jewish Committee

At the opening of the twentieth century, there was no single, respected agency comparable to the Board of Deputies of British Jews which could speak with assurance for American Jews, or on behalf of overseas Jews, on civil and religious rights. This was partly because the general American pattern of decentralization and voluntarism in religious and ethnic groupings made the successful transplanting of traditional, all-embracing, European-style communal organizations extremely difficult.

There were many Jewish organizations and institutions of stature, but none was sufficiently prestigious or broadly representative to undertake an unchallenged line of action in the name of American Jewry. The Board of Delegates of Civil and Religious Rights of the Union of American Hebrew Congregations, formed in 1878 by the incorporation of the older Board of Delegates of American Israelites into the Union, was the body which most closely resembled a central defense organization. Its role, however, was seriously limited, in an age of large-scale East European Jewish immigration, because it was an official arm of the German-Jewish dominated Reform movement.

The largest Jewish fraternal group, the Independent Order B'nai B'rith, was composed, at that time, mostly of middle class, Americanized Jews of German background. Not until 1913 did it establish a special defense agency, the Anti-Defamation League. This group concentrated on such efforts as attempting to persuade newspaper editors to discontinue the practice of referring to persons accused of crimes as Jews, stopping the caricature of Jews on the stage, and eliminating the *Merchant of Venice* from the schools. Still later, during the 1920's when the East European Jewish community was coming of age, the American Jewish Congress, under the dynamic leadership of Rabbi Stephen S. Wise, emerged as a prominent and aggressive champion of Jewish, and general, civil rights.

In the early 1900's, however, Jewish leaders, like Cyrus Adler and Jacob Schiff, believed that an authoritative, widely respected organization capable of speaking for American Jews and their co-religionists abroad was lacking. The impetus for the formation of such a group, interestingly, came not from the subtle threats to American Jews from native anti-Semitism, but from the hammer blows that Jewish communities overseas were being subjected to. It was impossible to unite American Jewry as a religious body, but was possible to unite it for the immediate purpose of aiding unfortunate persecuted Jews in Czarist Russia. Thus, the Kishinev massacre and the Russian pogroms of 1903 to 1905 provided the background for the formation of the American Jewish Committee in 1906. When established, it became the most important agency for intervention on behalf of foreign Jews and for the defense of Jews in America.

The early history of the American Jewish Committee was marked by severe and prolonged controversy.[1] Two basic

problems nearly killed it at the very outset. The original de-
sign had been to bring together representatives of all leading
Jewish organizations, but the B'nai B'rith and the Union of
American Hebrew Congregations, the two major old-line organizations, felt that they would lose their identities and become submerged in the new group if they accepted it wholeheartedly. The Committee, therefore, never enjoyed more
than lukewarm cooperation from them. Secondly, a debate
on the constitution of the Committee centered on the democratic nature of its composition. The initiators of the American Jewish Committee were almost exclusively uptown, or
German, Jews of considerable wealth and prominence. The
more broadminded among them felt some method had to be
established to secure the acquiescence and participation of
the broad masses of the Jewish community. The democrats,
led by Louis Marshall, called for a system of congregational
elections, but the oligarchs, led by Oscar Straus and Adolf
Kraus, favored the creation of a self-appointed and self-
perpetuating body. Kraus bluntly questioned the necessity
for democracy: "Is it necessary that this Committee represent
the riff raff and everybody? If this Committee represents the
representative and high class Jews of America, that is
enough." [2] The anti-democratic faction won, and it was clear
that the Committee, consisting of sixty members co-opted by
an original group of fifteen, could never hope to be more
than a voluntary group, lacking cooercive power, with only
the prestige of its members behind it.

The subsequent enlargement of the Committee's membership, the inclusion of prominent Jews of Russian origin, and
the establishment of regional Advisory Councils eventually
provided a more democratic framework, but the high standing
of such members as Jacob Schiff, Julius Rosenwald, Judge
Mayer Sulzberger, Louis Marshall, Cyrus Adler, and Oscar
Straus gave the Committee the most powerful voice in the
American-Jewish community. Although continually criticized by socialists and Zionists for its alleged velvet glove tac-

tics, super-patriotism, and non-democratic organization, the Committee acted effectively in the interests of American Jewry.

Marshall, the Defender

When Judge Mayer Sulzberger of Philadelphia, the first President of the American Jewish Committee, declined re-election for the 1913 term, the man chosen to succeed him was Louis Marshall. Marshall served as President and guiding spirit of the Committee until his death in 1929.

Energetic, determined, and possessed of a deep sense of responsibility toward the Jewish community, Marshall had risen from humble origins. His father, Jacob Marshall, was born in 1829 in the village of Neidenstein, Baden, Germany; he later moved to another town in the Palatinate, and at the age of twenty, penniless and barely able to read or write, arrived in New York on September 1, 1849.[3] Unable to speak English, alone and friendless, Jacob tried his hand at a dozen different occupations, including peddling and manual labor in railroad construction. In the early 1850's, he settled in the town of Syracuse, New York, which had a substantial German community, and eventually started a not too successful hide and fur business. There he married Zilli Strauss, who had emigrated from Germany in 1853.

Their first child, Louis, was born on December 14, 1856, the eldest of six children. His mother, a self-educated woman who taught her son to memorize long passages, in German, from Schiller, Scott, and Hugo, was the dominant figure in his early life. "Looking back seventy-two years," he later said, "I can say without any qualification that she was the greatest influence upon my life." As a boy, Marshall worked hard in the family business, keeping his father's books, and salting hides and calfskins. During the day, he attended grammar school (and later high school), while in the afternoon he studied at the religious school in the basement of the synagogue of the Society of Concord.

Books attracted the boy at an early age. "I read everything within reach," he remembered. By the time he was ten, inspired by participation in informal debates on constitutional topics, he had decided to become a lawyer. After graduation from Syracuse High School in 1874, Marshall served a two year term as apprentice in a law office, during which time he not only swept the floor but committed to memory every old case he could find. In 1876, he left for New York where he completed the two year Columbia (then Dwight) Law School course in one year, impressing both professors and classmates with his prodigiously retentive and sharply analytical mind.

Back in Syracuse, he was admitted to the bar and taken into the law firm headed by William C. Ruger, who shortly thereafter became Chief Justice of the Court of Appeals of New York State. Marshall stayed on as a partner, working diligently in the office from nine in the morning to midnight, with time out only for meals. His talents suited him especially for appellate work, and, from 1878 to 1894, he argued with great success over 150 cases before the Court of Appeals. In his leisure time, Marshall took a prominent role in the Syracuse Jewish community and was known to almost everybody in the town and in the surrounding area. By 1891, he was important enough to be included in a national delegation which visited President Benjamin Harrison on behalf of Russian Jews.

While engaged in a case bearing on Jewish philanthropy, Marshall met Judge Mayer Sulzberger of Philadelphia. Sulzberger was so impressed that he introduced Marshall to Randolph Guggenheimer. This, in turn, led to an invitation to join the well known New York law firm of Guggenheimer and Untermyer.* Marshall accepted and in 1894 became a full partner in the firm of Guggenheimer, Untermyer and Marshall. The following year, he married Florence Lowenstein, a relative of the Untermyers, and settled down to a happy family life as well as a successful professional career.

In New York City, Marshall joined the select company of the German-Jewish elite, led by Jacob Schiff, the Straus brothers (Oscar, Nathan, and Isidor), Adolph S. Ochs, the Guggenheims, the Warburgs, and the Seligmans. German in origin, these men were intensely American; as loyal Jews, they were adherents of social-justice, modernized Judaism, not old fashioned Orthodoxy. Remembering the anti-Semitism of the Old World, they did not want any recurrence in the New. Linked by origin, marriage, and political conservatism, they provided responsible, thoughtful, even if at times cautious, guidance for the Jewish community during a dramatic era. Marshall was an intimate friend of these German-Jewish leaders and, although there were occasional differences on tactics, they usually agreed on fundamentals.

Marshall specialized in constitutional and corporate law. During his career, he argued more cases in the U.S. Supreme Court than anyone except Solicitors- and Attorneys-General, and many of these were of major constitutional significance. His eminence in the legal profession was recognized by appointment or election to three constitutional conventions in New York State—in 1890, 1894, and 1915—where he was active in the formulation of conservation clauses. For many years Marshall was Chairman of the New York City Bar Association's Committee on the Amendment of the Law, keeping a close watch on legislative developments in Albany. In communal affairs, he participated in local and national politics, took a leading role in the establishment and management of the New York State College of Forestry at Syracuse University, and served on numerous committees and boards. Especially after he became President of the American Jew-

---

* Untermyer had been a law school classmate of Marshall's, and they had referred legal matters to each other in the interim.

ish Committee, his principal and favorite office, Marshall's primary interest was Jews and Judaism, both in the United States and abroad. From appearances before Congressional Committees to private conferences with Presidents, to such minor matters as informing the New York State Board of Regents of the dates of forthcoming Jewish holidays, the range and extent of his activities were truly staggering. Strike arbitrator, fund raiser, philanthropist, educator—Marshall wore many hats and wore them well. He ranked fourth— topped only by Einstein, Weizmann and Zangwill, none of whom were American—in a readers' poll conducted by the *Jewish Tribune* in 1923 to name the twelve outstanding Jews in the world.

Marshall greatly owed his eminence to his role *par excellence* of defender of the Jews. Almost all elements of American Jewry, despite differences of opinion, acknowledged his position as attorney-at-large for the Jewish people. Many would have agreed with the young Congressman, Rep. Emanuel Celler, who wrote him in 1924: "I have always considered you the greatest asset possessed by American Jewry. To me you have always been a sort of pater-familias."

Marshall's Ideology

In order to understand Louis Marshall the spokesman, one must consider the ideas which motivated him and determined his approach to basic issues confronting the Jewish community. Marshall was neither sophisticated or subtle in his ideology and style of life, but he did have strong, frequently passionate, convictions on certain subjects. He regarded his activities as part of an integrated pattern based on his status as a citizen of the United States, an adherent of the Jewish faith, and a member of the legal profession, all of which were intertwined in his mind. It is important to attempt an analysis of these elements.

"One of my first impressions," Marshall remembered late in life, "was thankfulness that I had been born in America. I used to hear my parents and some of their friends talking about the hard life in the Old World, with its privations and denials at the hands of autocratic governments." [4] As a son of German-Jewish immigrants, spending his formative years in the small town atmosphere of Syracuse in upper New York State in the decades after the Civil War, Marshall absorbed a deep and permanent Americanism. His sincere patriotism was apparent each Fourth of July; at his summer camp in the Adirondacks, following the reading of a chapter from the Bible, he led his family in a little parade, each carrying a flag and singing patriotic songs. Mixed with this Americanism was a good portion of home town loyalty; in later years, he sometimes acted as though no one from Syracuse could do any wrong.

To Marshall, the Constitution of the United States was a "holy of holies, an instrument of sacred import." It was "the hope and refuge of millions of the oppressed and persecuted . . . the guiding principle of the freest government on earth. Let no unhallowed hands be laid upon it." [5] His legal career was dominated by this attitude of respect and reverence for what he regarded as a body of law based on the Constitution, enacted by the legislatures, and interpreted by the courts without regard to personal bias or temporary circumstances.

Placing the Bill of Rights almost on the same level as the Ten Commandments, he consistently and fearlessly fought for the civil liberties and rights of all persecuted groups, not only Jews. Catholics, Indians, Japanese, Negroes, and socialists received his legal aid and support in important cases. Defending the right of the Civil Liberties Union (of which he was not a member) against the New York City Board of Education's refusal to allow it the use of a school building for a meeting; participating in a delegation to the Secretary of State on behalf of the rights of Haiti, then under the control of the U.S. Marines; accepting membership on the Board of Directors of the National Association for the Advancement of Colored People—all were part of Marshall's defense of civil rights, in which his Jewish activities played a dominant, though not exclusive role. Marshall clearly recognized that Jewish rights could be guaranteed only in a society where the rights of all were secure.

As a native of upper New York State, and as a very prosperous lawyer, Marshall was naturally Republican. Interpreting his beloved Constitution, in which he felt that Article X of the Bill of Rights was a key provision, he emerged with a generally conservative approach to social and economic innovations, especially those extending the power of the federal government. Much of his public activity and legal business was concerned with opposition to the introduction of such legislation as federal child labor laws, state minimum wage acts, workmen's compensation, and, consistently, prohibition—all of which, he believed, infringed on private rights as guaranteed by the Constitution. In New York City, he successfully blocked Mayor John F. Hylan's plans for a city run bus system and defended ticket speculators by winning a U.S. Supreme Court decision holding price fixing of theater tickets unconstitutional.

Despite victories in these and other cases, Marshall sensed that the trend was running against him:

> . . . When I read the decisions of the highest courts in the land and in the State, I sometimes feel that our Government is gradually being transformed into a Socialistic state. Study our legislation, consider the agitation in favor of municipalities going into every possible kind of private business, ponder the extension of the police power, so that the old-fashioned ideas of liberty and property are vanishing into nothingness from year to year.[6]

> . . . Congress is rapidly being transformed into a Soviet form of government. . . . There are really three Soviets, one resembling the

peasant Soviet of Russia—the farmers' bloc, one the soldiers' Soviet—the bonus hunters' bloc, and the third, the workingmen's Soviet—the trade unions bloc. To say nothing about an incapacity to think internationally, there is a woeful inability to think even nationally.[7]

Conservative on most social and economic matters, Marshall was never merely a paid corporation lawyer, and he resented being labeled as such. He helped establish many legal principles which limited the rights of corporations. On retainers from New York State, for example, he sustained, in the U.S. Supreme Court, the constitutionality of a special franchise tax on corporations, of an inheritance tax on non-residents, and of an act regulating private banking, which he had framed. Marshall took an enlightened view in labor-management relations, urging employers to treat employees as human beings, not as machinery, and placed most of the blame for labor unrest on management. As mediator or arbitrator in a number of disputes in New York's clothing industry, Marshall was influential in establishing collective bargaining procedures.

Marshall did, however, approve of government control over conservation. He was exceedingly devoted to the forests of the Adirondacks, where, since 1898, he spent his summers. As a founder and President of the Trustees of the New York College of Forestry, as a delegate to the Constitutional Conventions of 1894 and 1915, and as a prominent public figure, Marshall fought for the Forest Preserve concept tenaciously, resisting all efforts at commercialization. In New York City, he managed to find time to write to the Parks Commissioner, suggesting species of trees for planting in Central Park. While he opposed legislation giving federal aid to states for the purchase of forest lands as "bribery" which would destroy state sovereignty, he upheld the right of the federal government to regulate the flights of migratory birds.

Marshall's economic and political conservatism, and civil rights liberalism were two sides of his abiding respect for the Constitution of his native land. Whereas his legal training and social status resulted in a conservative interpretation of

the economic clauses of the Constitution, his religious background and position as a Jewish leader led to a liberal interpretation of its civil rights clauses.

Marshall's Judaism

With his professional career firmly established, the Jewish
communities in America and abroad increasingly became the
focus of Marshall's abundant energy. It is essential, therefore,
to understand his sense of what it meant to be a Jew in this
country. Marshall's religion was concerned primarily with
the institutional aspects of Judaism: the synagogue, education, and philanthropy. Personal piety and ritual observance
of the traditional Orthodox variety were not major elements
in his belief, but he did have a sense of God and of ethical
values, revered and studied the Bible, and attended Reform
services regularly.* He was simply a Jew to whom nothing
Jewish was alien. Contrasted with consciously formulated
Orthodoxy, extreme Reformism, or Zionism, his Judaism was
non-denominational, enabling him to play a mediatory role
in Jewish life.

In Syracuse, he had been a leading synagogue member;
when he came to New York he joined Temple Emanu-El. By
1903 he was Secretary and a leading member of the Board of
Trustees of this wealthiest and most important Reform congregation in the land, and in 1916 he became its President. It
was at Emanu-El that Marshall first met a promising young
rabbi, Stephen S. Wise, who had been invited from Oregon
in 1905 to try for the New York pulpit. Wise made no secret
of his wish to exercise complete freedom of speech if selected

---

* His son recalled that Marshall often wished that, as the president of
his congregation, he could be provided with a push-button that would open
a trap-door in the pulpit when the sermon seemed prolonged.

as minister of Emanu-El, but Marshall bluntly informed the impetuous candidate that the Board of Trustees would always remain the ultimate authority over the pulpit. Wise rejected this condition, released the story and the correspondence to the press, and a *cause célèbre* was created on the issue of muzzling. Wise declared he would have nothing to do with a congregation which lived, as he said, under Marshall law, but Marshall retorted that the real issue was Wise's penchant for preaching on highly controversial subjects. In any event, Wise went on to become the rabbi of his own congregation, the Free Synagogue, where he led many crusades, often in opposition to Marshall's wishes.

Marshall believed the synagogue to be central in Jewish life and urged a back to the synagogue movement. Although one of the leading Reform Jews in America, he rejected the use of divisive labels. Theological discussions between Reform, Conservative, and Orthodox were meaningless or distasteful to him: "This is not religion. This is not Judaism. It is nothing but vulgar bickering." [8] He regarded Jewish unity as essential, but not at the price of suppressing different opinions. Finding it impossible to effect a merger between the Conservative and Reform theological seminaries, he threw himself into the work of converting the Conservative establishment into a successful institution. He saw no inconsistency between his role in the Reform Temple Emanu-El and his chairmanship of the Board of Directors of the Conservative Jewish Theological Seminary; to him there was one Judaism.[9] Marshall also believed that the greatest weakness in American Judaism was its failure to create an up-to-date, widespread system of Jewish education, and much of his philanthropy and propaganda were devoted to correcting this.

Although he felt that Judaism was a faith, ethnic loyalty was not completely absent from his thought. The indifference and secularism of the college-educated second generation during the 1920's alarmed him:

> Our so-called young intellectuals are inclined to boast that they take no stock in religion. They have a sort of an idea that it is a symbol

of enlightenment if they can cut loose from our ancient traditions and from all that has made the Jew of the slightest importance in the history of the world. They are more familiar with Ulysses, and filth of that character, than they are with the Bible. Some of them even pretend that they are atheists and are ready to pass adverse judgement upon the generations of Jews who remained loyal to their faith, who were ready to die for it, and who guided their lives by those great ethical doctrines which Judaism gave to the world. They are making a dreadful mistake. No matter how high they may rise in their own esteem, they are, after all, compared with their humble ancestors, quite contemptible. . . . It is the coward who seeks to be something different than what he really is, the man who is disloyal to his past and a traitor to his ancestral faith who will be despised for what he is.[10]

Marshall was firmly attached to his roots and condemned the more radical Reform elements who zealously tried to eliminate some of the sentimental ceremonies he fondly remembered from his youth. Proud of his Jewishness, he objected to the prevalent non-Jewish practice of softening references to Jews by using such euphemisms as Hebrew and Israelite. Marshall asked his Gentile associates to use the word which expressed what he was—a Jew. But—as Marshall said in his utterances on the Russian passport issue—he was now more than a Jew; he was also an American citizen.

How were these two ideas related, and what was the place of the Jews in the United States? To Marshall, as to other Jewish leaders of his generation and background, there was no incompatibility between living as a loyal Jew and as a loyal American. They were two sides of the same coin, for America was indeed a promised land. Viewing Jews as a religious group, not a race, Marshall considered himself simply an "American Jew." Replying to those Jews who believed they were American citizens first and Jews in religion afterwards, Marshall stated:

It has always been my conviction that we were at the same time American citizens and religiously Jews, that there could be no possible incompatibility between these two facts, that neither had precedence over the other, that the glory of our country was that every citizen worshipped God according to his own conscience, and that there was no occasion for him to make any concessions to government by way of subordinating his religious beliefs.[11]

Confronted from the opposite side with extremist statements that the Jews of England, France, and America were neither Englishmen, Frenchmen, nor Americans, Marshall countered, "I would rather die than accept such a doctrine." [12] It was unthinkable to him that the American Jew might be considered a man without a country, for he felt himself to be an integral part of America. His faith in America was sincere, despite occasional disappointments. When his brother-in-law, Dr. Judah Magnes, who had emigrated to Palestine to head the Hebrew University, wrote that his children spoke Hebrew, Marshall replied, "I hope that they will not forget the use of the English language, and that they will retain a love for their native land, which, after all, will continue to constitute the best hope of the human race." [13]

Marshall resented the popular idea that the United States was a Christian country; this was in direct opposition to his view of America. He argued that since the Constitution contained no reference to the deity, and since it prohibited religious tests for office and included the First Amendment, there was no legal basis for the Christian country idea. The claim that the United States was in.fact Christian because the majority adhered to that faith was dismissed by Marshall as unsound because the majority was changeable.[14]

As head of the American Jewish Committee, Marshall was often troubled by official actions which tended to confirm the Christian nature of the United States. He secured the withdrawal by the Department of Commerce of a pamphlet for immigrants which referred to the United States as a Christian country, although Oscar Straus, then head of the Department and the highest ranking Jew in politics, found it inoffensive. When an Oklahoma Constitutional Convention considered inserting a clause in the State Constitution affirming Christ as God, he objected vigorously. After the World War, he opposed the placing of a cross upon or near the tomb of the Unknown Soldier. When a New York State law was proposed requiring county child welfare boards to be composed of Jewish, Catholic, and Protestant members, he saw it as unconstitutional and a dangerous precedent, even though it gave recognition to Jews. Religion was a private matter, and any governmental action which smacked of the establishment of Christianity was completely unacceptable to him.

Similarly, Marshall rejected the notion that American culture was a fixed, Anglo-Saxon entity that all Americans had to assimilate:

> If it is intended to convey the idea of being totally absorbed and of losing one's identity completely, then I am frank to say that I hope that the Jews will never be assimilated. They have retained their identity for fifty centuries and I harbor the fond belief that the world has benefited thereby. I have no patience with the idea that all men must be alike and that the dead level of uniformity must take the place of that variety created by the Almighty. Is a Jew any better after he has turned his back on his glorious tradition. . . ? Would the world be any better if Jews and Jewesses were to intermarry . . . as some of the assimilationists would have them do? I answer, a thousand times, No! [15]

Assimilation—what sociologists now call acculturation, that is, adjustment to the laws, customs, and standards of living of one's resident land—was nevertheless necessary. In this sense, Marshall observed, "there are no people on earth who more readily assimilate than the Jews." [16]

Marshall looked with disfavor on Zangwill's theory of America as a melting pot. To him, this concept implied the creation of a mongrelized, hybrid civilization which lacked the vitality and creativity of the original cultures. He did not approve, either, of the theory of cultural pluralism expounded by Horace M. Kallen and Randolph Bourne, though statements of his as, "A Jew can serve America best by preserving his identity," seemed to imply support for their views.[17] Marshall's complicated conception, never clearly or coherently formulated, was closer to religious pluralism: religious distinctions of the culture are maintained and encouraged, but ethnic elements are minimized.

At the same time Marshall, with Jacob Schiff and other

Jewish leaders, denounced any form of Jewish separatism as reprehensible.[18] Jewish identity had to be preserved, but this was a matter of religious identity, and anything that promoted self-segregation, politically or socially had to be avoided, if possible. When he helped form the American Jewish Committee, Marshall was apprehensive that the organization be regarded by Jews as recognition that their "interests [were] different from those of other American citizens." [19] Speaking before congressional committees or making public pronouncements on controversial issues, Marshall characteristically emphasized that he spoke as an American, and on behalf of Americans:

> . . . I would never in any discussion that I would undertake before any legislative committee ask anything for the Jews that I would not give to any other people. I know of no question of religious differences in this country and therefore, I have as much concern for any minority, for any race or nationality, as I have for my own flesh and blood.[20]

Asked for his opinion on the advisability of publishing a volume called *Who's Who in American Jewry*, Marshall opposed it because it would have been against the welfare of the Jews. Marshall regarded the establishment of Jewish parochial schools as a great mistake, both theoretically and practically. The ghettos of the past had been imposed by external pressures, and parochial schools would mean the creation of an unnecessary self-built ghetto wall between Jews and non-Jews. Referring to his experience in Syracuse, he believed the public schools to be the best antidote to bigotry and the best preparation for life in a heterogeneous society. Also significant to Marshall was the probability that Jewish acculturation would be hampered by parochial schools with inferior English instruction, from which students might emerge with "pronounced accents" and "peculiar grammatical constructions and intonations." [21]

Marshall realized that fear of self-segregation could be carried to extremes. In response to those who felt that Jews should not use the phrase, "our people," Marshall called it entirely proper. But in an era when hypersensitivity to racial and cultural differences was common, he generally displayed considerable caution by avoiding any possible action implying the political or social separateness of Jews.

Marshall and Anti-Semitism

As a fully integrated American citizen of the Jewish faith, Marshall saw anti-Semitism as a threat, both to his Jewishness and his status as an American, and as a throwback to the Europe before emancipation. As a boy, Marshall had heard stories from his father of beatings by gangs of Germans, and the memory of these episodes was engraved deeply in his heart. In the Syracuse public schools, Marshall remembered, relations between the Jewish and Gentile children were generally good, except when

> . . . the Bible was read every morning, by the teachers in charge of the various grades. Ordinarily the readings were from the New Testament, and usually I enjoyed them, although there were times when they were not what they should have been. . . . On Good Fridays, however, the readings always related to the crucifixion and the teachers seemed to have the habit of intoning their reading, and especially when the word "Jew" was mentioned, in such a manner as to convey the idea not only of contempt, but also of hatred. This was always followed during the recess and for several days after by the most hostile demeanor on the part of the Christian boys and girls of the school, some of whom resorted to physical violence and most of them to the calling of names and the making of scurrilous remarks.[22]

Childhood memories of anti-Semitism (while not reinforced by any serious difficulties in his personal career) were sufficient, in combination with his position as a Jewish leader and with his knowledge of European conditions, to convince Marshall that anti-Semitism in America had to be carefully watched.

Marshall never believed that anti-Semitism was a major social problem in the United States. This was partly objective, but it was also because of his desire to avoid stressing and thereby stimulating anti-Semitism. Similarly, he refused to admit the possibility that a Jewish problem on the continental European model might arise in America. At the height of the post-war anti-Jewish agitation, he flatly stated, "We do not recognize the existence of a Jewish question in the United States." [23] He was aware, of course, that there were bigots and fanatics in America, but the overwhelming majority was "one hundred per cent American" and understood the meaning of justice and fair play for the Jews.

Marshall was not greatly interested in theories about the origins of anti-Semitism. He believed it resulted from ignorance, malice, and senseless hatred because of religious intolerance and, occasionally, for political reasons. The crucifixion, associated in Marshall's mind with unpleasant childhood experiences, disturbed him as a potent cause of anti-Semitism. He recognized, without delving deeply, that anti-Semitic propaganda had psychological roots. On hate publications, he remarked,

> They are so patently the emanation of the disturbed minds of a lot of sad morons, that they can only arouse contempt in those who have average intelligence and an ordinary supply of human instincts. . . . I always suspect those who are boasting of their patriotism, their civic virtue, and their one hundred per cent Americanism. They are generally dishonest hypocrites, consumed by envy and jealousy, and with no room in their hearts for anything but hatred and cruelty.[24]

Marshall distinguished between two types of anti-Semitism: first, an "innate anti-Semitism, of which many of our citizens are unconscious." [25] This was the basis of much of the social and economic discrimination, and was a problem that could be solved, if at all, by the spread of liberalism, through years of education.[26] Deep-rooted anti-Jewish prejudice of this kind, he felt, was most prevalent among the ignorant and the dwellers in small towns or rural areas where Jews were unknown and ancient myths strongest. Marshall continued nevertheless to meet anti-Semitism among the, presumably, educated, and his sense of shock led him to suspect that prejudice of this sort might never yield to reason. During his last years especially, a note of disillusionment could be seen in his private communications.

The second kind of anti-Semitism was that fomented deliberately by mischievous groups or individuals hoping to stimulate the latent innate anti-Semitism for private gain, political purposes, or personal gratification. It was this overt anti-Semitic activity that Marshall and his associates concentrated their efforts on.

The tactics adopted to fight anti-Semitism varied according to the nature and seriousness of the specific case, but he favored the "sane method" of "quiet, deliberate and pacificatory means, rather than by agitation, newspaper headlines, slogans and alarmist publications." [27] Sensationalism, public demonstrations, and mass meetings were to be used only as last resorts, for these were inconsonant with the dignified image of the Jew that Marshall and those who shared his views wished to project to Americans.

This did not mean that Marshall would passively accept signs of anti-Semitism, especially when they originated from responsible or official sources, or when they affected the civil rights or integration of Jews in American society. He refused to tolerate even minor, sometimes unintentional, slurs. In 1924 he protested to leaders of the National Association for the Advancement of Colored People about their inadvertent use of the swastika as a decorative symbol in their journal. Marshall knew that its appearance was not deliberate, but, as he told Dr. W. E. B. DuBois, the swastika had been appropriated by Adolf Hitler whose policies on the Jews were "identical with those of the Ku Klux Klan," that is, "the elimination of the Jews socially, economically, politically, and even physically." [28] Similarly, when the *New York Staats-Zeitung*, perhaps unwittingly, printed a humorous tale poking fun at Jews, Marshall objected, saying there were many readers "whose sense of humor may be stunted." Of course, anti-

Semitic prejudice of this minor variety, if deliberate, drew from Marshall more vigorous denunciation.

Marshall held, however, that no good would come from constantly agitating about anti-Semitism. As President of the American Jewish Committee, Marshall received many letters from anti-Semites, but rarely allowed them to disturb his equanimity. "We are always talking too much about Jews, Jews, Jews and we are making a Jewish question of almost everything that occurs. . . ." [29] When the Yiddish press criticized President Coolidge for failing to mention the Jewish companion of a famous aviator in a telegram of congratulations, Marshall thought it ridiculous. Informed of a remark, at a jewelers' convention, that only Italians and Russian Jews were responsible for jewel thefts, he commented, "If the American Jewish Committee were to take up every case where remarks of this character are made about Jews it would be unable to accomplish anything." [30] In response to complaints calling for action against a crackpot anti-Jewish sheet, Marshall replied that it was so ridiculous it could not possibly make an impression on anyone who was not already fit for a lunatic asylum, and no countermeasures were necessary.

Carefully defending Jews against the canards of anti-Semites, Marshall did not exempt his brethren from some share of the responsibility for arousing anti-Semitism. Much of the hostility which Jews faced, he reflected, was due to their own conceit, arrogance, and chip-on-the-shoulder attitudes. He confessed, also, that he was not so much concerned about anti-Semites as he was afraid of "the consequences of Jewish indiscretions in dealing with these matters." [31]

For these reasons, among others, Marshall was often a carping critic of the Jewish press—particularly the Yiddish newspapers—and of Jewish organizations and individuals, such as Stephen S. Wise and the American Jewish Congress, which pursued more aggressive policies and tactics. When Maurice Samuel, a young Jewish writer, daringly published *You Gentiles,* which was a bitter denunciation of anti-Semitism and hinted that it was an incurable disease, Marshall furiously dismissed it as a "colossal piece of impudence" certain to accomplish great mischief. A facetious reference by a Jewish lawyer to the election of Israel brought forth Marshall's wrath, for what would Christians think of Jews if one of them indulged in "ribald jests intended to destroy with ridicule the millennial convictions of his own people?" [32] On one occasion, Marshall wrote with bitterness of "a class of Jews, erroneously referred to as 'Kikes,' whose name is legion. It is due to them that we are daily forced to blush for shame —not only men but also women, sensual vulgarians, who disgrace us." [33] As a Jewish leader, Marshall spent almost as much time and energy in guiding the reactions of Jews to anti-Semitism and in exhorting them to better behavior as he did fighting anti-Semitism directly. It should be remembered that Marshall's critical views of fellow Jews were expressed privately; in public, he remained their consistent champion.

Zionism

The rise of Zionism confronted Marshall with a very real challenge to his conceptions of Judaism and Americanism. In its early years, American Zionism was a downtown movement led by uptown Jews, but the greatest part of the older Jewish community looked on it with horror as negating everything that Jews had achieved in America. Marshall occupied a somewhat intermediate position between the two extremes. The vision of Theodor Herzl impressed him, but he did not care for the non-religious side of secular Zionism, and, more fundamentally, could not subscribe to the sovereign state idea explicit in Herzl's thought. "I look upon the United States as my home and my homeland, and the people of the United States as constituting the Nation to which I belong." [34]

Although he regarded the Jewish State idea as fallacious, impossible of achievement ("Neither you nor your children nor your children's children will live to see the formation of a Jewish sovereign state in Palestine."), he sympathized with the humanitarianism of the work done by the Zionists in Palestine.[35] With the increasing certainty of legislation barring access to the United States for Jewish immigrants from Eastern Europe, Marshall clearly saw Palestine as an alternative haven and refuge:

> There is no other outlet for them. . . . Where shall they go if they desire to better their condition? What objection can there be, therefore, to an effort to establish for them a home in the land of their fathers and to enable them . . . to build up the waste places of the Holy Land and to bring about a Renaissance? [36]

In the early Palestine pioneers, he saw a new kind of man who revived the Maccabean spirit and provided a ray of hope for the despairing Jews of Europe. Confessing to Nathan Straus that as he grew older his feelings of reverence and love for "the cradle of our race" increased in intensity, Marshall called for seizing the opportunity to perform large-scale practical work in Palestine. In cooperation with such philanthropists as Jacob Schiff and Julius Rosenwald, he supported the technical institute at Haifa, and a new agricultural experiment station.

Support for such humanitarian enterprises was in the tradition of American-Jewish philanthropy, but the issuance of the Balfour Declaration by the British government in 1917 posed a much more controversial problem for Marshall and the leaders of the American Jewish Committee. Marshall finally formulated a statement on it which he hoped would placate the Zionists without offending what he considered to be "the most influential part of American Jewry." [37] After submitting the statement to Secretary of State Robert Lansing for approval, it was issued to the public. Opening with a reference to the "axiomatic" allegiance of the Jews to the United States where they had their permanent home, it sympathized with the desire of those Jews who yearned for Palestine as their home. The Committee promised to cooperate in the realization of the Balfour Declaration with those who sought to establish in Palestine "a center for Judaism . . . and for the rehabilitation of the land." [38]

The statement, intended to please both Zionists and anti-Zionists, pleased neither. Marshall was accustomed to criticism from Zionists, but he also faced a strong anti-Zionist upsurge among the A.J.C. membership and within the older, Reform Jewish community. Confident that the majority of American Jews stood with him on middle ground, Marshall attempted to repress public displays on anti-Zionism. He felt that open opposition to the Zionist program would provide ammunition for the anti-Semites, divide the Jewish community, and alienate large numbers of East European immigrants from their more established brethren in America. As Marshall phrased it: "Zionism is a theory and anti-Zionism is a folly." [39]

His apprehensions about a nexus between the Zionist controversy and anti-Semitism were realized, for the cry of dual allegiance was soon heard. When this allegation was raised in Jewish circles, as an argument against Zionism, Marshall considered it unwise; when it was voiced by non-Jews, it represented potential danger. Cyrus Adler, his associate in the American Jewish Committee, believed that Zionist nationalism was "bound to bring about hatred of the Jew." [40] Marshall could manage Adler, but gentile accusations along the same lines were more serious.

Professor Albert Bushnell Hart, of Harvard University, believed a clear alternative faced the Jews of America: "The Jewish people must either fish or cut bait. They must either reject their American citizenship or renounce any such dangerous doctrine as Zionism." [41] Herbert Adams Gibbons, writing for *Century Magazine* (Sept., 1921), called on "every Jew who does not want to become a Palestinian to say so openly." In 1925, Professor Philip Marshall Brown, of Princeton University, spoke before the American Society of

Louis Marshall, Defender of Jewish Rights

International Law, and accused the Jews of not owing allegiance to any land.

Marshall angrily rejected these and similar statements. He asserted that loyalty to the United States by American citizens was no more inconsistent with help for the upbuilding of Palestine than was assistance to Ireland by Americans of Irish descent. Although this argument may not have convinced men of Professor Brown's inclinations, it indicated a recognition of American realities and an insistence on equal treatment for Jews. Marshall considered the very suggestion of divided loyalty as an insult, for it implied that unless the Jews surrendered important traditional attachments, their status as full Americans might be challenged. "Not even a Princeton professor," Marshall retorted to Brown, could frighten the Jews into accepting a complete, cowardly, and hypocritical assimilation in order to escape the label of dual allegiance.[42]

During the last decade of his life, Marshall continued his efforts to bridge the gap between Zionists and anti-Zionists, and became increasingly involved in work with Palestine and Zionist politics. He urged Secretary of State Charles E. Hughes to use American influence on the League of Nations in favor of the British mandate over Palestine, and he endorsed Senator Henry C. Lodge's resolution supporting the Balfour Declaration. Although the American Jewish Committee continued to insist that relief and constructive work for East European Jews was possibly more important than the immediate upbuilding of Palestine, Marshall contributed greatly to the latter.[43]

In reply to continued criticism from anti-Zionist Reform Jewish quarters, Marshall declared:

> I have belonged to a Reform Congregation for nearly sixty years. I have never understood that there is anything basically inconsistent between belief in Palestine and Reform Judaism. If there is then so much the worse for Reform Judaism. . . . Indifference to Palestine on the part of any Jew to me spells inconsistency with the spirit of Judaism.[44]

With the Mandate an established fact, Marshall felt it would be a disgrace if the Jewish settlement in Palestine were to fail. In time, he even sounded a note reminiscent of Zionist propaganda, as he spoke of Jewish industry and intelligence bringing prosperity for Jews and Arabs alike, and of the miraculous growth of Tel Aviv from a sand dune to a city of 30,000 with Jewish policemen.

Throughout these last years, Marshall cooperated with Chaim Weizmann in attempting to arrange a *modus vivendi* which would allow non-Zionists, such as Marshall and some of his wealthy American Jewish Committee associates, to share in the supervision and support of the Palestine endeavor without actually becoming Zionists. Weizmann was well aware that the economic contributions of the rich non-Zionists might be crucial. He recounted that Marshall once protested, "But Dr. Weizmann, you will need half a billion dollars to build up this country," to which the Zionist leader calmly replied, "You'll need much more, Mr. Marshall. The money is there, in the pockets of the American Jews. It's your business and my business to get at some of it." [45]

Weizmann's work, in which Marshall was a powerful ally, contributed to a split in the Zionist camp, with Stephen Wise leading the opposition to the inclusion of the non-Zionists. After many years of discussion, however, an agreement was reached. In Zurich, August, 1929, shortly before his fatal illness, Marshall and the Zionists ratified a pact for the establishment of a Jewish Agency—to include both Zionists and non-Zionists—for the management of Jewish colonization efforts under the terms of the British mandate. Marshall's participation might have assured the success of this venture; his death soon afterwards was a great blow. The Jewish Agency became almost identical with the Zionist Executive, but Marshall's labors had not been completely in vain, for he helped create a tradition of American non-Zionist support for Palestine that was of great value in the crucial decade after World War II.

Marshall and the East Side

American Zionism received its mass support from the large numbers of East European immigrants who settled in the United States from 1880 to 1920. This Russo-Polish group—crowded in the slums of the great cities, divided by conflicting ideologies of religious orthodoxy, secular radicalism and nationalist Zionism, and struggling to gain an economic foothold in America—upset the equanimity and the ethnic composition of the older American-Jewish community. Marshall and his friends, as leaders of that community, were deeply involved in the tremendous task of economic and cultural integration of the newcomers.

Marshall, profoundly interested in everything Jewish and firmly convinced of the need for unity within the Jewish fold, emerged as one of the key links between the two communities. Far more than most members of his social class, he sympathized with and understood the East Side Jews. A busy adult, he learned Yiddish after settling in New York and regularly read one or two Yiddish newspapers, especially the *Forward*. Service as Chairman of the New York Immigration Commission in 1908 increased his knowledge of immigrant life. There were few East Side leaders whom Marshall did not know and he assisted in bringing them into general Jewish communal affairs. He developed a fondness for the new immigrants, respected their industry and intelligence, and was quick to defend them against the prejudices of non-Jews and the snobbishness of Jews:

> Have you ever had opportunity to observe the intellectual life of the East Side? I fear not. I do not believe that you will find many of the native born Americans in this community who work for their daily bread, engaged in the evening hours in discussing questions of

philosophy, science and literature. But I can show you society after society on the East Side, of men who earn their living as pushcart peddlers, or as workers in what are called "sweatshops" who devote their evenings to these subjects.[46]

The difficulty with many of our Jews is that Jews who were born in Germany or Austria, or whose parents were born there, regard those whose cradle was rocked a little further to the East as men of an inferior race, when as a matter of fact, they are, intellectually and otherwise, in every respect equals.[47]

To me this phase of our life is tragic. For God's sake let us at least be united and eliminate this element of bitterness from the cup of sorrows that is pressed to our lips continually.[48]

Marshall upbraided his fellow uptown Jews for isolating themselves in a gilded ghetto and warned that social stratification could lead to the older community being outstripped by the newer. His outspokenness on this surprised even his relatives. "But one thing went through my mind," wrote one of them, "when I read your defense of the Polish Jews and that is what your father would have thought of anybody in his family trying to defend them." [49]

As a responsible leader of a minority group in which new immigrants were the overwhelming majority, Marshall had no choice but to defend them. The great Americanization crusade of the first two decades of this century, arising both from a nativistic fear and suspicion of Southern and Eastern European immigrants, and the idealism of certain social workers and officials, stressed the importance of rapid and thorough absorption by the new immigrants of American culture. Marshall, although he resisted the more hysterical demands of the later Americanization movement, accepted its early program, much as the immigrants themselves accepted it, in practice.[50] He never tired of saying that Jewish immigrants were prime examples of successful Americanization, especially the second generation. "The children of our Jewish immigrants," he proudly informed Senator James A. Reed, "are among the best scholars in the land." [51]

Marshall was careful to emphasize, however, that Americanization would never come by patronization, or by treating decent immigrants as problems. He carried this into his work with the Educational Alliance in New York's lower East Side. This institution, one of the most important of the private Americanizing agencies, was organized in 1893 by Jacob Schiff, Isidor Straus, and other uptown leaders.[52] Marshall was elected a trustee in 1897 and remained on the board until his death in 1929. With a fine building and able staff, well-financed by contributions from its sponsors, the Alliance conducted an unusually extensive program. It taught the immigrants English; prepared their children for public schools; presented adult education courses in science, American history, English literature, vocational subjects; and generally provided an Americanizing cultural center.

The impact of the Educational Alliance on the East Side was great and beneficial, but its policies, particularly its alleged neglect of specifically Jewish and religious activities, sometimes came under sharp attack by spokesmen for the immigrants. Marshall defended the Alliance against the strictures of outsiders, but within the Board of Trustees he deplored the fact that

> . . . we have been unable to make a tangible impression on the younger generation. In the meantime agnosticism, atheism, socialism, radicalism, and Bolshevism have grown to such an extent that they apparently overshadow the entire community. The Alliance is a thing apart. It has never succeeded in entering the life of those for whom it was organized. . . . Radicals and conservatives alike hold it in suspicion, the one on the theory that it is capitalistic and the other in the belief that it is seeking to destroy the traditions of Israel.

The blame for this situation he placed upon the uptown Americanizers:

> They held themselves aloof from the people. They did not associate with them, socially, religiously, or otherwise. They acted as Lords and Ladies Bountiful bringing gifts to people who did not seek for gifts. They frankly avowed the purpose of bettering those among whom they labored and of dealing with them as a problem. . . .[53]

In order to overcome these handicaps, Marshall worked to make the Alliance a real neighborhood organization and to bring the leaders of the East Side community into the Board of Trustees.

Marshall held that the Yiddish press was one of the most important ways of Americanizing immigrants. He saw it as fulfilling the necessary task of inculcating American ideas in the transitional generation through the medium of a language they understood and trusted. Rejecting the criticism of those Americanized Jews who believed it a danger, he publicly defended the right of the Yiddish press to exist.[54] Marshall felt it was, after all, a "temporary affair," and that the second generation would quickly master English and avoid using the ancestral tongue. At the New York State Constitutional Convention in 1915, he objected to the requirement of a literacy test in English for the right to vote, arguing that there was no reason why English alone should be chosen.[55] Learning of a dissertation on the Yiddish press as an Americanizing agency, Marshall saw that it was published in the *American Jewish Year Book.*

Contrarily, within the Jewish community, Marshall was often bitterly critical of certain aspects of the Yiddish press. He was dismayed by the radicalism of such papers as the *Forward*—their tendencies toward irresponsible yellow journalism, and attacks on uptown Jews. In 1902, he sponsored an abortive attempt to found a high class journal on the East Side comparable to the *New York Times,* one that would be "clean, wholesome, religious in tone; the advocate of all that makes good citizenship, and so far as politics are concerned, absolutely independent" (that is, anti-Tammany).[56] The *Yiddishe Velt* (*Jewish World,* as it was called), soon collapsed, and Marshall continued to criticize the "infinite mischief" performed by some Yiddish journalists:

> They regard themselves as the leaders of public opinion and have only contempt and contumely for those whom they describe as Jehudim. Where unity and harmony should prevail, they sow the seeds

of discord. Where calmness and self-control are required, they froth at the mouth. Where secret councils are indispensable, they demand mass-meetings, Jewish congresses, and loud vociferation. . . . If out of this ruck and bedlam anything can be accomplished for the Jews, it will be in spite of them.[57]

When a plan was broached for the publication of a daily Jewish newspaper in English, Marshall endorsed it, hoping that it would eventually put an end to Yiddish journalism, "a consummation devoutly to be wished."

In the eyes of the German-Jewish Americanizers, the crude religion of the Orthodox newcomers was a great hindrance to rapid absorption as well as a bad reflection on their own middle-class, enlightened religion. The support given by Marshall and such men as Jacob Schiff to Conservative Judaism and the Jewish Theological Seminary was motivated in good measure by their desire to create for the immigrant masses a modernized, Americanized Judaism that would be for them what Reform had been for the older group—a link with the past yet consonant with the present. Being themselves Reform Jews, they recognized the need and desire of the East European Jewish immigrants to retain their traditional faith, but felt that the Seminary, with proper guidance, would imbue that faith with the spirit of America, modernize it, and make it palatable to the Americanized second generation.[58] For these reasons also, Marshall urged the establishment of a model synagogue on the lower East Side which would cast out those practices "uncongenial to a mind influenced by American culture." [59]

The most pressing need of the East Side population was for economic integration, and Marshall knew that successful Americanization largely depended on a higher standard of living. One of the major recommendations of the State Commission on Immigration, of which he had been Chairman, was for the establishment of a Bureau of Industries and Immigration to help regulate economic conditions affecting the newcomers. Headed by Miss Frances A. Kellor, a leader of the Americanization movement, this agency performed an important function. Marshall was instrumental in creating a Legal Aid Bureau within the Educational Alliance to protect East Siders against oppressive speculators, extortion and fraud, as well as to promote arbitration instead of litigation among Jews.

A significant service of Marshall, and one which symbolized his attitude toward the immigrants and his role as a link between the communities, was his mediation in labor disputes involving the Jewish workers of New York. When the great women's clothing strike of 1910 threatened to become prolonged and to create irreparable animosity between the workers (mostly East European Jews), and the owners (some of them German Jews), Marshall, with the backing of Schiff and the cooperation of Louis D. Brandeis, helped settle the dispute through the adoption of the famous Protocol. Marshall personally prepared the final draft of this document which, by establishing a Board of Arbitration and a Joint Board of Sanitary Control, set a precedent for the labor movement. He later served in a similar capacity during other industrial disputes, including the strike of the Amalgamated Clothing Workers in 1919.

Marshall was linked to the East Side through still another medium. This was the Kehillah of New York City, an organization that attempted to unite the entire Jewish community into a federation which could deal authoritatively with problems of common concern. Inspired by New York City Police Commissioner Theodore A. Bingham's charges of Jewish criminality, Marshall's brother-in-law, Dr. Judah L. Magnes, took the lead in summoning East Side delegates to a conference at Clinton Hall in October, 1908, where the foundations were laid for the new communal council. Marshall declined an invitation to attend this conference, but by the time a Constituent Convention met in February, 1909, he had become involved.

Aware of the potential significance of the Kehillah, Marshall agreed that its Executive Committee should constitute the membership for New York City on the Executive Committee of the American Jewish Committee. This, in effect, made the Kehillah the local arm of the American Jewish Committee, a step which, if followed throughout the nation, would have made the Committee a central body speaking for a democratically organized national Jewish community. The Kehillah idea, however, did not spread very far, and even the New York organization was soon beset by ideological disputes and practical problems.

The Kehillah suffered a serious decline after 1918 and came to an end as an organization when Judah Magnes left for Palestine in 1921. Some of its agencies, including the Bureau of Jewish Education, continued to exist. Throughout the life of the Kehillah, Marshall defended it against attacks and pointed especially to its outstanding work in modernizing the curriculums of Jewish schools. Yet, he was concerned about the possibility of hostile criticism of the Kehillah as setting up an *imperium in imperio,* or political self-segregation. He constantly said that the Kehillah was thoroughly American. Explaining to Dr. Solomon Schechter, the most distinguished Jewish scholar and rabbi in New York, why he could not be included in the Executive Committee (because he was not an American citizen), Marshall said that the Jews otherwise would be placed in great peril.

One of the reasons for the demise of the Kehillah was the agitation brought into American-Jewish life by the World War. Questions of relief for the Jews in Europe, Zionism, and the post-war settlement in Eastern Europe dominated Jewish discussions, producing endless wrangling among radicals, nationalists, the Orthodox, and the uptown community. The arguments came to center on the necessity and advisability of calling a democratically elected American Jewish Congress to deal with the war problems. Marshall and the American Jewish Committee would have preferred to act traditionally, utilizing the influence of the small group of conservative leaders both in the United States and abroad to secure a satisfactory post-war settlement based on the emancipation of East European Jewry. The Zionists, however, led by Louis

Brandeis and Stephen Wise, gradually forced the Committee into participating in an American Jewish Congress.

Marshall opposed the Congress idea strongly, for, as he said, "The problems with which we have to deal are of so delicate a nature that the mob cannot grapple with them." [60] At the Congress, however, Marshall agreed to press for national rights for the Jewish minorities in Eastern Europe. Some American Jews and their upper-class counterparts in Western Europe objected to this terminology because it might adversely reflect on the emancipated Jews of the West who claimed to be merely a religious community. But Marshall respected the opinions of the Jewish leaders who knew European conditions best and who saw national rights as the only possible solution.

Marshall participated in the deliberations of the American Jewish Congress because he knew it would proceed with or without him and he wanted to prevent complete Zionist domination. For the same reasons, he went along as a member of the Jewish delegation sent by the Congress to the Paris Peace Conference in 1919. While there, he performed ably as a liaison between Western and Eastern Jewish leaders (he was for a time head of the Comité des Délégations Juives) in negotiations with the assembled diplomats, including Woodrow Wilson, and in the formulation of the minority rights clauses eventually inserted into the Constitutions of the newly created states of Eastern Europe. He regarded these treaties, perhaps immodestly and certainly over-optimistically, as "the most important contribution to human liberty in modern history." [61] Despite his best efforts throughout the 1920's, as head of the American Jewish Committee, to secure enforcement of the treaty clauses, the non-adherence of the East European governments became increasingly obvious.

The internecine quarrels of the war years had emphasized democracy in Jewish life, but the struggle had also involved issues lurking in the background, such as Zionism, and the possibility of a permanent American Jewish Congress. The eventual participation of Marshall in the Congress indicated he could not completely ignore the upsurge of popular sentiment which demanded more aggressive tactics. Still, when Wise and his associates permanently established the American Jewish Congress in 1920, Marshall refused to join. He abhorred mob rule, especially when the mob favored ideologies and leadership that he and his group did not sympathize with.

Marshall's Political Role

Marshall derived much of his importance and prestige from his position as leader of the Jewish community when it was becoming more significant in American politics. It is essential, to further understand his role, to see his place in American politics. Marshall was a staunch, and consistent, Republican, as were most of his contemporaries of German-Jewish middle-class background.[62] He respected and cooperated with such Democrats as Woodrow Wilson, and Alfred E. Smith, and occasionally voted for deserving Democrats, but he rarely swerved from party loyalty. His son recalled that Marshall was silent on his vote only once, in 1904, when Theodore Roosevelt ran against Judge Alton B. Parker. Next to Stephen Wise, Roosevelt—whom he regarded as a dangerous demagogue—was Marshall's chief target for invective, and Judge Parker he regarded as a boob. In the 1912 campaign, when Jacob Schiff deserted Taft to support Wilson, Marshall remained loyal, despite pressure from Schiff.

As a longstanding, dependable, and influential supporter and contributor, Marshall had access to the inner circles of the Republican hierarchy when the party was almost continually entrenched in Washington, D.C. He repeatedly used his high standing in the party to bring pressure on Jewish issues.

Marshall knew his power, as can be seen by a remark he made to President Coolidge's secretary: "I am not a politician, but you are possibly aware that a man's political influence is not to be measured by his blatancy or by his activity in seeking office." [63]

Marshall was equally determined in New York City municipal politics. By being friendly with Sam Koenig and other local Republican leaders, endorsing candidates for election and nomination, participating in intraparty squabbles, working with Republican Congressmen and State legislators, Marshall made his influence felt. He was a bitter foe of Tammany, yet even there his opinion was respected.[64]

Marshall was never interested in holding political office.* The only post that attracted him, and one for which he considered himself qualified, was that of Justice of the United States Supreme Court. When a vacancy on the Court occurred in 1910, Marshall was an active candidate. Jacob Schiff, Judge Mayer Sulzberger, and Col. Isaac Ullman (a power in Connecticut Republican circles), visited President Taft in the White House to urge Marshall's nomination. Taft reportedly replied, "Schiff, if you were President, would you name Sam Untermyer's partner to the Supreme Court?" whereupon Schiff lost his temper and left with the delegation. Taft, anyhow, had already received the acceptance of Charles Evans Hughes. Marshall later partly blamed his failure to receive the nomination on the opposition of Arthur Brisbane and the Hearst forces. After the war, when it was suggested that President Harding might appoint him as Ambassador to Turkey, Marshall rejected the idea with disdain: "I would regard it as a humiliation to have another Jew join the procession of Jewish ambassadors to Turkey. We have had enough of that bird. It might as well be understood that we are not Orientals. . . ." [65]

Marshall recognized the power of Jewish voters, neverthe-

---

* There is no clear explanation for this attitude, but it may be surmised that the hurly-burly of active office-seeking was distasteful to a man with Marshall's sense of dignity.

less he consistently refused to countenance any suggestion
that they voted as a group: "I am utterly opposed to any plan
whereby the Jewish people shall segregate themselves from
the remainder of the citizens of this country for political purposes." [66] Marshall's attitude was in line with the general
opposition to Jewish voting which was prevalent among the
old-time Jewish leadership—men like Oscar Straus and Simon
Wolf.[67] These men strongly believed that a Jewish vote
would not only be undignified and contrary to their view of
Jews as integrated citizens, but, as Marshall wrote, "there are
always two who can play at that game." [68] Jewish bloc voting
could be potentially dangerous by stimulating anti-Jewish
counter voting.

Marshall's ideas on voting were clearly illustrated by his
reaction to a speech of Israel Zangwill's at Carnegie Hall, October 14, 1923. The noted Anglo-American author had included in his remarks the provocative statement:

> If there is no Jewish vote today—and by a Jewish vote, I do not
> mean a vote for Jews—it is a disgrace, not a policy to be commended.
> If Jews will neither use their vote to protect themselves nor to ex-
> press their ethical conceptions, then they do but cumber the
> ground.[69]

Marshall was aghast at this public call for united political action by Jews for Jewish purposes, fearing it would supply fuel
to the anti-Semites. In reply, he issued a statement to the
press repudiating Zangwill's indiscretion and reassuring
Americans that Jews did not desire political self-segregation:
"Our fellow citizens need not fear that Mr. Zangwill's views
on this subject are shared by any appreciable number of the
Jews of the United States." [70]

Zangwill, in turn, rebutted Marshall's argument: "You
have the Ku Klux Klan against you. Have you not the right
to vote against them? Haven't the Jews the right to vote
against Henry Ford if he runs for President?" To this, Marshall optimistically replied,

We Jews are happy here and contented with conditions. We don't care for Ford and the Ku Kluxers. We don't notice them. If we did notice them we would commit a great mistake. We rely on our fellow Americans to protect their honor. We require no Jewish vote for any purpose. . . .[71]

Privately, Marshall termed the Carnegie Hall statement, "a terrible load for us to bear." Zangwill, he contended, misunderstood American conditions and had made his "utterly irresponsible" remarks under the influence of Stephen Wise and purely for the sake of publicity.

Not only did Marshall refuse theoretically to admit the existence of a Jewish vote, he usually declined to participate personally in any public activity that might be construed as such an admission. In 1920 the Republican National Committee asked him to lead a delegation of Jews to Marion, Ohio so Presidential candidate Harding could address them. Marshall refused, calling it an insult to the Jews and to himself. Again, in 1924, he was approached by a U.S. Senator who requested advice on how the Jewish vote could be reached. Marshall angrily replied that it could be done by the same methods that were used with all intelligent American voters.[72] He similarly opposed attempts to influence Jewish voters by references to the number of Jews appointed to public office by a candidate, or by the injection of the charge of anti-Semitism against certain candidates. Jewish political clubs were particularly distasteful to him, for a Jewish citizen could have "no distinctively Jewish interests with respect to matters of government." [73]

Marshall did concede that Jews had a personal interest as citizens in preventing discrimination or intolerance. After the abrogation of the Russo-American treaty of 1832, he warned that if the administration negotiated a new treaty which disregarded Jewish rights, "the Jews would be justified in voting as a man against the party which would be guilty of such an attack upon their citizenship." [74] Similarly, when an editorial containing slurring remarks about Russian Jews appeared in 1908, in the Cincinnati newspaper of Charles P. Taft (brother of the Republican nominee), Marshall openly warned that it would be most inexpedient to provoke the million Jews of New York, most of whom were voters.

Marshall deplored the concept of a Jewish vote; still, he knew there were Jewish voters who might be instructed and advised, and the politicians knew this, also. In 1919, Marshall sent a form letter to Jewish voters, written on reverse sides in English and Yiddish, urging the election of "my partner, Mr. Irwin Untermyer," who was running for Supreme Court Justice on the Democratic ticket. Marshall informed readers of the letter that "party lines should be disregarded in the selection of judicial officers." [75]

A recurring theme in Marshall's political life was a partiality for gentile friends of the Jews. In 1912, Marshall was faced with a choice for Governor of New York State between Oscar Straus and William Sulzer. Straus was his good friend and ally, and Sulzer was the sponsor of the congressional resolution abrogating the Russian treaty. Together with Schiff, Marshall resolved the dilemma by endorsing Sulzer, because it was important to have a non-Jewish champion of Jewish rights in office. Besides, Jews remembered their friends. Marshall wrote to Calvin Coolidge, after the latter had delivered his flattering speech at the Washington Jewish Community Center: "Your words will never be forgotten, because, as I can assure you, the Jews are a grateful people." [76]

Probably Marshall's chief political role was instructor and adviser to Jewish voters in national presidential campaigns, especially during the 1920's. In the post-war campaign of 1920, Marshall originally endorsed Herbert Hoover for the Republican nomination, praising him as "a sound man of affairs" with "transcendent ability." [77] After Harding's nomination, however, Marshall switched and soon was on excellent terms with him. When Harding died, Marshall, "speaking for the Jews of America," as the *New York Times* put it, eulogized the late President in glowing words.[78]

The election of 1924, from the point of view of many

Jewish voters, was notable because of the Ku Klux Klan issue, which all three parties handled gingerly. Marshall firmly believed that the best approach for the Republican Party on the Klan was to ignore it, and he therefore opposed efforts by some Jewish Republicans to insert an anti-Klan plank into the Party's platform. The great schism at the Democratic Convention, however, inevitably raised the Klan issue in the public mind, and Robert M. LaFollette and John W. Davis took strong stands against it.

Marshall then argued that unless Coolidge, whom he supported, took an equally unqualified anti-Klan position, the results in such pivotal states as New York might be affected. He pressed the President and Republican leaders for a "nonmealymouthed" statement which, by establishing unanimity among all candidates on the Klan issue, would take it out of politics. Displeased at Coolidge's silence, he informed the leaders that the statement issued by the President's secretary denying Coolidge's membership or connection with the Klan, was entirely inadequate. In the meantime, considerable dissatisfaction was emerging among some Jewish voters, even those normally Republican. A delegation of Jewish leaders in Chicago pledged support to Davis on the basis of his "brand of Americanism," and Nathan Straus, as well as Herbert Lehman, also backed Davis.

Marshall did his best to counter these trends. Coolidge, he informed his correspondents, was "extremely friendly" to Jews. He condemned a circular issued by the Hebrew American League of New Jersey calling on Jews to vote for Davis because of Coolidge's stand. Finally, Coolidge bestirred himself to appear before the Holy Name Society in Washington and to state his belief in religious toleration, without, however, specifically condemning the Klan. The Republican National Committee also issued an address given by Coolidge in 1918 in which he had stressed the heroic and conspicuous role of Jews in the making of America. Marshall was willing to accept the President's Holy Name Society speech as a sufficient answer to his demands for a statement. Other Jews, however, felt that Coolidge had not come out four square and had contented himself with pious platitudes pleasing neither Jews nor Catholics.

The Republican strategy in 1924, in which Marshall injected a Jewish twist, concentrated on LaFollette rather than Davis.[79] Marshall, despite his opposition to LaFollette's radical ideas, denounced attempts to brand him as a subversive.[80] But when LaFollette appealed strongly for Jewish votes by an unequivocal statement on the Klan and by a promise to use the President's good offices to alleviate anti-Semitism and eliminate the racial element from the immigration laws, Marshall counter-attacked. He publicized the fact that La-Follette had not opposed immigration restriction and had followed the labor line completely. Trying to head off any movement in which LaFollette might pose as a Jewish champion, Marshall announced that LaFollette had presented to Congress and inserted in the record of March 3, 1923, a document called "Justice for Hungary," which made reference to international bankers, Jews, and Rothschild. From the LaFollette camp came cries of outrage. The Northeastern director of his campaign stated that the Wisconsin Senator had presented the document at the request of another Senator, did not know its contents at the time, and had repudiated it as soon as he did. LaFollette himself called Marshall's attack a "last-minute political trick," but Marshall remained unmoved.

The value of Marshall's aid to the Republicans in 1924 is difficult to measure, for the results of the election indicated that they were still unbeatable. Albert Ottinger, who received Marshall's endorsement in his race for Attorney-General of New York, wrote that it had proved very helpful, especially upstate. Marshall's consistent support of Coolidge, in spite of the latter's noncommittal attitude on the Klan, may have caused a certain diminution in his influence, for, as Marshall contemptuously noted, there were "a large number of pin-heads" who now regarded him as more of a Republican than a Jew.

In the 1928 campaign, Marshall gave complete and warm support to the Republican candidate, Herbert Hoover. Knowing that Jewish voters might be influenced in favor of Al Smith as a reaction to the strong prejudice against Smith's religion, Marshall tried to repudiate allegations of Republican bigotry and to eliminate the religious issue from the campaign. He admitted that individual Republicans might be intolerant, but most were not, and Hoover was certainly free of any taint of prejudice. Taking issue with C. L. Sulzberger and others who claimed that bigotry was definitely being used to elect Hoover, Marshall pressed the attack to the other side by retorting that the most bigoted elements were the Southern Democrats. Speaking to large audiences in Boston, Brooklyn, and elsewhere, Marshall lauded Hoover's relief activities after the war, during which Hoover had displayed "supreme indifference to religion." [81]

There were strong indications, nevertheless, that many Jewish voters, following the advice of such leaders as Stephen Wise and Herbert Lehman, favored Smith.[82] A New York Jewish lawyer asked Marshall whether, in endorsing Hoover, he had acted as an individual, or wished the public to believe that he was speaking for American Jewry. When Marshall replied that the questions were insulting, impudent, and stupid, the lawyer instituted a libel suit which was subsequently withdrawn. Another revealing incident centered on an invitation Marshall received to address a nonsectarian meeting in Baltimore. The Republican Speakers' Bureau noted that Marshall's presence was particularly desired "because of the effect among the Jewish people." [83] When Marshall's acceptance became known, a distinguished Baltimore Jewish leader protested that invitations had been sent only to Jews and that the manifest purpose of Marshall's visit was to use his prestige to influence Jewish voters in a political campaign. Marshall was deeply offended and bitterly pointed out that he had always deplored the Jewish vote, had never spoken on a political issue to a specifically Jewish audience, or used arguments directly aimed at Jews. Still, he believed he had the right to express his opinions, and Jews, like others, had the right to listen.

In New York State—where Franklin D. Roosevelt was waging a strong campaign against Albert Ottinger, the Republican nominee for Governor—the religious issue also arose. Supporters of Smith and Roosevelt charged that Ottinger had been nominated as a sop to Jewish voters in order to draw them away from Smith. Marshall, who endorsed Ottinger, rebuked those who made this allegation: "With all your culture," he wrote to the editor of the *Nation,* "you are unable to get away from the atavistic urge which unconsciously causes your mental processes to culminate in the cry of Jew! Jew!" [84] Rumors also circulated on the East Side that Ottinger was not a good Jew, that he attended a Presbyterian Church. Ottinger answered these charges by announcing that he was "brought up in proper surroundings in a kosher home and . . . was bar mitzvah in the Central Synagogue." [85] Roosevelt, apparently concerned about this, sharply attacked religious intolerance: "I hope I do not receive one vote because my opponent, Mr. Ottinger, is a man who believes in a different Church of God." [86] Marshall, of course, consistently defended Ottinger's record and continued to decry the religious issue. But, despite Hoover's victory, Ottinger was defeated.

Marshall's Later Years

In the sense of a consistent, mass vote for one political party, Marshall was undoubtedly correct when he said there was not a Jewish vote. In the broader meaning of the term, however, there were Jews whose votes might be gained by appealing to their Jewish interests. This was quite normal in American politics. During the first two decades of the century, Jewish voters generally leaned slightly towards the Republican Party, but substantial numbers, especially of the newer immigrants, cast their ballots for Democrats, as well as for Socialists and other minor parties.* In the 1920's, especially in New York after the rise of Al Smith, the balance shifted, and Jewish voters tended to favor Democratic candidates. The last years of Marshall's leadership, therefore, represented a transition during which his forthright Republicanism became increasingly unacceptable to the majority of Jews of East European descent who were reaching voting age.[87]

Nevertheless, in an era when national politics was still dominated by the Republican Party, Marshall's dogged adherence to it and its philosophy was symbolic of his brand of Jewish leadership. Marshall worked to establish the image of the Jew as a full American with deep roots integrating him into the community. Emotionally, many men of Marshall's background regarded Republicanism as almost equivalent to real Americanism.

It was inevitable, in a period of mass immigration, that Marshall's leadership, identified more with the opinions of the older, more assimilated Jews, would be challenged. The very qualities of self-assurance and firmness which made him strong also aroused opposition. Marshall, as attorney-general for the Jews, often acted as if he neither needed nor desired any associate counsel. A contemporary observer remarked that he had "a profound disbelief in the principle of collective reasoning." [88] He was usually kindly, yet his friends and family knew him as a man of quick temper whose ability to hurl invective was unmatched when aroused. When a group of Jewish leaders ruffled his composure by adopting what he considered unwise tactics, he confessed he was "mad enough to kick a hole in a stone wall," and this feeling overcame him not infrequently. Stephen Wise and others like him were, naturally, "troublemakers." [89] Yet, as Chaim Weizmann ob-

---

* It should be noted that some Jews of German background, such as Samuel Untermyer, were prominent Democrats before the 1920's.

served, "Of a naturally autocratic habit of mind, firm if not obstinate on occasion, impatient of argument, he was, I felt, a man who, if convinced of the righteousness of a course, would follow it unswervingly."

It was evident that, as the Jewish community matured and new leaders developed, Marshall would face serious challenges. This was clear enough from the controversies during World War I over the American Jewish Congress, and Zionism. In both cases, however, Marshall was sufficiently flexible to work out compromises that maintained his standing. He could not eliminate, despite his efforts, feeling that his leadership was undemocratic, patronizing, and not completely in the interests of the immigrant masses. Marshall strenuously attempted to penetrate the psyche of the East Side but remained beyond and above it.

His leadership, to some people, represented a continuation of the outmoded *Shtadlan* or *Hofjude* approach of medieval and early modern times—a kind of benevolent paternalism exercised by rich and influential Jews who interceded with gentiles on behalf of their brethren. To Yiddish-speaking persons and their Americanized children, Marshall and the American Jewish Committee appeared as a rich elite of elderly wise men who undoubtedly had accomplished great good, but who no longer were as necessary as they had been.

Marshall rejected all such criticisms, terming them a "mass of lies and misrepresentation." Even his opponents recognized and respected his complete sincerity and his faithful, tireless devotion to Jews and Judaism. The well-traveled Chaim Weizmann found that "the most important Jewish groups in every city in America looked to him for the lead in communal matters, and his attitude went a long way, in fact was often decisive, in determining theirs." [90] When Marshall reached his seventieth birthday, congratulatory messages were received from President Coolidge, Governor Smith, and many Jewish and gentile leaders. Benjamin Cardozo saw him as a "great civic institution. . . . I do not know how we should manage without him," while Adolph S. Ochs called him "the foremost leader of American Judaism . . . the American Jew par excellence—spiritually and militantly." [91]

The sincerest tributes were mostly from men like Ochs, whose background and status placed them among the Jewish establishment of the day. They shared with Marshall common beliefs—not always consciously or clearly formulated—about the position of Jews in America, and the nature of Jewish faith and life. Dignified, eloquent, and completely American, Marshall was eminently qualified to be their chief spokesman and defender of the integrity and rights of American Jews.

In this capacity, Marshall adhered to the generally cautious, traditional tactics of Jewish leaders, but his position was strengthened because of America's democratic heritage and the political importance of an increasing Jewish population. Marshall's correspondence, and relationship, with the non-Jewish press and with public officials reflected his firm diplomacy. With fellow Jews, especially trusted friends and relatives, he was usually more frank. With Jewish individuals and groups who competed with him in defending Jews, he was often impatient and harsh.

Non-Jews regarded Louis Marshall as one of the foremost, if not the leading, spokesman for his people, and this, in turn, reinforced his standing and usefulness among Jews. In the 1917–1918 *Jewish Communal Register of New York City,* Marshall's sketch included the encomium, "He is the acknowledged champion of Jewish rights." [92] Jonah J. Goldstein expressed a fairly common Jewish opinion of Marshall's abilities: "When I think of Louis Marshall, I think of Gibraltar." [93]

Chapter three

marshall
and pre-war defense
of jewish rights

Marshall's defense of Jewish rights before America's entry into World War I established his reputation as champion of the Jews. The incidents he was involved in illustrated both the range of problems confronting American Jews and the nature of official Jewry's response. Marshall endeavored, at this time, to counter growing social discrimination, to combat an apparent threat to the full citizenship rights of Jews, to oppose restrictive immigration laws, and to rectify an atavistic, anti-Semitic miscarriage of justice. In these campaigns, Marshall and his associates did not apply uniform, preconceived tactics but varied their responses in relation to each problem. Petitions for redress of grievances, intercession with public officials, judicial and legislative action, mobilization of public opinion, hints of political retribution—all were among the tactics used, with diplomatic moderation usually dominant. Marshall, however, never sacrificed what he regarded as a vital principle affecting the equal rights of the Jews, and, when necessary, diplomacy was abandoned for open pressure.

Social Discrimination

Marshall and his associates, including Jacob Schiff, Adolf Lewisohn, Daniel Guggenheim, Isidor Straus, and Adolph S. Ochs, initiated one of the most aggressive and successful defense actions of 1904. The target was Dr. Melvil Dewey, founder of modern American library science, State Librarian of New York since 1899, and head of the Lake Placid Company. In the latter capacity, Dewey had been responsible for distributing advertising circulars announcing Jews were barred from the Lake Placid Club.[1]

This was intolerable to Marshall and his friends. Social discrimination against Jews by exclusion from summer hotels and clubs was not new, and while resented by most Jews, did not arouse calls for drastic retaliation. In this instance, however, the Jewish leaders saw a high official of the state education system, a public servant cloaked with the dignity of his official rank, engaged in prejudicial activities. As long as Dewey remained in public office, some Jews might suspect the State of New York of being indifferent or hostile to their full integration into American society.

A petition was therefore submitted to the Board of Regents of the State University of New York on December 20, 1904, demanding the dismissal of Dewey as State Librarian. Hinting that what happened today to Jews might happen tomorrow to Catholics or others, the petitioners bluntly stated that the 750,000 Jews of New York deserved to be respected.

Dewey lessened his reputation by adopting a defiant attitude toward the charges. In written and public statements, he explained that the Lake Placid Club's original Board of Trustees had adopted the no-Jews policy and his behavior was merely in accord with that rule. Contrarily, President Nicholas Murray Butler of Columbia University, who had been a member of the Board, denied to Jacob Schiff the existence of such a policy decision. Under continued pressure, the Board of Regents unanimously censured Dewey for his anti-Semitic expressions and behavior; he resigned in February, 1905.

Marshall was exultant: "I have succeeded in getting Dewey's scalp. The result is most gratifying." [2] Ignoring the possible infringement of Dewey's own private rights, Marshall maintained that a most valuable precedent had been set, establishing the principle "that a public officer could not, directly or indirectly, identify himself with any movement that smacked of anti-Semitism." [3] Some Jews, however, regarded the affair with distaste, claiming it would only stir up old prejudices. Marshall adamantly replied that "he who would be free, himself must strike the blow." Turning the other cheek was "an exercise to which we have become accustomed, by the practice of centuries. It has, however, grown somewhat monotonous." [4] Rejecting accusations that the attack on Dewey had political implications, he claimed it would show "the weaklings" in Jewish ranks that the "cowardly Ghetto spirit" must be abandoned, for only those who were willing to fight for their rights were entitled to enjoy them.

The Lake Placid Club retained its anti-Jewish restrictions even after Dewey's resignation as State Librarian, and Marshall subsequently refused all invitations to attend conferences there. Nevertheless, he felt he had proved his point. Public officials could not engage in discriminatory practices, with impunity, even in their private affairs. To some extent, Marshall's success could be attributed to the growing political importance of the Jewish community in New York, a factor which was suggested by the reference to 750,000 Jews in the petition to the Board of Regents.

Marshall's aggressive behavior in the Dewey incident indicated not only that Jewish political influence was rising, but that social discrimination was becoming more vexing to many Jews. Hotel advertisements such as "Hebrews, consumptives or dogs not taken" were growing more annoying as Jews rose in socio-economic status. Because of the successful use of pressure in the Dewey case, Jewish leaders, including Schiff and Marshall, felt the time was ripe for passage of state legislation prohibiting offensive advertising, and the refusal of accommodations for religious reasons. The possibility of getting Congress to prohibit the sending of discriminatory advertising materials through the mails was also considered.[5]

As early as 1907, an amendment to the Civil Rights Law, which would accomplish these ends, was entered into the legislature at Albany and Marshall began to press for its passage. Warning the Republican leaders that the 850,000 Jews in New York were seriously concerned and would resent further non-action, he urged the passage of the proposed legislation so that it might serve as a model for laws in other states.[6]

Several years elapsed before the New York State Legislature succumbed to the arguments of Marshall and his friends. Finally, in 1913, an equal rights statute was passed prohibiting discrimination because of race, creed, or color in any place of public accommodation or amusement, or advertising such discrimination. Hotel men were not overly disturbed. "We never discriminate," smiled one clerk; unwelcome guests were simply told the house was full. Marshall recognized this weakness in the law, but, as in the Dewey affair, he was satisfied that a principle had been affirmed. A law was now on the statute books of the State emphatically declaring that manifestations of social prejudice in public places would not be tolerated; the question of possible evasion was secondary.

Within the Jewish community, however, dissenting voices were heard, challenging on theoretical grounds the justice and wisdom of adopting a legal approach to the solution of problems of discrimination. A Reform rabbi, later to become head of the Hebrew Union College, suggested that the motive for such legislation was, at least in part, the desire of social-climbing Jews to gain entrance to exlusive hotels where they were not wanted. Jews must protect their rights as American citizens, but should not seek punitive legislation in order to settle social problems or root out prejudice. Time and education, he asserted, were better remedies for anti-Semitism than laws. When Marshall threatened to invoke the new law in the case of an offensive magazine advertisement, similar protests were heard.

Marshall agreed that social discrimination was not solved by direct legislative action, but he also felt that an issue of public policy, involving the civil rights of Jews, was at stake. In answer to his critics, he explained that education was admirable, but

> Legislative protection of the rights of citizens, is after all, infinitely more important and effective in its operation upon the present generation. Some of us are getting older and are weak enough to fancy that we have a right to be spared from insult and ignominy, as well as our grandchildren.[7]

Marshall did not believe that the new law encroached on anyone's rights. Basing his argument on the status of hotels as public places, he held that American citizens must be guaranteed the right to dwell in or be received in such places without discrimination. The law, he granted, would not eradicate anti-Semitism. It was meant solely to prohibit open and public insult to the equal rights of minorities.

In following years, Marshall, with the cooperation of the B'nai B'rith and its affiliated Anti-Defamation League, secured the enactment of similar laws in several of the more heavily populated states, including Illinois and Pennsylvania. This early legislation, now almost forgotten, helped establish the legal principles subsequently used in more intensive attempts to fight prejudice.

Russo-American Treaty

Marshall's qualified success in the defense of Jewish rights against social discrimination was surpassed by a dramatic triumph in the campaign for the abrogation of the Russo-American treaty of 1832.[8] This seemingly innocuous commercial treaty had guaranteed the right of individuals from one country to enter and conduct business in the other, "with the same security and protection as natives of the country . . . on condition of their submitting to the laws and ordinances there prevailing." When discrimination against Jews became a fixed part of Russian governmental policy, the Czarist regime began to insist that American Jews entering its territory would be subject to the same restrictions applying to native Russian Jews. Refusing to recognize the right of expatriation, the Russsian government discriminated against Russian-born, naturalized, American-Jewish citizens who returned to Russia on business; expulsion, imprisonment, and refusal of the privilege of acquiring real property resulted. In 1881, Secretary of State James G. Blaine protested, but without avail. By the end of the nineteenth century, the Russian government would not, with some exceptions, issue visas to American Jews, whether naturalized or native.

This was clearly different from the exclusion of Jews from summer resorts. Social anti-Semitism might very well be considered "purely a matter of individual taste, judgment, and predilection," but the construction by the Russian government of its contract with the United States in a manner which placed American Jews in a position of second-class citizenship, could not go unchallenged.[9] The Russian government, however, could defend its stand by interpreting the treaty to mean that American citizens of Jewish faith would be accorded no greater rights than Russian subjects of the same class, or by invoking its doctrine of permanent allegiance, under which American citizens of Russian birth were still regarded as Russian subjects.

It was certainly true that American Jews were not the only ones discriminated against by Russia. British subjects of Jewish faith and other European Jews were also sometimes denied visas. The Czarist government, moreover, claimed that only a tiny number of American Jews who applied for visas were turned down, but this was probably a reflection of the unwillingness of Jews to apply in the first place. In any event, Russia viewed her anti-Jewish policies as essential to her internal security and doggedly refused to alter them.

The point of view of the American Jewish Committee leadership was that the treaty could not properly be an excuse for discrimination against certain American citizens, and that, besides, the American government traditionally upheld the right of expatriation. Congressional resolutions, throughout the 1880's, 1890's, and early 1900's—revealing a growing disenchantment with Czarist autocracy in general, as well as reflecting the increasing political importance of American Jewry—condemned Russia's passport policies.

Marshall at first advised caution on the Russian question. Suggesting in 1903 that it would be unwise to try to force President Theodore Roosevelt into taking a vigorous stand on the treaty, he urged tact, patience, perseverance, and diplomacy. His feelings and those of his associates in the American Jewish Committee changed, however, when the State Department, at first under John Hay, began to display signs of sympathy for the Russian point of view. A directive of May 28, 1907, issued under the aegis of Secretary of State Elihu Root, announced that the State Department "will not issue passports to former Russian subjects or to Jews who intend going into Russian territory, unless it has assurance that the Russian Government will consent to their admission." Marshall and his friends, thoroughly aroused, strongly protested this American capitulation, whereupon Root informed them that the circular would be withdrawn. The State Department's attitude was apparently based on continuing hopes of settling the matter by quiet negotiation and on the opinion of the Department's legal experts that Russia's strict interpretation of the treaty was valid. Foreign affairs specialists felt also that it would be unwise to endanger economic ties for the sake of Jewish visas and that American relations with Russia in the Far and Near East would suffer.

Marshall was unconcerned about such matters. When some Jews expressed doubts to him about his vigorous initiative in responding to Root, he replied that the American-Jewish community had no choice but to officially protest violations of its rights. "I fear," he remarked, "we are getting to be too damned diplomatic." [10] Early in 1908 the President of the American Jewish Committee, Judge Sulzberger, asked President Roosevelt to terminate the treaty in accordance with a provision therein. The best that could be obtained, however, was a Republican Party platform plank pledging equal treatment of all citizens. Working with Oscar Straus, Roosevelt's Secretary of Commerce, Marshall then put pressure on presidential candidate William Howard Taft to secure Jewish support by an explicit statement during the 1908 campaign. Taft succumbed, and, in his campaign speeches, committed the new administration to solve the Russian passport problem.

There was now some hope on the horizon and Marshall angrily rebuked Congressman Henry M. Goldfogle of New York who introduced a resolution on the passport question in January, 1909, warning him that "ill-advised haste will kick over the entire kettle of fish." Nevertheless, no positive action was forthcoming from the Taft administration, and the patience of Marshall and his co-leaders was rapidly exhausted. "I am utterly disgusted," Marshall wrote to Schiff, "with the manner in which we have been treated. . . . We have been so diplomatic as to hide our light under a bushel." [11] Schiff, the most influential figure in the American Jewish Committee, agreed that more decisive action was necessary. The Jewish leaders believed that the passport matter was the only existing instance in which the full citizenship rights of American Jews were impaired. In addition, Schiff hoped that the solution of the passport matter along American principles, by opening a crack in Russia's anti-Jewish wall, might result in the Czarist government adopting more liberal policies towards its own Jews.

The American Jewish Committee decided to abandon its customary restraint in favor of a public campaign of agitation aimed at helping the President make up his mind. Schiff mentioned this plan to the President's Secretary, who did not object. At this point, Marshall assumed the most prominent role in the Committee's efforts and began its campaign by delivering the keynote address at the convention of the Union of American Hebrew Congregations on January 19, 1911.

Explaining that the painfully slow methods of diplomacy had been tried for thirty years and that congressional resolutions and party platforms were ineffective, he called on the President "to abrogate every treaty now existing between the United States and Russia." This would fulfill Taft's campaign promises to make the American passport respected throughout the world. As for possible damage to American trade which might result from the suspension of commercial relations, Marshall argued, "I have a higher opinion of the American people than to believe that they are so destitute of idealism, so devoid of a sense of honor, as to regard a matter of this supreme importance with the eyes and souls of mere shopkeepers." The much publicized historic friendship of Russia for America he dismissed as a fable. Finally, playing down the element of Jewish pressure, he placed particular emphasis on his belief that this was a basic question of American citizenship:

> As a Jew he might look down upon his persecutors with pity and contempt, and suffer in silence as his ancestors did for centuries. But he is now more than a Jew—he is also an American citizen, and the hand that smites him inflicts a stain on his citizenship. It is not the

Jew who is insulted; it is the American people. And the finding of a proper remedy against this degradation is not a Jewish, but an American question.[12]

Reprinted in 35,000 copies and distributed to leaders of government, press, and pulpit, Marshall's speech had immediate repercussions. Deluged with protests, Taft decided to call outstanding Jewish leaders for a conference. Marshall, warning that the Republican Party was likely to lose New York State if it failed to redeem its pledges, looked forward determinedly to concrete action: "The time is past when sweet words will butter our parsnips." [13] On February 15, 1911, Marshall, Schiff, Adolf Kraus of B'nai B'rith, Congressman Goldfogle, and other representatives met with President Taft and Secretary of Commerce, Charles Nagel.

After a pleasant White House luncheon, Taft took from his pocket a prepared statement and read it to his guests. He respected his campaign promises and the importance of upholding national principles, but abrogation of the Russian treaty, he affirmed, would seriously endanger American property without accomplishing anything constructive. Implying he might feel differently if he were Jewish, Taft pointed out that he had to act as President of the whole country.

Marshall and Schiff, recovering from their astonishment, attempted counter-arguments, but the President cut them short, and as a final gesture, gave the delegates an opportunity to read part of a dispatch from Ambassador William W. Rockhill in St. Petersburg, which repeated the standard arguments about loss of trade. There was obviously no further room for discussion. Schiff, furious, was sufficiently incensed to refuse to say goodbye to the President, and on the way out remarked to Marshall, "This means war." [14]

No other course was available to the Jewish leaders but to intensify the public campaign for abrogation of the treaty, to press for adoption of abrogation resolutions in Congress, and, if necessary, to carry the fight into the political conventions of 1912 and the election. Coordinating their activities through a special central committee, the American Jewish

Committee, B'nai B'rith, and the Union of American Hebrew Congregations increased their efforts. A National Citizens Committee, headed by Andrew D. White and William G. McAdoo, was organized and, within a short time, fifteen state legislatures had passed resolutions condemning the Russian treaty. The campaign reached its climax in a mass meeting at Carnegie Hall, on December 6, 1911, addressed by Governor Woodrow Wilson of New Jersey, House Speaker Champ Clark, President Jacob Gould Schurman of Cornell University, and William Randolph Hearst.

Meanwhile, Marshall was pressing the attack through Congress. In addition to personal appearances before the House and Senate Committees on Foreign Affairs, he worked with congressmen who were then introducing abrogation resolutions. In line with his frequent reiteration that the passport problem was an American issue, Marshall preferred to deal with non-Jewish Congressmen, such as Representatives Herbert Parsons, Francis Burton Harrison, and William Sulzer, of New York, rather than through Jewish Congressmen. Congressional Democrats, eagerly making partisan propaganda, attacked the Taft administration for its inaction.

Marshall also made effective use of the argument that Russia was discriminating not only against Jews, but also against Protestant and Catholic clergymen. Early in 1911, Congressman Morris Sheppard of Texas introduced a resolution protesting Russia's exclusion of some Christian missionaries. Together with Oscar Straus, Marshall led a delegation of distinguished Jews in a private hearing on the Russian passport issue before Senators James A. O'Gorman and Elihu Root of New York. O'Gorman agreed with their arguments, but Root remained noncommittal.

As pressure mounted steadily, ex-President Theodore Roosevelt, possibly inspired by Oscar Straus, launched a proposal which threatened to halt the abrogation movement. Roosevelt granted that the Russian treaty ought not to be continued under its present interpretation, but urged that the question be submitted to international arbitration before the final step of abrogation was taken. Marshall immediately announced his opposition to the idea, rejecting Straus's words of caution on the wisdom of attacking the ex-President. Arguing that the rights of American citizens were not arbitrable, that the arbitrators might be prejudiced, and that Russia would probably not adhere to an adverse decision, Marshall privately wrote that he "took no stock in promises that come from St. Petersburg. Everything that emanates from there is a lie." [15] Marshall found the arbitration scheme completely unacceptable and worked, through intermediaries, to convince Roosevelt to reconsider.

Congressional action finally forced the administration's hand; on December 13, 1911, the House passed a joint resolution, introduced by Congressman Sulzer, instructing the President to notify Russia of our intention to abrogate the treaty. The vote, 300-1, demonstrated overwhelming national support for abrogation. Taft did not wait for Senate concurrence and ordered Secretary of State Knox to issue a notice of termination to the Czarist government.

Marshall was overjoyed:

> I feel as though I had won the greatest law suit in which I have ever been engaged, or ever will be engaged. It operates as the removal of the last civil disabilities to which the Jews of this country have been subjected. . . . It is a lesson to all the world, by showing the regard in which Jewish citizens are held by this country.[16]

Cautioning Jews against public celebrations that might give Russia and "Americans of anti-Semitic proclivities" an opportunity for propaganda, he simultaneously shrugged off the alleged possibility that the victory on the passport issue would in itself stimulate anti-Semitism. No one who was not already an anti-Semite would become one because Jews stood up for their rights.

> We will have at last acted the part of men, and will at least have indicated that we no longer possess the cringing Ghetto spirit. . . . We cannot get rid of anti-Semitism merely by speaking with bated breath.

. . . I care not for what the anti-Semites, or the University Club, or the Union League Club, or Columbia University may say, do, or think, so long as I am true to my citizenship and to my manhood.[17]

It was a resounding victory; not only Jacob Schiff, but the entire American Jewish community recognized that Marshall deserved much of the credit. He had conducted an aggressive campaign, shrewdly utilizing the implied political strength of Jewish voters while openly emphasizing the ethical principles involved. Abandoning the soft approach when it proved ineffective, he had fearlessly applied sufficient pressure to achieve his goal. In this success, Marshall was aided by widespread American sentiment that responded adversely to the cumulative record of Czarist atrocities; by the crusading mood of American Progressivism in 1911; by resentment of Russian treatment of Christian missionaries; and by the lack of overriding *raisons d'état,* which were to be prominent in the somewhat analogous case of restrictions by Arab states on American Jews in the 1950's.*

In practical terms the passport victory left much to be desired. In Russia, the abrogation of the treaty was considered an insult and brought on a strong wave of anti-Americanism. The status of Russian Jewry did not improve; American Jews received even less consideration, and trade declined. In the context of America's general foreign relations with Russia, the agitation on Russian-Jewish issues, including pogroms and the passport question, was one of the most important contributions to the decline of traditional "good will" between the two countries.

Marshall nevertheless was convinced that upholding the citizenship rights of Americans was worth these adversities. Planks were placed in the platforms of all three major parties in the 1912 campaign pledging them to work for treaties that did not discriminate against citizens because of race, creed, or previous nativity, and that allowed the right of expatriation.

---

* In the latter case, some important Jewish leaders, while opposing the official policy, hesitated to risk a struggle which might be interpreted as damaging America's foreign relations at a time of great international crisis.

Periodically, American diplomats tried to reverse the Russian treaty decision by negotiating a new treaty that would avoid explicit guarantees of full rights to all American citizens. Taft himself, before leaving office, attempted to arrange a *modus vivendi* with the Russians, but Jewish leaders opposed any pact which did not concede their viewpoint. Implications that the interests of 100,000,000 Americans had been sacrificed for the sake of the Jews, and that great profits awaited the resumption of commerical relations with Russia, infuriated Marshall. He denounced any plan for a commercial treaty with Russia unless it fully guaranteed the rights of all American citizens.[18] During World War I, he opposed American financial aid to Russia as long as it continued its anti-Jewish policies. When Lee, Higginson and Co. launched a loan to the Czarist government in 1916, a letter from Marshall appeared as part of a Hearst editorial opposing it. Marshall agreed with the prophetic warning of the *Evening Journal:* "When the crash comes, those that hold Russian bonds will own interesting souvenirs of their own folly." [19]

Immigration Restriction

Marshall and American-Jewish leadership faced an even more serious issue in the decade before America entered the European War. The movement for immigration restriction was not new but was becoming more influential.[20] As far back as the 1880's, during the anti-Oriental struggle on the West Coast, the idea existed that "there were categories of humanity altogether unfit to become Americans." [21] The notion that American culture was a fixed entity from its beginning and that non-English, or non-Teutonic immigrants were shut off from this culture by their innate nature, and therefore should not be admitted to America, gradually took root in the American mind as the nation passed from the open, agricultural society of the nineteenth century to the conflict-ridden, industrial, urban society of the twentieth. The social insecurity, economic anxiety and aggressive nationalism at the turn of the century were exploited by restrictionists led by the Boston Brahmin-dominated Immigration Restriction League, until an almost irresistible ground swell of anti-immigration sentiment had been created.*

The fears expressed for the preservation of traditional American culture had some factual basis. Between 1901 and 1910, 2,104,209 Italians, 967,263 Jews, and 873,660 Poles came to the United States—the three largest groups of new immigrants.[22] A growing number of Americans of older Anglo-Saxon and Teutonic stocks were influenced by racial propaganda; the hordes of outlandish newcomers seemed not only economically threatening, but socially and culturally undesirable.

Eminent American intellectuals—often of New England background—joined the handful of race-conscious Yankee patricians in urging restriction of immigration as a necessity for avoiding a collapse of American ideals and morals, and for saving the American economy. John R. Commons, Henry Pratt Fairchild, Edward A. Ross, and others argued that the melting pot was not working, could not work, and should not be allowed to work. Ross's book, *The Old World in the New,* revealed its point of view in the blunt chapter headings, such as: "Endless Inflow of Neediest," "Our Standard of Living Crumbles," "Illiteracy," "Overgrowth of Cities," "Pauperism," "Insanity Among the Foreign Born," and "The Loss of Political Like-Mindedness." [23] Racial thinking was apparent from such comments as:

> The blood now being injected into the veins of our people is "subcommon.". . . It is reasonable to expect an early falling off in the

---

* See Barbara Miller Solomon, *Ancestors and Immigrants* (Cambridge, 1956), for a perceptive analysis of the views and influence of the Boston school of immigration restrictionists.

frequency of good looks in the American people. . . . That the Mediterranean peoples are morally below the races of northern Europe is as certain as any social fact.[24]

Attributing many social ills, some temporary and others deep-seated, to the new immigrants, these men wanted immigration to halt so that the nation could catch its breath. The choice between free and restricted immigration, they warned, would determine "the kind of civilization that is to have its home in the United States for coming generations." [25]

American racists and immigration restrictionists rarely singled out the Jews as the exclusive or even the major object of their attacks. Yet, their doctrines were formulated to put an end to all Southern and Eastern European immigration, and the Jews loomed large in their thoughts. Henry Adams, whose thinking anticipated that of other New England Brahmins, vented his anger on the Jew as symbol of the grasping, industrial society he despised. Using social snobbery to resist the advances of upper-class Jews, American patricians also transferred their hatred to the poor immigrant Jew.

According to Edward Ross, Jews rarely participated in basic production, taking to the pack as the Italian to the pick. No one could stop the aggressive Jews who were even crowding the Irish out of political jobs in New York. Prejudice against them was growing, he intimated: "The situation is— honey above, gall beneath." If the Czar sent the rest of his Jews to the United States, it would mean the "rise of a Jewish question here, perhaps riots and anti-Jewish legislation." [26]

Thoroughgoing racists, such as Madison Grant, later added to the condemnation of the Jewish immigrant. The Polish Jew, according to Grant, possessed "dwarf stature, peculiar mentality, and ruthless concentration on self-interest." The melting pot did not change them; it merely mongrelized the nation, for a cross between a European and a Jew was a Jew. Men of the older stocks were being driven off the streets by "swarms" of Polish Jews. "These immigrants adopt the language of the native American; they wear his clothes; they steal his name; and they are beginning to take his women; but they seldom adopt his religion or understand his ideals." [27]

Particularly vexing to the restrictionists was what they termed a Jewish-inspired campaign to keep America's doors open to immigrants. Ross noted that "Hebrew money" was behind the National Liberal Immigration League, and, indeed, some was. Prescott Hall, masterminding the restrictionist campaign from Boston, exploded when President Taft vetoed the literacy test bill in 1913, "To Hell with Jews, Jesuits and Steamships!" [28]

An important restrictionist charge was an alleged increase in the criminality of Jewish immigrants. This received official substantiation when Police Commissioner Theodore A. Bingham of New York, writing in 1908 in the *North American Review,* stated that whereas "Hebrews" were 25 per cent of the city's population, they supplied 50 per cent of the criminals. A wave of indignation swept the Jewish community in response to this allegation. Marshall and other Jewish leaders barely managed to keep their anger in check while presenting contrary evidence to Commissioner Bingham, who thereupon wrote a formal apology in the next issue of the *Review.* Notwithstanding Bingham's retraction, the criminality charge continued to appear in restrictionist propaganda.

Generally, however, anti-Semitism in this period emphasized the private misbehavior of Jews rather than their public crimes. The stereotype of the ignorant and dirty Jewish immigrant—congregating in cities where he performed no useful labor, practiced low business ethics, crowded his way into the professions, and generally behaved in an unassimilable manner—was a useful weapon of immigration restrictionism. Gone were the days when a Judge, Noah Davis, stood before a mass meeting and voiced such sentiments as:

> Let them come! I would to Heaven it were in our power to take the whole three million Jews of Russia. The valley of the Mississippi alone could throw her strong arms around and draw them all to her opulent

bosom, and bless them with homes of comfort, prosperity and happiness.[29]

The established, middle and upper-class, Americanized
Jews had originally viewed the mass East European Jewish
immigration with some trepidation, but the immigration restriction movement, with its anti-Jewish overtones, made it
clear that attacks on Russo-Polish immigrants might involve
their own status and well-being. Responsible Jewish leaders,
with Louis Marshall and the American Jewish Committee at
their head, were convinced that restrictionism, if successful,
might not only represent a possible danger to themselves, but
would also shatter the greatest hope of masses of oppressed,
poverty-stricken European Jews. Appointed by Governor
Charles E. Hughes as Chairman of the New York State Immigration Commission in 1908, Marshall knew and sympathized
with the plight of newly arrived immigrants. He was himself
but one generation removed from immigrant status, and
Schiff had been born in Germany. It was not surprising, therefore, that Jewish leaders were significantly opposed to the restrictionist movement.*

These men, in addition, sincerely believed that any severe
limitation of immigration would injure the whole nation. To
Marshall, the immigrant was the foundation for all the material and moral progress of the United States from its incep-
tion. Contrary to the wails of the restrictionists, immigrants
made excellent citizens; in fact, he claimed, there was more
electoral corruption among native-born elements. Each succeeding immigrant group, he pointed out, had been considered objectionable, and yet, in a generation's time, the children of the immigrants became integral parts of the nation.
Countering the economic arguments in favor of restriction,
he asserted that it was still economically beneficial. Immigrants worked at tasks not ordinarily sought by natives or
older immigrant groups and did not depress wage levels or

* For a comparison with a similar situation in England, see Lloyd P.
Gartner, *The Jewish Immigrant in England, 1870–1914* (Detroit, 1960), pp.
50–55.

damage trade unions—witness the organization of Jewish unions in New York. Ironically, he asked if it were honest to propose measures that would allow immigration from countries whose immigrants no longer wished to come, while those who did want to come would be barred.

Marshall was particularly concerned with the proposal requiring that all immigrants pass a test demonstrating their reading knowledge of some language. This idea, advocated as early as 1887 by Edward W. Bemis, became the chief measure sponsored by the newly formed Immigration Restriction League. For Henry Cabot Lodge, who introduced the plan in Congress in 1891, as well as for its other advocates, the chief purpose of the literacy test was to discriminate against alien races, that is, to keep out undesirable immigrants from the countries of Southern and Eastern Europe, where literacy was low. In its propaganda, however, the League maintained a dignified tone, stressing the importance of literacy in preserving the American character and American citizenship.

The literacy test passed both Houses of Congress in 1896, only to be vetoed by President Grover Cleveland. In 1898, 1902, and 1906, the same measure was re-introduced, but did not succeed because of considerable opposition from big business interests and from immigrant groups. Then, in 1907, a well-financed Immigration Commission was established by Congress, and after three years of work, presented a forty-two volume report.[30] The Commission's most important legislative recommendation, hardly unexpected, was that restriction was needed for economic, moral, and social reasons, and that a reading and writing test would be "the most feasible single method." [31] The suggestion of the American Jewish Committee, and other Jewish organizations, that no changes were necessary in the current immigration laws, other than a few amendments on administrative details, was unheeded.

Marshall and his associates intensified their efforts to prevent the literary test. Seeking to avoid the appearance that the immigration question solely concerned Jews, they co-operated with representatives of Italian and Slavic groups; but the Jews played the most important role. As a reply to the imposing statistics of the Immigration Commission, the Committee privately sponsored the publication of a scholarly treatise by Isaac Hourwich (*Immigration and Labor* [New York, 1912]), which presented an equally impressive argument that immigration had benefited the economy and that restriction was economically unnecessary.

On the surface, the literacy test proposal could be defended as a sound measure insuring the maintenance of America's cultural standards and, in this sense, it may have appealed even to part of the American-Jewish community. Nevertheless, Marshall maintained a running correspondence with Washington officials, and other influential figures, arguing strongly against it. He believed the literacy test would keep out vital unskilled labor groups, but would not exclude a well-educated, violent socialist. He agreed that immigration should be regulated in order to bar criminals, the insane, paupers, and suchlike, but restriction was another matter.

On tactical questions, Marshall was wary of any Jewish action that might add fuel to the restrictionist campaign. He advised against any attempts to secure admission of children of naturalized citizens who had been excluded on physical or mental grounds. Cautioning sponsors of the Jewish National Farm School, he warned against use of scare words on urban Jewish congestion as likely to play into the enemy's hands. He asked the President of the Alliance Israélite Universelle to refrain from assisting any large number of Jews to immigrate to the United States at a time of depression.

The elaboration of racial theories, and an upsurge of nativism in the South and West after 1905, made immigration restriction more likely to succeed. Allowing for the strong possibility the literacy test would finally be passed, Marshall tried to soften its impact on Jewish immigration. Hebrew and Yiddish were recognized by the sponsors of the literacy test as languages, knowledge of which would satisfy the requirements, but this did not solve the problem.* The Immigration Commission's report had revealed that 26 per cent of Jewish immigrants over fourteen years of age could not read or write, a figure only slightly below the average for all immigrants. Marshall estimated that 18 per cent of Russian-Jewish male immigrants and 30 per cent of the female immigrants might be excluded by a literacy test even if Hebrew and Yiddish were included as standard languages. He therefore urged the insertion of a provision in the proposed bill which would exempt from the literacy test those immigrants escaping religious or political persecution. Marshall anticipated that this exclusion would almost nullify the effect of the literacy test on Jewish immigration.

Marshall's precautions were well-founded, for the literacy test recommendation of the Immigration Commission was embodied in the Smith-Burnett Bill and passed by Congress, only to be vetoed by President Taft shortly before he left office in 1913. Two years later, practically the same legislation was passed once again and placed before President Wilson. After hearing three hours of arguments on the bill—Marshall was one of the speakers for the opposition—Wilson vetoed it with a ringing warning of the danger of such a radical departure from the country's traditional policies. The bill passed again in 1917 but was once more vetoed by Wilson. This time, however, the presidential veto was overridden by a substantial vote and the bill finally became law as the Immigration Act of 1917.

Included in the law was a clause exempting aliens from the literacy test who could prove they were fleeing religious persecution. Marshall, and his American Jewish Committee associates, had achieved this limited law, but they had been unable to include political persecution in it.[32] The victory of the restrictionists, and the limited achievement of Marshall,

---

* Marshall asserted that the recognition of Hebrew and Yiddish as languages for purposes of the literacy test was not the result of Jewish pressure, but was done by the sponsors of the legislation themselves. It may, however, have been meant to allay Jewish resistance.

were largely meaningless, for the war effectively precluded the possibility of mass immigration. The law, however, was symbolic of a major change in American history and paved the way for stricter post-war immigration legislation.

The war helped in securing the final passage of the literacy test in 1917, yet Marshall placed most of the blame on labor and the South. Organized labor, represented by the American Federation of Labor, had endorsed the literacy test as far back as 1897 and was strongly behind restriction after 1905. Ironically, it was Samuel Gompers—the son of Jewish immigrants, and an immigrant himself—who led labor in its campaign for immigration restriction. The A.F. of L. took this position ostensibly on economic grounds, to prevent lowering of standards by big business use of unskilled immigrant labor, but there are indications that racial snobbery may also have influenced Gompers's attitude. Marshall (who, incidentally, strongly resembled Gompers in physical appearance) actively opposed the creation of a separate Department of Labor, principally because immigration would be transferred from the Commerce Department to the control of a possibly hostile Secretary of Labor. All his efforts to obtain a veto by President Taft of the Labor Department law were unsuccessful.

Marshall held the South responsible even more than labor for the rising strength of restrictionism. When the New South ideology was at its height, immigration to the South was considered desirable to stimulate industry and the economy. The rhetoric of this period found its way into such documents as the Alabama State Constitution, which Marshall liked to quote to the effect "that immigration shall be encouraged. . . ." [33] But Southern immigration promotion was never more than superficial and passing in a section that remained basically xenophobic and racist. The revival of Anglo-Saxon nationalism during the imperialistic turn of the century, and the gradual realization that native poor white sources of labor would satisfy all of the South's demands, demolished any existing sympathy for European immigration. During a visit to his home town of Van Buren, Arkansas, in 1911, Cyrus Adler was shocked to hear anti-Semitic talk among the residents. They did not want to live with any Jews or Italians: "We have one race question in Arkansas and that is all we can stand." [34]

After 1910, it was obvious to Marshall that the South was solidly for restriction. He referred to the Burnett bill as "purely a Southern Democratic measure." [35] Still, Marshall rejected a suggestion that the American Jewish Committee participate in defeating Congressman Burnett for reelection: "It would be a great mistake, would be misinterpreted, and would in the end react most seriously. . . . For us to invade Alabama . . . seems to me the height of audacity." [36]

The immigration restriction movement, especially after the realignment of the South, might have resulted in even speedier enactment of legislation had it not been for the opposition of certain business groups (that still felt a need for cheap immigrant labor), and, most important, immigrants themselves. The effectiveness of immigrant opposition was largely based on recognition by the major parties of the growing importance of foreign-born voters, particularly in large, pivotal states. The official Republican Party platform, that previously included the literacy test proposal, omitted it from 1904 to 1912. When the B'nai B'rith held its 1910 convention in Washington, President Taft, Speaker Joe Cannon (who had fought the literacy test), and a galaxy of other political guests attended. Taft, flattering his audience, commented, "You represent the oldest race in the world—the race that is entitled to be the aristocrats of the world, and yet who make the best Republicans. . . ." [37] Marshall was well aware of this and often used political pressure in his skirmishes for Jewish rights.

Marshall and his associates could not prevent the adoption of the first major legislation restricting the right of entry to the United States, but their struggle had been well-conducted and substantially helped delay that adoption until 1917. Marshall exaggerated somewhat when he claimed, "We have, practically single-handed, fought the battle of all immigrants, irrespective of creed or nationality," yet his activities as a leader of the American Jewish Committee were of great importance in the fight against immigration restriction.[38]

Leo Frank Case

"At 3:30 on the morning of April 27, 1913, the body of Mary Phagan, a fourteen year old girl, was discovered in the basement of an Atlanta pencil factory. She had been horribly murdered." [39] Thus began the classic case of Leo Frank that ended two years later in his equally horrible lynching near Mary Phagan's home town, Marietta, Georgia. A high point of pre-war nativism, this incident involved economic resentment, frustrated progressivism, and race consciousness. Dramatically demonstrating the smoldering resentments that could be aroused here in America, it marked a transition to a new kind of anti-Semitism.

The state of Georgia had a Jewish population of about 20,000, less than 1 per cent of the total. Still, this was considerably higher than the percentage of Jews in some of the neighboring states, and every Georgia town had its familiar Jew store. The Atlanta Jewish community, consisting of several thousand, was quite prosperous and felt comfortably integrated, despite social segregation. One of its rising young men was twenty-nine year old Leo Frank, a graduate of Cornell University who had settled in Atlanta five years before as manager of a pencil factory established by his uncle. Intelligent and ambitious, if somewhat reserved and nervous, Frank had recently been elected president of the local chapter of B'nai B'rith. All seemed well, when suddenly he was taken into custody by the police and charged with the murder of one of his employees.

Under different circumstances, Frank might never have been charged with the crime, much less convicted, but in the Georgia of 1913–1915, a combination of factors sealed his doom. The city administration and police department, faced with a rising tide of public criticism due to corruption and the failure to solve a number of previous murders, seized upon Frank; after committing themselves to his guilt, they could not reverse themselves and resorted to the collection of dubious evidence. The Phagan murder came also when the Atlanta press was locked in a vicious circulation war, promoted by a newly acquired Hearst paper. For months, the Atlanta newspapers sensationally exploited the Frank case, rousing public opinion to a fever pitch. Rumors that Frank was a sexual degenerate and had acted in accordance with the tenets of the Jewish faith, which supposedly condoned the violation of Christian women, were widely believed.[40] Frank was also an ideal culprit, for he was not only an alleged pervert, but a Jew, a Northerner, and an employer of cheap, Southern, female labor. The *New York Times*, pointing to the "many esteemed citizens of Atlanta" who were Jewish, editorially stated that racial prejudice was only an "incidental feature" of the case; most observers disputed this: "It is ridiculous to protest that there has been no prejudice against 'the Jew' in this Frank case. The whole atmosphere reeks with it." [41] In Louis Marshall's understatement, the "fact he was a Northern Jew did not help."

Frank's trial, held before Judge L. S. Roan in Atlanta during the summer of 1913, demonstrated the influence of mob psychology. Solicitor-General Hugh M. Dorsey made the most of incriminating, but basically circumstantial, evidence, and relied heavily on the testimony of a Negro ex-convict, Conley, to implicate Frank. Although it was apparent to outsiders that Conley was perjuring himself, the prosecution did not abandon its case, with the unusual result that the word of a Negro was taken as truth against that of a white man. A poor Negro would not suffice as a victim when a more substantial, yet still vulnerable, one was available. On the final day of the trial, the jury deliberated to the accompaniment of a mob outside screaming for Frank's conviction. The judge, fearful of violence if Frank was acquitted, advised the defendant and his lawyers to retire without waiting to hear the verdict. In the absence of Frank and his counsel, the jury returned and declared Frank guilty. An appeal to the Supreme Court of Georgia was turned down in February, 1914, by a 4-2 decision based on technical grounds.

Throughout the proceedings, Frank did not lack for defenders. Not only did he have good lawyers, but his relatives and supporters spent freely, hiring private detectives, including William J. Burns, to locate information damaging to the state's case. A good deal was turned up, including material implicating Conley, but still the Georgia courts refused to grant a new trial. The expenditure of large sums, rumored to have been sent from the North, and the importation of the disliked Burns had the negative result of further antagonizing Georgia public opinion, especially among the poorer whites and the working class. It was generally believed, for example, that Nathan Straus had brought a $40,000 fund into Georgia in an attempt to buy up the state's Supreme Court.

Marshall followed the Frank case closely and was aware of its dangerous overtones. He refused, however, to see it as exclusively Jewish, and the American Jewish Committee decided to take no official action on it. Believing the case to be basically a police frame-up, forced by a yellow press, Marshall wrote to Judge Irving Lehman, ". . . it would be most unfortunate if anything were done in this case from the standpoint of the Jews. Whatever is done must be done as a matter of justice, and any action that is taken should emanate from non-Jewish sources." [42] He urged Jewish leaders not to promote public campaigns on behalf of Frank, for this was a "delicate matter" which had to be handled in a "quiet, unobtrusive manner." Any criticism from Northern quarters, Marshall warned, would be resented fiercely by the sensitive Georgians. The best technique would be to work through native Georgian non-Jews. Marshall therefore advised Jews to avoid protest meetings and similar tactics, and, in general, to "suppress themselves."

Marshall privately viewed the Frank affair as "almost a second Dreyfus case." He offered legal counsel to Frank's lawyers during their appeals, raised substantial sums among his New York friends for their expenses, appealed to eminent Southerners to create a better climate of public opinion, and maneuvered to influence the press within Georgia. All these measures unavailing, Marshall joined Frank's legal staff, gratuitously, and initiated an appeal to the Federal Supreme Court. Arguing that the Frank trial was permitted by the court to degenerate into a judicial lynching, and that the defendant and his counsel had been absent during the reading of the verdict, Marshall called for a writ of habeas corpus and a new trial. The Court, however, with Justices Charles E. Hughes and Oliver W. Holmes dissenting, rendered a long and highly technical decision denying Marshall's plea.[43]

Even before the failure of the final appeal, national interest in the Frank case was high, with almost unanimous sentiment in favor of a new trial. Frank partisans included such diverse figures as Eugene Debs, Billy Sunday, Jane Addams, and Senator William E. Borah. The state legislatures and governors of a dozen states, including Texas and Tennessee, appealed on behalf of Frank. Northern newspapers and magazines reported the story of Frank fully and sometimes sympathetically. Georgia was not slow in reacting to these challenges from outsiders. When the *Atlanta Journal* on March 10, 1914, timidly suggested that Frank be given a retrial, its voice was drowned by an outburst of vituperation emanating from the master politician of the state, Tom Watson, who sensed that most Georgians would agree that Northern interference was responsible for pro-Frank sentiments.[44]

Watson, who had previously adopted anti-Catholicism, now added anti-Semitism to his arsenal. His organ, *The Jeffersonian,* indulged in an orgy of sensationalism for over a year, whipping its readers into a highly emotional state. Referring to a "gigantic conspiracy of Big money" and to Frank as "a Jewish libertine" and "lascivious pervert," Watson played on Southern chivalry, race prejudice, state pride, and class consciousness: [45]

> Our little girl—*ours* by the eternal God! has been pursued to a hideous death and bloody grave by this filthy perverted Jew of New York. . . . It was determined by the rich Jews that no aristocrat of their race should die for the death of a working-class Gentile. . . . How much longer is the innocent blood of little Mary Phagan to cry in vain to Heaven for vengeance? . . . RISE! PEOPLE OF GEORGIA! [46]

It seemed that Watson had struck a rich vein, for the circulation of *The Jeffersonian* rose sharply, from 25,000 at the start of his crusade, to 87,000 at the time of Frank's lynching. Efforts of the American Jewish Committee to silence Watson's journal by barring it from the mails were unsuccessful.

After the refusal of the U.S. Supreme Court to grant a new trial, the only hope of the Frank forces was a commutation of the death penalty by Georgia Governor, John M. Slaton. Slaton's term of office was due to end shortly before the scheduled execution of Frank and intense pressure was put on him. Marshall, working vigorously together with Jacob Schiff, used his influence discreetly, interceding through prominent non-Jewish Southerners. At the same time, mass meetings were held by local groups in Northern cities, a Frank Committee in Chicago sent a petition with 415,000 signatures to Governor Slaton, and leading figures from the North sent messages urging clemency.

In Georgia, an Atlanta ministers' group appealed for commutation and the Governor later revealed that he had received 10,000 letters from Georgians alone asking for mercy. Tom Watson, on the other hand, intensified his campaign and sent an emissary to Slaton promising a Senatorship if Frank were allowed to hang. Slaton's answer came on June 21, 1915, when he courageously announced that he was commuting Frank's sentence to life imprisonment.

Marshall immediately sent Slaton a letter of thanks: "You have earned the eternal gratitude of the good people of Georgia and the admiration of every lover of justice in America." [47] At that moment, 10,000 of the people of Georgia were marching on the Governor's mansion that was ringed by soldiers protecting Slaton from the infuriated mob. Respectable opinion in Georgia upheld the Governor, but Tom Watson, and those for whom he spoke, felt bitter and betrayed. Anti-Semitic feelings came out into the open as threats of boycott were received by Marietta Jews, many of whom were asked to leave town. Thousands of cards were distributed in downtown Atlanta: "Can't you buy clothing from an American? Can't you buy shoes from an American? . . . American Gentiles, it is up to you." Slaton was hanged in effigy in many Georgia towns, and the placard on the Marietta effigy bore the inscription, "John M. Slaton, King of the Jews and Traitor Governor of Georgia." [48]

On the night of August 16, 1915, Frank was kidnapped from the State Prison Farm at Milledgeville, Georgia—where he had been sent for safekeeping—by twenty-five armed, masked men. At that time, Frank had not yet fully recovered from a near-fatal wound inflicted by a crazed fellow prisoner. The following day, his lynched body was found near Marietta, where it was taken from the crowd and shipped to his parents in Brooklyn.[49] The killing, C. Vann Woodward noted, "for audacity and efficiency . . . was unparalleled in Southern history." [50] Protests poured forth from the North, and Marshall announced that Tom Watson was "the murderer of Frank." He called on Georgia to apprehend the lynchers and, if that could not be done, to indict Watson for murder in the first degree.[51]

There was little chance that the lynchers would be caught, much less punished, for the crime was generally approved by the populace. An observer reported seeing intelligent Atlantans, after the Frank lynching, "fight their way to newsboys and pay from twenty-five to fifty cents a copy" for *The Jeffersonian*. That journal defended the lynchers:

The next Leo Frank case in Georgia will never reach the Courthouse. THE NEXT JEW WHO DOES WHAT FRANK DID, IS GOING TO GET EXACTLY THE SAME THING THAT WE GIVE TO NEGRO RAPISTS. . . . The voice of the people is the voice of God.[52]

Marshall called on the federal government to stop Watson, but when Attorney-General Thomas Gregory planned to initiate prosecution, he was dissuaded by Georgia political leaders. Solicitor-General Dorsey, Frank's prosecutor, was elected Governor of Georgia in 1916, running under Watson's tutelage. During his primary campaign, Dorsey kept the Frank issue alive, attacking Slaton and charging that the Jews of the United States, headed by Marshall, had raised a large fund for the purpose of defeating him. Of the Jews, Dorsey remarked, "The attitude of that race in the Frank case and in every criminal case in which a Hebrew is the defendant has demonstrated the fact that the successful prosecution of a Hebrew is regarded by the members of that race as persecution." [53] Marshall, of course, immediately issued a blanket denial of Dorsey's insinuations. It was apparent, however, from Dorsey's behavior that the impression made by the Frank case lingered in some Southern minds.*

The Frank atrocity indicated to Jews in the United States that they were far from secure in the New World. Mendel Beilis, the victim of a determined Czarist ritual murder frame-up, had finally been acquitted in Russia, but Frank had been convicted and lynched in America. As one rabbi dolefully remarked, "It only shows that the Jew is born to suffer." [54]

Marshall's intervention in the case was discreet and without propagandistic emphasis on its Jewish aspects, although he was fully aware of them. Even after the lynching, he tried to avoid publicity by urging the family to conduct a quiet funeral without any demonstrations by the Jews of Brooklyn.

* C. Vann Woodward has noted the coincidence of the lynching of Leo Frank and the inauguration of the modern Ku Klux Klan at a ceremony on Stone Mountain, ten miles from Atlanta (Woodward, *op. cit.*, pp. 449–50).

The strategy of Marshall and his associates, combining legal efforts and behind-the-scenes pressure, almost averted the final tragedy, only to be frustrated by the failure to suppress Tom Watson or to calm the outraged instincts of the plain people of Georgia whom Watson represented.

The Frank case was a violent outburst of mass emotion in which anti-Jewish feeling had a prominent part, especially in its later stages. It exposed the hatred and passion that could be aroused in the American population. It did not, in itself, have immediate, national consequences, but it was more than an isolated, local episode. When Tom Watson thundered:

> From all over the world, the Children of Israel are flocking to this country, and plans are on foot to move them from Europe en masse . . . to empty upon our shores the very scum and dregs of the Parasite Race.[55]

he mirrored, in exaggerated form, the pure, unthinking nativism that possessed many Americans and contributed to the successful immigration restriction movement.

When Marshall and the American Jewish Committee led the triumphant fight for the abrogation of the Russian treaty, they eliminated an official, if unintentional, form of discrimination against the equal citizenship of American Jews. Although foreign policy considerations slowed the process, this success was achieved fairly easily because it was in harmony with American traditions and popular sentiment, and it did not seriously harm any substantial domestic interests. On the other hand, the battle against immigration restriction was less successful because large numbers of Americans, for prejudicial or economic reasons, were prepared to reverse long-standing American policies.

Marshall and his associates had demonstrated by 1917 that a new, vigorous sense of power existed in the American-Jewish community. Issues affecting its status had been met with dignity. Caution predominated in the Frank case, where one individual was immediately at stake; in the struggle against immigration restriction, diplomatic argument was joined with political pressure; in the Dewey affair, involving a public official in a state where Jews were numerous, a more aggressive stand was taken; in the Russian treaty episode, where Jewish leaders felt that an important and unchallengeable civic right was affected, caution was abandoned for outright pressure-group tactics.

Marshall still spoke primarily for the prestigious, economically powerful American Jewish Committee, but in the relative absence of outstanding leaders from the newer immigrants, he spoke for them as well. He attained considerable stature from his pre-World War I campaigns and, when problems facing the Jews of America intensified during the war and post-war years, the experienced Marshall was to speak with assurance in their name.

Chapter Four

anti-semitism:
the
war
years

The anti-Jewish feeling that emerged in America during the last decades of the nineteenth century had developed by World War I into observable, if not alarming, symptoms of hostility and exclusion that affected both the older and newer Jewish community. This embryonic pattern was solidified and broadened during the war years and the immediate post-war era. The primary manifestations of anti-Semitism before the War were genteel, social discrimination and certain unpleasant implications in immigration restriction; however, the war years saw the growth of a more rigid social anti-Semitism, the beginnings of damaging economic discrimination, and most seriously, the propagation of the international banker-Bolshevik stereotype. Outright governmental anti-Semitism and pogroms remained taboo in America, but the increasing agitation of the Jewish question did have immediate results and laid the foundations for the ominous anti-Semitism of the 1930's.

This upsurge of anti-Jewish feeling and expression was related to disturbances within the structure of the American economy, society, and psychology. During this period, there

was a recognizable loss of confidence, by many of the population, in some of the traditional American ideals. The arti-
ficially stimulated unity of the war years cracked under the
impact of post-war disillusionment, and a sense of imminent
danger from internal and external subversive forces seized
the nation. The old way of life appeared to be disappearing
under the onslaught of the foreign-born, the city, the new
moral relativism, and liberal religion. Faced with post-war
deflation and depression, the decline of farm prices, the
sharpening of the labor-management clash, and the success of
the Bolshevik Revolution, many Americans adopted ideologies fiercely resistant to change; they stressed a coercive political and religious fundamentalism and sought satisfactory
scapegoats for the ills, real and imaginary, that beset them.
Isolationism, immigration restriction, high tariffs, the Ku
Klux Klan, prohibition, and anti-Semitism—all were part of
this reaction.[1]

While anti-Jewish social discrimination increased among
the urban middle class during these years (due in part to the
rapid upward mobility of Jews), far more disturbing was the
anti-Semitic nativism that saw the Jews as an alien, conspiratorial, sinister race, desiring and wielding inordinate power
over real Americans. This theme, major in European anti-
Semitism, crystallized in the international Jew-banker-Bol-
shevik motif, and became a staple of American nativism. It
added fuel to social discrimination and was itself reinforced
by racism which—although men like Marshall regarded it as
"unmitigated humbug"—was widely accepted in respectable
American society.

American conditions may have produced the need for
anti-Semitism, but the Jews and their alleged misbehavior
provided the rationalizations. For example, the presence in
the great Eastern cities of large masses of partially assimilated
Jews continued to arouse feelings of antipathy. A native,
Anglo-Saxon Protestant recalled the Jewish community of
Dorchester, in Boston, during the 1920's: "To walk along
Blue Hill Avenue always seemed to me like paying a visit to a

foreign country." [2] Jewish success in business or in education did not remove the stigma:

> All down the ages it has been the same; first the three thousand ducats and then the pound of flesh. The centuries are resonant with the outraged cries of the Gentile as he finds himself outmaneuvered by the Jew.[3]

> We hated the Jews because they worked so hard, because they were so relentlessly competitive, because their one thought was to force themselves ahead, to win the prizes at the year's end, to get top College Board marks and then admission into Harvard.[4]

> A greater percentage of Jews than of other races are over-boastful, over-loud, aggressive, sordid, lacking in consideration for others, and without the finer graces. . . .[5]

> Jews virtually control certain businesses—for example, the clothing trade, the theatre, and the department store. . . . Thoughtful Jews have no defense for the condition in which the theatre finds itself today; the drama gone, driven out by salacious and gaudy spectacle; the moving picture keeping just within the law. . . . In too many cases, when Jews control an industry, they do not improve it; they merely make it more lucrative.[6]

It seemed, as one observer noted, that "the very rapidity with which the Jew adjusts himself to the primary conditions of life in America is his chief handicap."

Jews accepting what America had to offer, while at the same time maintaining their cultural identity, led to reiteration of charges of racial solidarity and obstinate hatred of all others. The existence of Jewish Zionists, Socialists, and Bolsheviks was used as an argument to prove this allegation:

> . . . the Jew is restless, and by nature detached from most nationalistic interests because of his sense of racial solidarity that militates against his taking deep root in any community.[7]

> In habit, custom, and social life they choose to remain apart from the mass, and then complain that they are unwelcome, forgetting that exclusiveness is all their own. . . . Invited in, they do not melt, but mass.[8]

> The New York Times is an organ of Jewish propaganda. A Gentile cannot advertise in that paper his desire for a servant of Gentile or-

igin, nor can a word be said in that journal that is disparaging to the Hebrew race. How absurd is this; and how naturally it antagonizes the Gentile and seems to point to a cabal bent upon controlling society.[9]

As a solution for the Jewish problem, critics advised the Jews to exercise extreme caution in their demands, to avoid politics, to remember that they were living in a hostile land, and, in general, to practice a standard of behavior higher than that demanded of their neighbors. "This is the fundamental fact of Jewish life. . . . What is forgiven to others will not be forgiven to Jews." [10]

Few Americans confessed to being anti-Semites, even when expressing anti-Jewish sentiments. The plea of the English anti-Semitic author, Hilaire Belloc, that Jews and gentiles agree on a policy of mutual segregation, was never widely accepted in the United States.[11] Responsible Americans agreed that anti-Semitism was an infantile sickness and a monstrous survival of the past. Nevertheless, the agitation of the Jewish question could not be dismissed as insignificant. Marshall felt distaste at "this constant discussion of the Jew as though he were a corpse upon a dissecting table or a pathological specimen," but he knew it was aroused by pressing issues that could not escape the serious concern of the Jewish community.

Americanism during World War I

The stage was set for anti-Semitism during the 1920's by the impact of World War I on the attitudes and behavior of most Americans. The war brought a new wave of nativism and gave it a nationalistic tinge that had profound implications. The preparedness campaign, anti-hyphenism, the metamorphosis of Americanization from social welfare to social solidarity—all indicated the United States was entering a period of unprecedented emphasis on national conformity, from which dissent would be unwelcome.

The one hundred per cent Americanism of the war years, enforced through state action and private vigilance, provided not only an impetus to the 1917 Immigration Act, but to the more severe post-war legislation. National differences and Old World ties, now in the foreground, created fear of disunity and demands for compulsory unity. At the expense of certain ethnic groups and political dissidents, a sense of national unity was indeed achieved. During America's participation in the war, incidents of anti-Semitism were sporadic and apparently unrelated. Nevertheless, a momentous shift was occurring in the mood of the American people, and Jews were not immune to the dangers implicit in this change.

From the very beginning of the war, the great majority of American Jews, especially those of recent East European origin, favored the Central Powers. This pro-Germanism was a result of the deep hatred of Czarist Russia, and the faith in Germany as progressive and culturally advanced. As the *Jewish Daily News*, August 12, 1914, put it, "The Jews support Germany because Russia bathes in Jewish blood." Top level American Jewish leaders, however, were not quite so unanimous. Jacob Schiff freely admitted he was a German sympathizer and a good friend of the German Ambassador, but most of his colleagues in the American Jewish Committee favored the neutrality that the Wilson administration at first fostered.

Marshall, while admitting that "Russia is the enemy of civilization, the foe of the Jew," felt that American Jews should be absolutely neutral.[12] One of the arguments he used against the calling of a wartime American Jewish Congress was that it would inevitably be critical of Russian policies, and it might react adversely on the Jewish citizens of the Entente powers. In his heart, however, Marshall was strongly pro-Ally from the day Germany declared war. The unfortunate experiences of his parents in Germany, and his admiration of the English and French governments, made him hope for a German defeat.

The old-line Jewish leaders privately agreed with Marshall. As the war progressed and the United States began to commit itself to the Allied cause, the pro-Germanism of the Jewish masses became embarrassing. Men such as Oscar Straus were at pains to prove that American Jews were really pro-Ally. The Russian Revolution and the formation of a liberal government in St. Petersburg was hailed with joy by American Jewish leaders, not only because it promised a new era for Russian Jews, but because it transformed American-Jewish public opinion. When the United States entered the war in April, 1917, there was no longer any question as to the reaction of American Jews; this was reinforced in November, 1917 by Britain's issuance of the Balfour Declaration.

On New York's lower East Side, editors and publishers of Yiddish newspapers formed the Jewish League of American Patriots to aid recruiting of Jews for the armed forces. Jacob Schiff, by now a staunch supporter of the Allies, opposed this "grouping of Americans into separate nationalities." Marshall and the American Jewish Committee felt it advisable to adopt a special resolution pledging their loyalty, lives, and possessions in the great struggle for humanity and liberty. A *New York Times* reporter observed that "the reading of the resolution brought the assembled delegates to their feet in a great outburst of patriotism." [13] When the United States officially declared war on Austria-Hungary, the Directors of the Federation of Galician and Bukovinian Jews sent a statement of loyalty to President Wilson, through Louis Marshall.

Jewish leaders plunged into patriotic activities with enthusiasm. Marshall served uner Charles E. Hughes as a member of the New York District Draft Appeals Board, devoting most of his time for the duration of the war. Realizing the traditional antipathy of East European Jews to the draft, Marshall and others spoke to large Jewish audiences, urging registration and compliance as a patriotic duty. When a member of a Brooklyn draft board publicly remarked that the third great event in a Jewish boy's life, after circumcision and confirmation, was exemption, he was dismissed from his post. A New York street-corner agitator who provoked riots by inveighing against Jewish socialists and slackers, was sentenced to thirty days in the workhouse after Marshall's intervention.

Publicly avoiding controversy, Marshall did his best to restrain Jewish association with radicals and pacifists who persisted in opposing the war. Marshall wrote to his brother-in-law, Dr. Judah Magnes, urging him not to participate in a protest rally with such people as Scott Nearing and Emma Goldman. This was, to Marshall, a "defensive war," and talk of Wall Street instigation was mere "claptrap." [14] Anything that might be used to justify a charge of disloyalty against Jews was potentially explosive. Long after the war ended, Marshall was still writing, "We must be extremely cautious lest we might be charged, even unjustly, with the taint of Germanism." [15] At the same time, Marshall openly upheld the right of free criticism, even in wartime, as a safeguard against government absolutism.

The administration and the nation at large, however, were increasingly intolerant of criticism. Particularly suspect was the immigrant press, part of which was not wholeheartedly for the war. Word reached Marshall in 1917 that the *Forward,* the leading leftist Jewish newspaper, might be excluded from the mails. Wishing both to protect the paper and prevent a slur on Jewish loyalty, Marshall obtained a pledge from Abraham Cahan, the *Forward's* publisher, that his newspaper loyally supported the war effort. With this, Marshall went to Washington and gave his personal guarantee to Postmaster-General A. S. Burleson that he would read the *Forward* regularly and report to the government anything which seemed unpatriotic. This promise to act as quasi-official censor was accepted, and Marshall thus helped to prevent possible government action against the Yiddish newspaper. In his wartime reports to the government and in later comments, Marshall proudly pointed to the "burning patriotism" of the Yiddish press.

The hysteria bred by anti-hyphenism and anti-Germanism affected not only the foreign language press but threatened to spread to any form of non-American expression. In May, 1918, Governor W. L. Harding of Iowa issued a proclamation outlawing the use of languages, other than English, in all public and parochial education, conversation in public places, and religious services. This decree would have been impossible to enforce, but to Marshall it was a serious ideological issue. He objected vigorously to the Governor, emphasizing that such chauvinistic action was beyond his constitutional power and that it contradicted the fact that Americanism was "not the product of one but of many civilizations, not of one but of many traditions." [16] Governor Harding, under pressure from others as well as from Marshall, finally admitted that his proclamation was merely a request, not an order.

Marshall was aware that many Americans shared Governor Harding's view and he therefore handled this problem carefully. When a Yiddish newspaper condemned the Jewish Welfare Board for sponsoring entertainment in English rather than Yiddish for immigrant Jewish soldiers, Marshall was alarmed that such remarks might lead to the outlawing of Yiddish journals. His sensitivity was not unwarranted, for the clamor over foreign languages persisted even after the war. In 1919, the legislature of South Dakota considered a bill to prohibit religious teaching in languages other than English, and again Marshall protested, expressing shock that the nation had reached the point when "a man can be suspected of treason, sedition, or disloyalty . . . because he prays to God in a language other than English." [17] The following year, a bill was introduced in Congress which would have excluded foreign language newspapers from second class mailing privileges unless they contained full English translations of their contents and conformed to other harassing regulations. This time, Marshall was sent to Washington by the Inter-Racial

Council and the American Association of Foreign Language Newspapers in order to defend the loyalty of the foreign language press and denounce the unconstitutionality of the proposal.

One of the chief methods Marshall and his associates used to establish Jewish loyalty was the collection of statistics on the participation of Jews in the armed forces. In December, 1917, the AJC's Executive Committee, deciding that this was a matter "of the highest importance," established a Division of War Statistics, with a special office in Washington. For three years, this agency labored heroically, collecting hundreds of thousands of individual biographies, compiling lists of decorations, and issuing periodic reports to the press on the war conduct of Jewish servicemen. Under such headlines as "JEWS ACTIVE IN WAR" and "JEWS POINT IN PRIDE TO RECORD IN WAR," statistics were presented to prove that Jews contributed proportionally more men to the armed forces than the population as a whole (5 per cent as against 3 per cent), that they served in greater numbers in the combat services, and that they had performed numerous deeds of heroism.[18] Marshall was enthusiastic over this project, feeling it would provide "material which will enable us to laugh to scorn any question as to the patriotism of the American Jew." [19]

Marshall was also concerned with defending Jews against discrimination in the services. Disclaiming any intentions of going out of his way "to look for exhibitions of prejudice or to see it where it does not really exist," Marshall did not hesitate to use pressure on Secretary of War Newton Baker, Secretary of the Navy Josephus Daniels, or their subordinates when he felt a situation warranted action. One of the more widely publicized discriminatory cases concerned a sentence in the Manual of Instructions for Medical Advisory Boards issued by the War Department, which read, "The foreign born, especially Jews, are more apt to malinger than the native born." Marshall protested strongly when he learned of the offensive remark; calling it a demoralizing insult, he demanded its excision and the disciplining of those responsible for its insertion. In response, President Wilson ordered Secretary Baker to expunge the accusation.

World War I was the first American war that large numbers of Jews served in, and it was expected that there would be resistance to Jews by the traditional military hierarchy. After receiving numerous complaints from Jewish soldiers, Marshall protested bitterly to Secretary Baker against "continuous unjust, unfair, and discriminatory treatment." [20] The hazing of a Jewish private brought from Marshall a demand for immediate punishment of the guilty party, otherwise it would "dampen the ardor and enthusiasm of a large number of the American people." [21] Jews who volunteered for aviation duty were made to feel unwelcome, Marshall reported. Out of the large number of commissions awarded to men from the ranks in Europe, Marshall charged, not one was given to a Jew. In fact, there was considerable hostility in the officers' corps to Jews who were commissioned. In November, 1918, about 100 Jewish students at New York University's Students' Training Camp were placed under arrest on charges of mutiny and disobedience. An investigation revealed that their drill sergeant had been guilty of anti-Semitic remarks and he was ordered to apologize.

Fewer Jews served in the naval services than in the Army, but here, too, Marshall was not lax. In 1916, the American Jewish Committee secured the reinstatement of a Jewish midshipman to Annapolis after he had been dismissed. When it was learned that anti-Semitic verses had been posted at the Naval Reserve Camp at Pelham, New York, Marshall's protest brought a Navy Department emissary to his office with assurances that no reflections on the Jews would be permitted.

Facetious remarks about Jewish soldiers, whether made by Jews or non-Jews, were not tolerated by Marshall. To a small town Iowa newspaper which had printed a story about a mythical Jewish chaplain who was court-martialed for requesting the three ball insignia instead of the cross, Marshall fumed that this was preaching the Prussian doctrine of hate. When a Jewish actor, working for a Jewish producer in a Broadway show, made jokes about Jewish soldiers, Marshall accused them both of dragging "the name of the Jew through the mud and mire in order to coin a few dirty shekels." [22]

The mobilization of American industry for war production created a situation of full employment, but Jewish workers sometimes faced resistance when they tried to share this prosperity. Marshall admitted it was extremely difficult to root out discrimination practiced by private employers, but when government departments or contractors were involved, he did not hesitate to call them to account. He was particularly concerned with preventing discrimination by government contractors in military construction and shipbuilding. His protests to Newton D. Baker and Bainbridge Colby brought strong pledges that the government would not permit discrimination by contractors against Jews. Marshall repeatedly said that anti-Semitism was a "Prussian invention and importation and should be weeded out from our soil before the insidious poison contaminates it." [23]

An article appeared in the *Americanization Bulletin* issued by the U.S. Bureau of Education, in which the amounts subscribed to the Third Liberty Loan by people of foreign birth or extraction were classified by ethnic group; Marshall disputed the accuracy of the figure ascribed to Jews. More seriously, he challenged the entire concept of such classification: "What is meant by men of foreign extraction in this connection? How many generations must a family have lived in the United States before they cease to be of foreign extraction?" [24]

Fear and suspicion of Germans, generalized to include all foreigners in the United States, gripped many Americans during the war. The American Red Cross fell victim to the pervasive atmosphere.* According to Marshall, every effort

* Red Cross leaders warned that German–Americans had infiltrated the organization in order to put ground glass into bandages.

was made to keep Jews out of Red Cross service abroad. He had to defend the appointment of the distinguished scholar Prof. Israel Friedlander (to a Red Cross Commission to Palestine) against charges he had been pro-German. At home, the situation was not much better. The niece of Marshall's law partner was refused a job as file clerk in the New York Red Cross office because no Germans were wanted.

A State Department ruling that no naturalized citizens of German or Austrian birth, or children of such, should be sent abroad for service in Red Cross hospitals was fought energetically by Marshall and Jacob Schiff. "Have we lost all sense of humor? Have we forgotten the fundamental principles of Americanism . . . ? Is it not time that this chauvinistic nonsense should cease?" [25] Protests were ineffective, and, in Marshall's opinion, the actions of the Red Cross remained glaringly anti-Semitic. At the end of the war, he accused Red Cross officials of discrimination in the distribution of relief to Polish Jews, and summed it up by saying, "There have been many people connected with the American Red Cross who have not even made a decent effort to conceal their hatred of Jews." [26]

Marshall and his colleagues were especially hurt by the attitude of Red Cross officials because they had been large and loyal contributors. Generally, the individual instances of anti-Semitic feeling that appeared during the war were not very alarming. More dangerous, potentially, was the creation of a climate of opinion in which conformist loyalty was regarded as the acme of Americanism; undertones of this affected the Jews to some extent during the war—as was evident by their passionate desire to demonstrate Jewish patriotic deeds. Nevertheless, no serious, concerted agitation that might threaten the Jewish position in the United States had yet appeared.

Post-War Red Scare

The fear of radicals, important in American nativism, was heightened by wartime emphasis on stability and conformity. After the war, the xenophobia that had been directed toward Germany was transferred to radicals, especially those of foreign birth or background, who now became the chief enemies of America. In part a natural tendency to seek an outlet for the unsatisfied emotions aroused by the abortive crusade for democracy, it was mainly because of the simultaneous appearance of a threatening Bolshevik regime in Russia and an upsurge of labor-management strife in the United States. These combined to produce the post-war Red Scare, an era of almost hysterical fear.[27]

Louis Marshall, interviewed after the first Russian Revolution of March, 1917, hailed it as the greatest world event since the French Revolution. Anticipating the establishment of a western-style parliamentary democracy in which an emancipated Jewry would flourish, Marshall, Schiff, and Oscar Straus even formed a committee to raise a loan among American Jews on behalf of the liberal Russian government. Their high hopes for Russian Jewry, however, were dashed when the Bolshevik regime took power in November, 1917. In addition, American nativists, sounding the alarm over post-war Communist uprisings in Central Europe and the formation of the Third International, soon found that the Jew offered "the most concrete symbol of foreign radicalism." [28] The disturbing development of a Bolshevik-Jew image became a major feature of post-war American anti-Semitism.

The key themes of the attack on the Jew as Bolshevik were sounded during the hearings of a special subcommittee of the Senate Judiciary Committee, in February and March,

1919, on Bolshevism in Russia and the United States.[29] Headed by Senator Lee S. Overman of North Carolina, the subcommittee heard a parade of prominent experts, among them Dr. George S. Simons, a Methodist minister who had supervised his church's missionary activities in St. Petersburg since 1907. His testimony particularly stressed the role of Jews in the Bolshevik Revolution. Hundreds of agitators from the lower East Side, Simons testified, had followed Trotsky back to Russia, and these men were responsible for the present turmoil. "A number of us were impressed with the strong Yiddish element in this thing right from the start, and it soon became evident that more than half of the agitators in the Bolshevik movement were Yiddish." [30] Petrograd, he reported, was swarming with Jewish troublemakers. "I do not want to be unfair to them, but I usually know a Jew when I see one." [31] To prove his contention, Simons presented statistical evidence; out of 388 members of the Petrograd Soviet, only sixteen were "real Russians," the rest Jews. He also presented a list of pseudonyms of the Bolshevik leaders, giving their original Jewish names, for example, Zinoviev-Apfelbaum.

Simons was not only certain that Bolshevism in Russia was Jewish-controlled, but there was similarly no doubt in his mind that "the predominant element in this Bolsheviki movement in America, is, you may call it, the Yiddish of the East Side." [32] In fact, Simons stated, his discussions with Harris A. Houghton of U.S. Army Intelligence had indicated that there seemed to be a concerted Jewish effort to attain world power. Simons, nevertheless, disclaimed personal anti-Jewish prejudice. "I am not anti-Semitic and have no sympathy with any movement of that kind, and some of my best friends in Russia and America are Jews." [33] During his testimony he asserted several times that Jewish Bolsheviks were really apostate Jews.

The testimony of Dr. Simons was front-page news in the *New York Times* the following day. Jewish leaders were worried that his remarks would be construed as government-sanctioned, and Marshall issued an official reply on behalf of the American Jewish Committee. In a letter to Senator Overman, which he asked to be inserted in the Committee's records, and in a statement to the *New York Times*, Marshall took issue with Simons's testimony. Vigorously denying the alleged Jewish-Bolshevik connection, Marshall noted that "the term, 'Bolshevist,' as now used means anything or everything to which the speaker may for the moment be opposed." Since an attack on East Side apostate Jews in this context might redound unfavorably upon all Jews, Marshall emphasized the patriotism of the East Side. "Bolshevism, with gnashing teeth and scraggly beard and dripping dagger, is pictured as stalking through the noisome alleys in the imaginary East Side," but Marshall with twenty-five years of experience in New York, vowed this was a bugaboo.

As further proof, Marshall investigated Simons's list of Jewish Bolsheviks and informed Senator Overman that some of the men who were Bolsheviks—such as Lenin—were not Jews, while some who were Jews—such as Martov, Dan, and Axelrod—were bitter opponents of the Bolsheviks. Using data supplied by A. J. Sack of the Russian Information Bureau, Marshall emphasized the recent attempt on Lenin's life by Dora Kaplan, a Jewish Social Revolutionary. His protests were reinforced by statements from such prominent Jews and non-Jews as Governor Smith, Mayor Hylan, Charles Evans Hughes, and Jacob Schiff, condemning Simons's testimony. Simon Wolf—Chairman of the Board of Delegates on Civil Rights of the Union of American Hebrew Congregations, and Washington representative of the B'nai B'rith—sent a statement to the Overman Committee endorsing Marshall's stand and upholding the valor of American Jews. When a Jewish expert on Russia, Herman Bernstein, took the witness stand at the Overman Committee hearings, he pointed out that it was no more fair to call Bolshevism a Jewish movement than to call it a Christian one because its major leaders in Russia and America were non-Jews.

Senator Overman, in reply to the outburst of criticism,

said Dr. Simons had tried to be just. "He only spoke of the Apostate Jews who went over to Russia from this country." [34] As Marshall knew, however, this was an evasion, for the bulk of the testimony had emphasized to the American public that Jews predominated in the Bolshevik movement. Subsequent testimony by other Russian experts before the Overman Committee also raised the Jewish-Bolshevik spectre, with such remarks as, "In Russia it is well known that three-fourths of the Bolshevik leaders are Jewish." [35] Simons himself stood by his Senate remarks on the Jewish role in Bolshevism, and his words later supplied ammunition for anti-Semitic elements. His testimony was included in an edition of the Protocols of the Elders of Zion published in 1920. [36]

Implications of a Jewish-Bolshevik nexus disturbed Jewish leaders well before the Overman Committee hearings. As early as September, 1918, the American Jewish Committee prepared a draft statement on this charge that would have been released if the Simons testimony had not provoked Marshall into an immediate counter-blast. His statement may have softened the impact of the anti-Semitic allegations, but similar charges continued to vex American-Jewish leaders throughout the Red Scare period and long afterwards. Union difficulties were attributed to radicalism of the Russian Jew type, Bolshevism was called a Jewish device for gaining economic control of Russia, and Jews were accused of being involved in the execution of the Russian Czar and his family. The Better America Lecture Service, Inc., which supplied materials for lectures on world affairs, captioned its slides with comments on the role of the Jews in Bolshevist Russia, offering such statistics as "sixty-eight Russian Hebrews and 264 Hebrews from the Bowery district of New York" were in the Bolshevik government. [37] Arthur Brisbane publicly announced that "more than half the ruling minds in Russia are Jewish," while Lothrop Stoddard called the Bolshevik regime "largely Jewish." [38] From abroad, it was reported that Winston Churchill, a member of the English cabinet, had referred to "the international Soviet of the Russian and Polish Jew." [39] Trotsky's role in Russia was frequently discussed in the American press, his features being described by *Current Opinion* (December, 1920) as "sallow, Mephistophelian, and distinctly Jewish."

Marshall believed that the constant references to Jewish Bolsheviks were the "unconscious expression of an innate prejudice." [40] Why else were the shortcomings of a few Jews visited upon the others who abhorred them? Some years back, Marshall recalled, a friend had lamented to Judge Sulzberger about the existence of Jewish criminals, whereupon the Judge indignantly exclaimed, "Damn it! Have we not the right to have criminals of our own as well as other parts of the American public?" [41] While he admitted the existence of Jewish Bolsheviks and was aware of the harm they did to other Jews, Marshall repeatedly stressed

> the unfortunate tendency of men of education and of leadership to do what they would not do in respect to any other part of our population, namely, to describe as Jewish any malefactor or abnormal individual who happens to have had Jewish ancestry.[42]

Most Jews were essentially conservative, anti-Bolshevik, and supporters of property rights and capitalism, Marshall asserted. American-Jewish workers desired proper compensation, suitable sanitary conditions, and, in general, to be treated as self-respecting human beings who might rise in the social scale; these were hardly Bolshevik traits. A certain amount of social and industrial unrest was necessary to progress, and if there were Socialists, the capitalists had created them. "Many of the employers of labor have been unreasonable, tyrannical, brutal. Some of them have told me, in so many words, that they were carrying on their business in a manner which amounted to industrial slavery." [43]

On the sensitive point of Jewish prominence among Bolshevik leaders, Marshall countered that Trotsky and his associates had repudiated Judaism and were completely unconcerned with its fate. A subsidiary argument was that Lenin, not Trotsky, was the key man in the Bolshevik Revolution and the real leader of the Russian regime. Marshall also claimed that 95 per cent of Russian Jewry was anti-Bolshevik, and had good reason to be because of property confiscation and pogroms. As an authority, Marshall cited Prince Lvoff, the former Russian Prime Minister, whom he had spoken to in New York. At the same time, the American-Jewish press published such reassuring articles as, "Russian Jews Against Bolshevism," as well as a statement from the Berlin representative of the Soviet Government that Jews were enemies of Bolshevism: "Russian Judaism is condemned to annihilation. It is not our ill-will, it is an historical fact." [44]

When Attorney-General A. Mitchell Palmer began conducting raids and deporting alien radicals, Jewish leaders were worried. Simon Wolf wrote to Palmer requesting the number of Russian Jews among the deportees; Palmer replied that there were a large number. Adolf Kraus, President of the B'nai B'rith, who reported this correspondence to the order's members, confessed it was serious, although he approved of Palmer's actions. Marshall, on the other hand, felt that the Palmer raids might lead to bloodshed, that they were undertaken because of Palmer's presidential ambitions, and that "so long as there is no overt act, so long as people merely talk and write what they have to say, there is no danger." [45] Jews should not be especially concerned; they had a right to a quota of radicals. Marshall, nevertheless, regarded the Jewish-Bolshevik issue as one of great potential danger: "The air is filled with suspicion. The first word upon the lips of these modern know-nothings is Bolshevism, I.W.W.ism and Socialism." [46] He knew that the Bolshevik threat, real or imagined, was of great concern to the American people, and that counter-arguments were necessary to absolve Jews of the charges hurled at them. At one point, he had A. J. Sack prepare a manuscript for a book about Bolshevism, but later decided it was inadvisable to publish it.* He called, unsuc-

* By that time, the joint statement of American-Jewish organizations on Bolshevism and the Jews had been issued, and Marshall thought it unwise to continue agitating the matter. See Chapter 6.

cessfully, on the Postmaster-General to withdraw mailing privileges from a publication issued in Brooklyn called "The Anti-Bolshevist," subtitled, "A Monthly Magazine Devoted to the Defense of American Institutions Against the Jewish Bolshevist Doctrines of Morris Hillquit and Leon Trotzky."

Marshall knew the defense of Jews against the Bolshevik charge could not be successful unless the entire atmosphere of the Red Scare was changed. For this reason, and because he continued to be a strong believer in a strict constitutional approach, he took a firm and prominent part in the case of the five Socialist New York State Assemblymen who were expelled in January, 1920 from their elected seats. A peak of hysteria was reached when these men, duly elected representatives of a legally recognized party, were summoned to the Speaker's stand in the Assembly, lectured on their party's treason, denied their seats, and herded out of the chamber by the sergeant-at-arms.

Responsible opinion, including the *New York Times's*, at first upheld the Assembly's action as a patriotic act. Charles E. Hughes, however, at a special meeting of the Association of the Bar of New York City, called for a defense of the Socialists' right to their seats. After full discussion and a close vote, a committee of five, headed by Hughes and including Marshall, was appointed to protest the expulsion. The committee went to Albany and prepared to testify before the Assembly's Judiciary Committee, which was investigating the expulsion; when the legislators refused to hear their testimony, Marshall submitted a brief in the name of the committee's members. The Judiciary Committee nevertheless upheld the expulsion, and when the same Socialists were reelected in September, 1920, they were expelled again. Despite this unsatisfactory outcome, the intervention of a man of Hughes's stature, supported by Marshall and other noted legal figures, dealt a heavy blow to the prevalent anti-Red hysteria.

Marshall's interest in the Assemblymen was not limited to his participation in the Bar Association committee. In letters to friends, politicians, and newspapers, and in public statements, he consistently and vigorously urged a sane and rational approach. Disappointed at the action of the Republican dominated legislature, he exclaimed, "Has our Party been stricken with blindness?" [47] It was clear to him that persecution aided the Socialists. He knew, also, that the expulsion of the five men might destroy vital constitutional principles and set a dangerous precedent:

> The greatest peril to our democratic government is the tyranny of the majority. . . . Every citizen is concerned in defeating the action that has been taken because he may at some time be one of an unpopular minority, just as in the past abolitionists, prohibitionists, freetraders, protectionsts, and men of serious religious beliefs have been opposed by the majority of their fellow citizens.[48]

> I regard it as especially important . . . that no religious or political test shall ever be imposed upon those chosen by the people to represent them. . . . If such a test can be applied to one school of political, religious, or non-religious thought, it can with equal right be applied to any. Safety lies in the absolute negation of the power to apply any test other than that expressly declared by the Constitution. To do otherwise would be to follow the example of the Bolshevists and to adopt the very principles we are seeking to combat.[49]

When a movement was begun to bar Socialists from law schools, Marshall was exasperated:

> This sitting in judgment on other people's ideas is becoming absurd and silly. . . . Suppose a man were Catholic or Methodist or a Democrat and the people who passed on his admittance to law school were Episcopalians or Republicans, what then? . . . If Americans cannot be trusted to deal sanely with economic questions, and if the only way to save them from heretical notions is to deport or lynch them, then I say we are entering a plea of national intellectual bankruptcy.[50]

Marshall strongly opposed the legislation proposed by New York State's Lusk Committee, including the outlawing of the Socialist Party and the institution of a teacher loyalty oath. Denouncing the Committee for its "un-American method of inquisitorial investigation," he charged that its bills were

. . . so reactionary that no parallel can be found in American history. The Socialist doctrines are unsound. That, however, is not the question. The question is whether the thought of the State of New York shall be put in a strait jacket. In a moment of hysteria shall we forget all that America stands for and adopt the Russian system? [51]

Marshall realized the implications the Socialist furor had for the Jews of America. Three of the Socialist Assemblymen were Jews and they had been elected from Jewish districts. When the *New York Times,* supporting the expulsion, urged the voters of those districts to become Americans, Marshall sharply reminded the *Times* that if they were not Americans, they could not have voted. Expressions of fear from Jews that Marshall's stand might intensify the Jewish-Bolshevik stereotype were derided by him. He regarded his action as the highest patriotism; it was to him the only position that could be taken to defend long-range Jewish interests:

> We have fought against the right of a majority to sit in judgment not only of political parties, but of religious organizations. The same reasons which underlie the action of the New York Assembly in respect to the Socialist members whom it has expelled, would constitute a precedent for the exclusion of Catholics and Jews. . . . Let it be said when I am gone, that I never feared to do what was right merely because it was momentarily unpopular among people who have become crazed by their hatreds and their prejudices and their stupidity.[52]

Protocols of Zion

The concern of Marshall and Jewish leaders over the Bolshevik charges was heightened greatly by the appearance of a curious document titled the Protocols of the Elders of Zion.[53] This spurious work, which became the most important documentary weapon of twentieth century anti-Semites, purported to reveal a gigantic Jewish plot to destroy Christian civilization and seize control of the world. Consisting of twenty-four sections supposedly read by an unnamed Elder to a secret gathering of the other Elders, the Protocols set forth the alleged Jewish plot: 1) the gentile states had already been weakened by liberalism and class war; 2) Jews, using the weapons of gold monopoly, control of the press, immorality, and economic crises, would gain complete control of the gentile world; 3) in this work, the Jews would be aided by Freemasons, certain political parties, atheists, speculators, and corrupt politicians; 4) the peoples of the world would finally succumb to domination by the House of David that would then establish a prosperous society based on police terror.[54] According to some editions of the Protocols, this conspiratorial scheme had been read by Theodor Herzl to the First Zionist Congress in August, 1897.

It is fairly certain that the Protocols were concocted by Russian secret police officials at the end of the nineteenth century on the basis of a tract written anonymously in 1864 by Maurice Joly, a Parisian lawyer and opponent of Napoleon III. Joly's work had been used in an 1868 German novel in which the machinations originally attributed by Joly to Napoleon III were transposed and alleged to be the substance of a secret meeting of Jewish elders in Prague. The document, in its Russian version, was published and propagated by a group of reactionary extremists who wished to discredit progressive influences on the Czar by associating new ideas with a Judeo-Masonic plot to overthrow the established government. George Butmi and Sergius Nilus published editions of the Protocols to explain the Revolution of 1905. Not until the 1917 Revolution, however, did the work become a major political weapon. Then its thesis was seized upon by the counter-revolutionary forces as excellent propaganda explaining the Bolshevik success. White Russian refugees carried the work from Russia to Germany where monarchists, and later Nazis, made use of it during the post-war chaos.

In February, 1920, an English edition of the Protocols appeared under the title, *The Jewish Peril*. Significantly, the publisher was Eyre and Spottiswoode, official printers to the British government.[55] The *London Times* expressed editorial approval, and the *Morning Post* (May 8, 1920) began a series of seventeen articles under the title, "The Cause of World Unrest," elaborating upon the original Protocols. Lucien Wolf, the eminent Anglo-Jewish scholar who attempted to expose the forgery, felt that Lord Northcliffe, publisher of the *Morning Post,* was not really anti-Semitic, but tolerated the material as good, yellow journalism. Wickham Stead of the *Times,* on the other hand, was characterized by Wolf as "quite a dangerous anti-Semite, absolutely monomaniacal." [56] The Protocols were useful Tory propaganda because of their anti-Red enthusiasm. When Eyre and Spottiswoode did not wish to publish a second edition of the Protocols, the work was taken over by an extreme nationalist, anti-Semitic group known as The Britons. In a prefatory note to the second edition, the new publishers explained that the world had fallen into a

> Jewish "Peace" . . . strikes, revolutions, high prices, shortage, speculation, and unrest everywhere. . . . The Kaiser was not the real enemy, egregious sinner though he was. The Learned Elders of Zion were behind him, and it is they who have now to be squarely met.[57]

Even before the publication of the first English edition of the Protocols, typewritten copies were circulated and seriously considered by Allied military intelligence officers and by government bureaus in London and Washington.[58] The extent of the distribution can be seen from the report of Dr. Ales Hrdlicka (of the Smithsonian Institution) that in 1918 he had been approached by the Czech Legation in Washington for advice on the document and had himself received copies. A Washington journalist who ran an editorial research service revealed that since 1917 he had been approached at least twenty times verbally or with typewritten documents proving the danger of the Jewish peril. A high official of the U.S. Secret Service disclosed to Cyrus Adler that President Wilson had seen the Protocols in Paris and had

ordered an investigation. Other delegates to the Peace Conference were also shown copies.

The prime movers in this propaganda campaign were
Russian émigrés operating in the United States under the
leadership of Boris Brasol, a Czarist officer who came to
America in 1916 ostensibly on behalf of the Russian Red
Cross.[59] Brasol, a former official of the Russian Interior Min-
istry, Police Department, and Justice Department, attained
considerable influence in Washington and New York. As part
of the White Russian effort to discredit the Bolshevik Revolution and restore the Romanovs, Brasol and his associates
sought to convince American leaders by the Protocols that
the Revolution was the result of an international Jewish
conspiracy. Brasol was able to foist the Protocols on Military
Intelligence and enter the good graces of Attorney-General
Palmer as an expert on Russian and American radicals.[60]
Closely allied with Brasol in the distribution of the Protocols
was Dr. Harris A. Houghton, a physician who headed the
New York office of Army intelligence during the war. Brasol
was also able to infiltrate two one hundred per cent American organizations—the National Civic Federation, and the
American Defense Society.

Louis Marshall and the leaders of the American Jewish
Committee knew since early 1918 that a typescript version of
the Protocols was being circulated secretly in Washington
and New York. Marshall believed nothing could be done to
prevent this and that no reputable publisher would dare put
it into print; he therefore took no action beyond keeping
close watch through Cyrus Adler's Secret Service friend. In
the summer of 1919, Casimir Pilenas, a Lithuanian who had
worked for U.S. Intelligence during the war and had collaborated with the Brasol group, made contact with Jacob Schiff,
Cyrus Adler, and Marshall about the Protocols. Having had a
falling out with Brasol, Pilenas announced he was prepared
to sell a copy of the Protocols and other important anti-
Semitic documents for $50,000. The offer was considered by
Marshall and his friends, but finally refused. Pilenas was re-

garded untrustworthy, and in any case, Marshall had already received a manuscript copy of the Protocols gratis.

At this point, the Brasol group decided, because of the Overman Committee hearings and the general Red Scare, to release the Protocols to the public. A few weeks after the publication of the Eyre and Spottiswoode edition in London (1920), the Boston firm of Small, Maynard and Company published the first American edition of the Protocols titled, *The Protocols and World Revolution.* The book had a lengthy preface written by Brasol, stating that the Bolshevik Revolution was Jewish in origin and control and was part of the international Jewish power conspiracy to destroy Christendom. Anti-Jewish portions of the Overman Committee testimony were included in appendices, as was a call to American Jews to repudiate Bolshevism and plans for world domination.

Marshall was shocked, especially when he learned that copies of the book were being sent to newspapers throughout the United States. He requested influential Jewish leaders in Boston to check on the publisher and the circumstances of publication. Later, the B'nai B'rith hired two detective agencies to investigate Small, Maynard and Company. Jewish leaders were greatly dismayed when, shortly after the Boston publication of the Protocols, the reputable New York firm of G. P. Putnam brought out an edition of *The Cause of World Unrest.*[61] A publisher's note disclaiming any desire to accuse the whole Jewish race was followed by a new preface written by H. A. Gwynne, editor of the London *Morning Post.* Gwynne stressed the danger of Jewish allegiance throughout the world to an independent foreign policy; he also endorsed the anonymous author's views blaming a Jewish-Masonic conspiracy for the Russian Revolution, the failure of the Peace Conference, the disorders in Ireland, the impending destruction of the British Empire, and "the increasing demands for more money and less work on the part of the labouring classes." [62]

This was damaging enough, but when Marshall learned

that Putnam's planned to issue an edition of the Protocols, he protested vehemently to Major George Haven Putnam. This "stupid drivel," Marshall exclaimed, was "calculated to make the Jew repulsive in the eyes of his fellow men and to exterminate him, not figuratively, but literally." [63] Putnam, who was bombarded by other Jewish leaders as well, took refuge in the publisher's right to print a variety of books on topics of public interest and pointed out that he had many personal friends among leading Jewish citizens. Marshall refused to countenance this kind of argument. Freedom of the press did not include the right to publish facts which were really criminal libels:

> Whoever touches pitch is defiled. . . . It will not do to say that you have many friends among the Jews whom you respect and that these books are not intended to reflect upon all Jews. The world is not so discriminating. People whose passions are aroused do not differentiate. . . . To say that Bolshevism is a Jewish movement is as ridiculous as to say that the Jews are responsible for capitalism. I am not a Zionist, and yet I regard the slurs that these books are attempting to make against Zionism to be unworthy. The very Zionists whom these books are attacking have been persecuted by the Bolshevists, just as the mass of the Jews of Russia have been pursued as members of the bourgeoise. . . . I had never believed that a Jew in this country would ever be called upon to occupy the humiliating position of defending his people against charges such as those which are being spread. . . .[64]

Major Putnam was probably not convinced by Marshall's arguments. More than a year later he was reported by a Jewish visitor to have remarked that Bolshevism was Jewish and the Jews murdered the Czar. Nevertheless, bowing under pressure from Marshall, Oscar Straus, and others, Putnam decided not to proceed with publication of the Protocols. At the same time, Rabbi Isaac Landman, editor of the *American Hebrew*, told Marshall that Putnam had agreed to publish a polemic against the Protocols to be written by him. Marshall, furious, rebuked Landman for "upsetting the apple cart," since such a publication would serve to condone Putnam's original shameful act of having published *The Cause of World Unrest*, and would therefore be a "betrayal of the

Jews." Landman did not write the book, but as late as 1927 Putnam informed Marshall that he was interestd in publishing a volume exposing the Protocols.

The edition of the Protocols Putnam had wanted to publish was a new translation emanating from Dr. Houghton's circle. After Putnam declined to go ahead with it, Houghton published it in New York under the imprint of the Beckwith Company.[65] It turned out that this mysterious firm was an ad hoc organization established principally for the purpose of publishing the Protocols, although it was suspected Putnam was using Beckwith as a front.

The Protocols were now available in a strictly American edition. The frontispiece of the new volume informed its readers that it had been

> translated from the Russian to the English Language for the Information of All True Americans and to Confound Enemies of Democracy and the Republic also to Demonstrate the Possible Fulfillment of Biblical Prophecy as to World Domination by the Chosen People.[66]

Handbills were distributed advertising the Beckwith edition as "The Red Bible . . . the most remarkable document uncovered in the turmoil of war."

In the turbulence immediately after the war, this anti-Semitic propaganda made headway. Marshall wrote,

> One would suppose that it is so infantile in its character that men of intelligence would laugh at it. The war has, however, tended to such a degree to the destruction of reason and the sense of humor that any assertion presented in melodramatic form, however stupid it may be, finds ready lodgment in the minds of men and women whom one would regard as immune to the prejudices sought to be engendered.[67]

Copies of the Protocols were distributed to Congressmen, cabinet members, newspaper editors, and other influential figures. Marshall called it silly; it was not selling well in New York bookstores, but he knew it had to be reckoned with. Judge Brandeis told Marshall that a socially prominent Washington hostess was circulating the Protocols and holding parlor meetings discussing the document. An occasional review favorable to the Protocols appeared in the press; a

Philadelphia newspaper published sensational articles head-
lined "Red Bible Counsels Appeal to Violence," and "Reds
Plot to Smash World and Then Rule with Universal
Czar." [68] Brasol himself continued to stir the fire, producing a
volume called *The World at the Cross Roads,* in which he
reiterated the old themes of Jewish responsibility for the
world war and the Russian Revolution.[69]

The bulk of responsible public opinion in America, however, did not accept the Protocols. Articles in such journals as
Current Opinion, Independent, and *Outlook* generally decried the conspiracy phobias, and the *New York Times*
remarked that the chief offense of the Protocols was that the
attribution to the Jews of such a false and feeble document
was insulting to their learning and mental power. The negative reaction to the Protocols was partly due to prompt and
effective exposés that appeared in England and the United
States. Israel Zangwill's, and especially Lucien Wolf's, essays
on the falsity of the Protocols provided an early and useful
basis for later, similar works, including an eloquent pamphlet by William D. Hard written originally for *Metropolitan Magazine*.[70] Hard satirically pointed out that if there
were a real international conspiracy, it was centered in the
drawing rooms of London, Paris, and Washington for the
purpose of helping certain persons in Eastern Europe.[71]
After *The Cause of World Unrest* was published, Marshall,
who had been following these exposés closely, hired the Jewish editor and Russian expert, Herman Bernstein, to assist
him in dealing with the propaganda. The result of this relationship and of Bernstein's diligent research was the thoughtful, well-written *The History of a Lie,* published in February,
1921.[72]

At about this time, Marshall was approached by Princess
Catherine Radziwill, a Russian exile living in New York,
who offered to provide from first-hand knowledge the origin
of the Protocols.[73] The account she gave of Russian secret
police fabrications dating back to the 1880's substantiated
Bernstein's findings, and for a while the Princess was quite

popular in Jewish circles. It was then discovered that Princess Radziwill, although she denied it, had been arrested and imprisoned for forgery in South Africa some years back. This revelation destroyed her usefulness, although Marshall did not doubt the accuracy of her tale.

Additional direct evidence of the spuriousness of the Protocols came from Paris in 1921. Count A. M. du Chayla, a Frenchman and former Cossack commander who had lived in Russia for many years, gave a detailed account in a Russian émigré newspaper of the machinations involved in the early history of the Protocols. His story corroborated that of Princess Radziwill in many respects.[74] Later that same year, what should have been the *coup de grâce* for the Protocols appeared in the *London Times* in the form of dispatches from its Constantinople correspondent, Philip Graves. He had been given a book by a Russian friend, and, after examining it closely and noting the striking parallels between it and the Protocols, was convinced the latter was a clumsy plagiarism. After checking in the British Museum, Graves identified the earlier work as Maurice Joly's 1864 tract, *Dialogue aux Enfers entre Machiave et Montesquieu*. The *Times* was convinced and Marshall was overjoyed. Copies of the *Times's* editorial of August 18, 1921, "The End of the Protocols," were sent by Marshall to the press throughout the country. At his suggestion, the *New York Times* reprinted Graves's dispatches and commented editorially upon them.[75] Seemingly, the end of the Protocols had indeed come.

If men behaved logically and rationally, it would not have been necessary to present counter-arguments and documentation to demonstrate the falsity of the Protocols.* On

---

* In later years, Marshall negotiated with Herman Bernstein on the possibility of a revised edition of the latter's *History of a Lie,* to include newly revealed documentation. Eventually, Bernstein wrote a new edition published in 1935, after Marshall's death, titled *The Truth About "The Protocols of Zion."* Marshall's struggle against the Protocols was entwined with the battle against Henry Ford. The official statement of American-Jewish organizations on "The Protocols, Bolshevism, and the Jews," was issued both as a denunciation of the Protocols and an answer to Ford's campaign. See Chapter 6.

the surface, the Protocols were glaringly preposterous. They fulfilled, however, a deep need in the disturbed atmosphere of post-1917 Europe and America, and were therefore unscrupulously exploited. The Protocols, fantastic though they obviously were, supplied a tried and tested scapegoat that could be blamed for the evils of a rapidly changing world beset by war and revolution. In America, the Protocols reinforced the anti-Jewish stereotype that already stressed the international, conspiratorial, immoral, and Mammon-driven Jewish nature.

No overt anti-Semitic movement appeared in the United States during World War I, but the national psychology had grown accustomed to demanding strict conformity and to attributing difficulties to alien conspirators. In the post-war era, the milder nativism was jolted by economic and political circumstances into being more determinedly anti-alien and anti-radical. The Red Scare, the Ku Klux Klan, intensified immigration restriction—all were characteristic of the new mood. Louis Marshall fought this change, but with only limited success. The Protocols were academically discredited, but in the hands of Henry Ford could easily amalgamate into anti-Semitism that reached far beyond social discrimination —into an embryonic political and ideological force.

Chapter five

henry
ford's
anti-semitism

On May 22, 1920, the *Dearborn Independent,* a weekly magazine published in Dearborn, Michigan by the Dearborn Publishing Company, launched an anti-Semitic propaganda campaign without precedent in the United States. Inaugurated soon after the U.S. publication of the Protocols, this campaign lasted, with varying intensity, for almost seven years. The serious nature of the attack on the Jews was underscored because the *Independent* was owned by Henry Ford, the richest man in America. It was Ford who personally initiated and ultimately suspended the severe barrage unloosed by his journalists.

A front-page editorial entitled, "The International Jew— The World's Problem," initiated this full-scale propaganda onslaught. Published weekly for almost two years and continued sporadically thereafter, the series played endless variations on a theme proclaimed in the first article:

> The Jew is again being singled out for critical attention throughout the world. His emergence in the financial, political, and social spheres has been so complete and so spectacular since the war, that his place, power and purpose in the world are being given a new scrutiny, much of it unfriendly. . . .

In America alone most of the big business, the trusts and the banks, the natural resources and the chief agricultural products, especially tobacco, cotton and sugar, are in the control of Jewish financiers or their agents. Jewish journalists are a large and powerful group here. . . . Jews are the largest and most numerous landlords of residence property in the country. They are supreme in the theatrical world. They absolutely control the circulation of publications throughout the country.

The question is, If the Jew is in control, how did it happen? There is a super-capitalism which is supported wholly by the fiction that gold is wealth. There is a super-government which is allied to no government, which is free from them all, and yet which has its hand in them all. There is a race, a part of humanity, which has never yet been received as a welcome part, and which has succeeded in raising itself to a power that the proudest Gentile race has never claimed. . . . It is becoming more and more the conviction of men all over the world that the labor question, the wage question, the land question cannot be settled until first of all this matter of an international super-capitalistic government is settled.[1]

Clearly, the inspiration of the article derived from the Protocols, with their fantastic allegations of a Jewish world conspiracy. The *Dearborn Independent* series used the raw materials of the Protocols, but adapted them to suit the American audience. Recognizing the possibility of readers disputing charges drawn from the forged Protocols, the *Independent* cautioned that "the document is comparatively unimportant, the conditions to which it calls attention are of a very high degree of importance."[2]

What were those conditions that the *Independent,* after innocently protesting its freedom from anti-Semitism, went on to expose? Behind the theorizing about an international Jewish conspiracy, the *Independent* primarily emphasized the alleged role of the Jew in destroying hallowed American traditions. Ford, in his autobiography, spoke of a "nasty Orientalism" that caused "a marked deterioration in our literature, amusements, and social conduct . . . a general letting down of standards."[3] Considering race as "the key to nearly every difficulty in the world today," Ford's writers saw the "unassimilable" Jews as the source of the corruptive and anti-American ideas that were destroying our Anglo-Saxon civilization: [4]

> If you take a map and mark off a thin strip half way down the eastern coast line, you will have designated that part of the country which is in a constant ferment, not because it is more "progressive," but because it is continuously receiving poisonous infections of revolutionary doctrine from its tremendous over-population of Eastern Jews. From this thin eastern strip of the United States the poison spreads throughout the country upon the wings of "liberal" publications subsidized by Jewish money, assisted by the voice of "professors" who have made themselves agreeable to the Judaized colleges of the East, and various organizations of destructive intentions whose stationery bears the date line of New York.[5]

The Jew was thus allegedly penetrating the labor movement with socialistic ideas, infiltrating the churches with higher criticism and liberalism, infecting the colleges with the virus of Red propaganda, and generally undermining American morality.

The fear of "Jewish ideas" was supported by constant reiteration of Jewish solidarity in a conspiratorial attempt to seize power. The Jewish attempt at subversion of America was connected with the substantial success alleged to have been achieved already. The drive to power, according to the *Independent,* placed Jews in the presidency of both France and the League of Nations, and even put the United States into the hands of a Jewish dictator, Bernard Baruch, during the war.[6] Not content with hidden control, Jews had tampered with the Presidency of the United States, so that such men as Taft and Wilson had become "gentile fronts" of the Jewish conspiracy. Jews not only controlled the press and the land, among other things, but achieved domination of Alaska. In fact, the articles accused, Jewish power had risen to the point where Jews, insisting on their so-called rights, had become persecutors of Christians, not their victims. It was charged, for example, that brazenness and arrogant interference had led to the Jewish debacle in the Leo Frank case.

A variation of the power motif charged that Jews concealed the extent of their strength by deceiving the American people with false estimates of the Jewish population. The Jews not only prevented the authorities from conducting a census of religions or a count of Jewish immigrants, but the figure of 3,500,000 Jews in the United States was entirely inaccurate. Based on the consumption of Passover "bread," the Ford mathematicians calculated there were at least 6,000,000 Jews.[7] Another disturbing stratagem widely used by Jews, the Ford magazine claimed, was the practice of changing their Judaic names to Anglo-Saxon sounding ones.[8]

The *Independent* did not neglect the double-barreled threat to America from Jewish bankers and Bolsheviks. They operated in a two-pronged offensive, but were both part of the same Jewish plot. Schiff, Loeb, Warburg, Kahn, and Guggenheim were names frequently mentioned in its pages, but special attention was given to the supposed machinations of Paul Warburg, who, in addition to being Jewish, suffered by being of German origin and a naturalized citizen. Warburg was accused of having masterminded the Federal Reserve System in the United States, along with Baruch and another "Jewish tool," Col. House. Their objective was to control American industry, to suck money to New York and ruin the productive sections of the country.

"Touch a Rothschild, and the revolutionary Jew from the ghetto utters his protest," claimed the *Dearborn Independent,* attempting to show the interrelatedness and solidarity of financier and Red.[9] The Russian Revolution, contrary to popular opinion, was neither political nor economic in origin, but was a maneuver by Jewish capitalists to take over Russia and use it for purposes of racial imperialism. This explained the prominence of Jews in the Bolshevik cause. Kerensky's real name was Adler, and as for Lenin, "Why do his children speak Yiddish?"[10] Jewish labor union leaders, such as Sidney Hillman, were "Sovietists" who received orders from Moscow and from Jewish capitalists in the United States and were attempting to Bolshevize the American Negro, through such fronts as A. Philip Randolph. Bernard Baruch and his capitalist fellows had plans prepared and waiting for the conversion of the United States into a communistic state immediately upon the outbreak of a new war.[11]

Active control of the Jewish plot in the United States, according to the *Dearborn Independent,* resided in the Kehillah in New York City. This organization, led by the pro-Bolshevist rabbi, J. L. Magnes, was linked with the odious activities of the American Jewish Committee, headed by Magnes's brother-in-law, Louis Marshall. Together, the Kehillah and the Committee constituted the shadow government of New York, if not the nation.

Jewish control of New York was a constantly recurring theme in the *Independent:*

> The Jewish problem in the United States is essentially a city problem. . . . In no other city of the United States can the Jewish problem be studied with greater profit than in the city of New York. . . . As a population, the Jews exert more power in New York than they have ever exerted during the Christian Era in any place, with the exception of the present Russia. The Jewish Revolution in Russia was manned from New York. . . . Politically, while the rest of the country is entertained with the fiction that Tammany Hall rules the politics of New York, the fact is rarely published that the Jews rule Tammany.[12]

Henry Ford, in his magazine, carried out a promise to teach Americans some history not taught in schools by delving into the past and emerging with sensational charges of Jewish treason and turpitude. Benedict Arnold was suddenly revealed to have been the associate of early Jewish Americans in treasonous activities and shady speculations with contraband. More fantastic was an article written by Conrad Siem; he alleged Bismarck revealed to him that Jewish financial circles were responsible not only for the American Civil War, but also for plotting Lincoln's assassination.

Jewish political and economic power were dangerous enough according to Ford's propaganda machine, but more insidious was the threatened Jewish subversion of American culture and social traditions. The Jews were charged with having destroyed the great age of the American theater and substituting frivolity, sensuality, and indecency. Controlling the movie industry, the Jews devoted it to sex and crime, disregarding the protests of "real Americans" who wanted to censor this filth. Moronic Jewish jazz was rapidly becoming the national music of America and the Yiddish popular song trust was allied with the movies in spreading degeneracy. Movies, theaters, night clubs, jazz—all were seen as part of a diabolical plot to narcotize the moral modesty of Anglo-Saxon Americans. The Jews did not stop at anything, the *Independent* said, in degrading the morals of the country; their gamblers corrupted even the national sport, baseball, in the Chicago Black Sox scandals.*

It was supposedly well known that Jews controlled the whiskey distilling industry and adulterated its products. Appealing to its rural audience, the *Dearborn Independent* charged that Jews had been in the forefront of the struggle against prohibition, which had finally been won by the gentile majority. With the victory of prohibition, the Jews turned to exploiting Christian Americans through bootlegging of spurious liquor. The exemption Jews enjoyed from the workings of the Constitution (the allowance of wine for ritual purposes) was merely a subterfuge for bootlegging. It was clear to Ford's editors that Jews were still the chief propagandists on the stage and in books for the "idea of drink."

The message of the *Dearborn Independent* series was exemplified by a special article devoted to Louis Marshall, entitled, "America's Jewish Enigma—Louis Marshall: Some Facts About American Jewish Committee's Head, Whose Name Is not very Jewish, but who Heads Anti-Christian Campaign." [13] After speculating on the origin of Marshall's non-Jewish name, the article said he was the head of the American Jewish Committee which was in charge of all official activities of American Jews. Marshall's power was so strong that

---

* The Ford writers were aware of the stimulus to reader interest in spicing their disclosures of Jewish influence with descriptions of Jewish moral immodesty. Marshall was aroused by implications in the series that Jews influenced American Presidents by pandering to their sexual appetites. See Marshall to A. C. Ratshesky, March 5, 1921, MP-AJA.

Col. House had been his "chief aid" at the Versailles Conference. His defense of Leo Frank in "a peculiarly vicious murder" of a Georgia girl illustrated the way Jews tried to prevent gentile law from being enforced against fellow Jews— witness also Dreyfus. The article conceded that Marshall was not the world leader of Jewry, but he was very high up. During the war, he collaborated with Bernard Baruch in running America. Marshall's denials that Jews were Bolsheviks were untrue since it was obvious that "Bolshevism is Jewish in its origin, its method, its personnel and its purpose."

Marshall's activities in the so-called defense of Jewish rights, the *Independent* charged, were the real cause of anti-Semitism:

> His propagandas have occasioned great resentment in many sections of the United States. His opposition to salutary immigration laws, his dictation to book and periodical publishers . . . his campaign against the use of "Christological expressions" by Federal, state, and municipal officers; all have resulted in alarming the native population.

Marshall was criticized for daring to say the United States was not a Christian government; for interfering in America's political affairs by protesting the Russian treaty of 1832; for leading the movement to "force the Jew by law into places where he is not wanted," thus Bolshevizing property; finally, he was charged with being the head of the Jewish "foreign office" through which the Jews negotiated with the government of the United States.

In January, 1922, the *Dearborn Independent* suddenly concluded its original series on the Jews. The final articles were called, "A Candid Address to Jews on the Jewish Problem," and, "An Address to Gentiles on the Jewish Problem." In the first address there was again a disclaimer of anti-Semitic motivation, and a protestation that the series purposed to awaken Jews to a sense of social responsibility. The substance of the two articles, however, revealed the fears and hatred at their root:

> Will any Jew deny that the civilization of the United States before the advent of the Jews thither was superior to the highest civilization

ever achieved by the Jews anywhere at any period of their history? There are two ideas in conflict—that is certain. The Jewish idea has a tremendous infiltrating force and a serious degenerative power. . . . It eats the substance out of the civilization which it attacks, destroys its moral virility, throws down its reverence, saps its respect for authority, casts a shadow on every basic principle. . . . Men are thinking ideas today that poison them morally, socially, and economically. Our mental hospitality has been grossly abused, the public mind has been made a sewer. The time has come for a custom barrier to be raised for the examination of imported ideas. Unrestricted immigration of ideas has been as bad for the American mentality as unrestricted immigration of people has been for American society.[14]

With a concluding warning to "Keep our life American and Christian," the *Dearborn Independent* asked its gentile readers to keep at hand the "bunch of keys" it had provided for the illumination of the Jewish question.

Ford's Motives

The propaganda dispersion of Ford's *Dearborn Independent* was one aspect of the loosely organized anti-Semitic agitation that struck the United States after World War I. Part of a world-wide phenomenon, this American variety of anti-Semitism was related also to the nativist upsurge of the early twenties that culminated in the Immigration Act of 1924. To many Jews, however, it was Henry Ford who symbolized, in obvious and dramatic form, the threat to their security as American citizens.

The origins and motivation of Ford's anti-Semitism, which Allan Nevins called the "darkest blot" on his career, are of more than passing interest; they largely explain the nature of his appeal to certain groups.[15] In 1923, the Ford Motor Company, incorporated a bare twenty years earlier, had accumulated assets of over $500,000,000 and a monthly gross revenue of $8,000,000. Ford's wealth was unique, not so much in size, but in the qualities attached to it; "he resolved the moral dilemma of a Puritan-capitalist society. He achieved material success without losing his primal innocence." [16] Ford's popular image, somewhat tarnished by his performances at the Mount Clemens trial and on the Peace Ship, was of a wizard who could handle almost any problem. Assiduously promoted by dozens of books and articles, the legend of Henry Ford, made concrete by his omnipresent motor vehicles, assumed almost Lincolnian proportions. Narrowly defeated for the U.S. Senate in 1918, Ford was a popular contender for the presidential nomination in the early 1920's.

Allan Benson, a sympathetic Ford biographer, once attributed to him a "mulish streak." Louis Marshall termed the same quality a thick skull, but the mule simile was quite apt because of Ford's rural background. His mechanical genius and production techniques were revolutionizing old America and Fordismus was sweeping the world, but the master himself remained in many ways a son of the soil. Born and raised on a farm, Ford typified many of the attitudes of rural America which resented and resisted the fundamental changes that he, among others, was bringing about. In Greenfield Village, Ford built a replica of an old farming community. He subsidized a back-to-the-soil movement, paid for printing selections from the McGuffey readers, condemned modern dance, and revived folk dancing.

Ford's social ideas corresponded to the milieu he came from. Monopolies, cities, and Eastern bankers were anathema to him. The East Coast was regarded as "a miasmatic place whence rises the fetid drivel of all that is subversive in public thought," and New York was "an unassimilated province on the outskirts of the nation." [17]

One biographer called Ford "just the sort of rural Protestant American who joined the northern wing of the Ku Klux Klan," for he shared many of the prejudices of those who did.[18] In his search for panaceas and scapegoats, and in his relatively simple-minded approach to social issues, Ford was very much part of the Populist tradition of his youth; this explains his appeal to the masses outside the large cities.

A cardinal point of Populist dogma was suspicion of banks and bankers. With Ford, the bank phobia amounted to an *idée fixe*. He constantly referred to the forces of finance as a threat to creative industry, especially his own. Accepting the popular stereotype, bankers were equated in his mind with Jews. Ford spoke, for example, of Morgan's gentile associates as "Jews." In an interview revealing his proposed policies if elected President, Ford was asked, "What do you mean by Jews?" and answered without hesitation, "The international financiers." When the *Dearborn Independent* series broke on the American scene, speculation was intense that Ford had been motivated by resentment at the refusal of New York Jewish bankers, especially Kuhn, Loeb and Co., to grant him a large loan. There was no evidence for this rumor, although Ford did borrow a substantial sum in 1919 when buying out minority stockholders in his company.[19]

In December, 1921, Ford explained the origin of his *Dearborn Independent* crusade by saying that two prominent Jews who were aboard his Peace Ship had informed him that the "international Jewish bankers" were responsible for starting the war, that they controlled the world's gold, and that only they could stop the war. Herman Bernstein, the Jewish editor who was aboard the Peace Ship, vigorously denied Ford's statement, and later made it the basis of a libel suit. Louis Marshall, representing informed opinion on Ford's allegation, termed it "merest moonshine" and "the figment of a diseased imagination." It may be, however, that Ford blamed the failure of his Peace Ship on the Jews. He also may have resented Mme. Rosika Schwimmer, a Jewess, for bringing him into the whole episode. On the other hand, Mme. Schwimmer disputed Ford, charging he was prejudiced against Jews long before the Peace Ship set sail. She recalled that at her first meeting with Ford, in November, 1915, he had suddenly said, "I know who caused the war—the German-Jewish bankers." Slapping his coat pocket, he had exclaimed, "I have the evidence here. Facts. I can't give them out yet because I haven't got them all. But I'll soon have them." [20]

It was claimed that Ford's anti-Semitism was a tactic he seized upon to exploit the prejudices of gentile voters for his personal political career. Allegedly, Ford had planned to attack the Jews during his 1918 Senatorial race in the hope of gaining votes, but was dissuaded. After his defeat in that election by Truman Newberry, Ford explained it had been contrived by Wall Street and an "influential gang of Jews." Newberry, Ford charged, was a "Jewish Tool," and "New York" and the "Jews" had made a fool of him.[21]

In 1927, Ford publicly disclaimed direct knowledge of the *Dearborn Independent's* crusade, but his personal feelings toward Jews were known to intimates and to strangers. Harry Bennett, Ford's secret service chief, recalled that when Ford liked a Jew, he would say, "Oh, he's mixed, he's not all Jewish." [22] Sharing the prejudice of many rural Americans, Ford considered Jews non-productive:

> The Jew is a mere huckster, a trader, who doesn't want to produce, but to make something out of what somebody else produces. Our money and banking system is the invention of the Jews, for their own purposes of control, and it's bad. Our gold standard was founded by Jews; it's bad. . . .[23]

He saw the Jews poised, ready to pounce on industry, with labor unions doing the dirty work on behalf of Jewish bankers:

> The Jews are ordained by God to clean up the things that are ready to disappear. These Jew financiers are not building anything. They wait until things begin to decay, then get into them. . . . You probably think the labor unions were organized by labor, but they weren't. They were organized by those Jew financiers. . . . It's a great thing for the Jew to have on hand when he comes around to get his clutches on an industry.[24]

Ford felt personally threatened by the power of finance capitalism and by labor unrest. His answer, in part, was to identify the two as one, and to equate both with the Jews.

This feeling was not kept private, but was made the basis of Ford's course of instruction, as he called it, awakening the American people to the danger in its midst. Having failed in his Mount Clemens trial appearance on the basic facts of American history, Ford decided to "tell the people, among other things, some American history they don't teach in the schools." [25] The *Dearborn Independent's* crusade, Ford always claimed, was meant as education for Americans rather than open anti-Semitism.

Ford repeatedly denied he felt any antipathy toward the individual Jew, with the possible exception of "moneyed" Jews. In support of this, he cited the thousands of Jews employed by Ford Motor Company, although he admitted "we see that they work, too, and that they don't get into the office." [26] Anti-Semitism was a charge that annoyed Ford:

> We are not anti-Semitic. . . . It is my desire to bring about world peace. There can be no world peace until the international Jewish bankers cease providing money for wars. . . . We do not blame the Jew for his earnestness and alertness, but we do blame the poor gentile boob for not waking up. . . .[27]

In his autobiography, written in 1923 by Samuel Crowther, Ford pretentiously called his anti-Jewish campaign, "studies in the Jewish Question." Prejudice against persons, he said, was neither American nor Christian:

> Our opposition is only to ideas, false ideas, which are sapping the moral stamina of the people. . . . Let the American people once understand that it is not natural degeneracy, but calculated subversion that afflicts us, and they are safe. The explanation is the cure.[28]

Ford was able to convince himself that he was acting as a true friend of the Jews in pointing out their weaknesses and urging reform. He even hoped that his campaign would be endorsed by "good Jews." This was evident from his behavior toward Rabbi Leo M. Franklin of Temple Beth-El in Detroit, a former neighbor of his, and one of his few Jewish friends. Ford, who was in the habit of giving Franklin an annual present of a custom-built car, was surprised and hurt when the Rabbi turned down the gift after the *Dearborn Independent's* campaign started.[29]

Ford's rationalizations could not conceal his anti-Semitism, which was becoming an obsession. Visitors to his Dearborn office reported he seemed to be suffering from a persecution complex. References to Jews were sprinkled liberally through his conversations. One of his friendly biographers told of Ford's anger when challenged on his Jewish theories. Handing the astonished writer a pile of *Dearborn Independent* propaganda, Ford exclaimed, "Read them right away and then if you do not agree with me, don't ever come to see me again." [30] A Ford executive remembered that in late 1919 Ford was eating a piece of a candy bar and complained about its quality: "The Jews have taken hold of it. They're cheapening it to make more money out of it." [31] At a luncheon for the Detroit, Toledo and Ironton Railroad, Ford rose during a discussion of technical issues and proclaimed, "We will never get rid of our troubles until we get rid of the Jews." [32] An Englishman who interviewed Ford quoted him as having said, "The Jews are the scavengers of the world. They are necessary when there's something to be cleaned up. Whenever there's anything wrong with a country, you'll find the Jews on the job there." [33]

Unable to fathom the revolutionary times he lived in, frustrated by his failures on the political scene, fearful of bankers and unions, Ford vented his aggression on a traditional target—the Jews. His anti-Semitism was directly related to the troubled social atmosphere of post-World War I America:

> For this was the same America which had produced the Ku Klux Klan, filled the card-index files of the Department of Justice with the names of sixty thousand "suspects," started the Lusk Committee on its labours, using the Espionage Law to establish a federal spy system, . . . made the question of Bolshevism an issue between neighbors,

broadcast suspicion, intolerance and ill will, and attempted to explain all the unexpected and unwelcome disarrangements of the old order, following in the wake of a world war, on the simple theory that since something was plainly wrong with things as they used to be, obviously there must be a villain.[34]

To Henry Ford, the villain was easily identifiable: it was the Jew.

Management of Ford's Campaign

The *Dearborn Independent,* a somnolent country weekly until Ford purchased it in 1918, became the mirror of his personality and the vehicle for the spread of his anti-Jewish attitudes. It had been bought by Ford to overcome what he thought was the anti-Ford bias of the banker-controlled press. Ownership of the paper was vested in a Ford instumentality, the Dearborn Publishing Company, with Ford himself as President. During its decade of existence, Ford's publishing venture cost him almost $5,000,000 in losses, but he seemingly was unaffected.

It was clear from the early issues of the *Dearborn Independent,* under Ford auspices, that its readers were to be regaled with a strange mixture of outmoded Populism and Fordian capitalism. Accepting no advertising, and calling itself "The Chronicler of the Neglected Truth," it inveighed against big business, Wall Street, monopoly, and the gold standard. Yet, as Keith Sward has observed, its bark was worse than its bite, for the emphasis tended to rest on such panaceas as cheap money and such scapegoats as the Jews. Combining muckraking with fundamentalist morality, the *Independent* found its audience primarily in rural areas and small towns where Ford's dated, eccentric radicalism was familiar to old-timers.

Ford spared little effort to make the *Dearborn Independ-*

ent successful. For its first editor, he chose Edwin G. Pipp, formerly of the *Detroit News,* an experienced journalist with progressive ideas and faith in Ford's liberalism. Pipp's chief assistant, also from the *Detroit News* where they worked together for over seventeen years, was William J. Cameron. Almost immediately, Pipp became aware of an anti-Semitic atmosphere, with Ford and members of his staff urging the publication of articles on the Jews. Pipp, a man of conscience, resigned on April 1, 1920 and soon founded his own journal, specializing in Ford news.

Pipp suspected that Ford's anti-Semitism was reinforced, if not actively stimulated, by the man closest to him in the organization—his private secretary, Ernest Liebold. Pipp attributed the same opinion of Liebold to Ford's son, Edsel. According to Allan Nevins, Liebold was a man of "cold, ruthless intensity" with a "rigid mind and the disposition of a Prussian martinet." Harry Bennett remembered that Ford once attended a banquet at which Liebold was seen to whisper to his chief, "See that man over there? He's a Jew," whereupon Ford looked at the man and scowled.

Pipp's theory had a basis in fact, for it was Liebold who organized and directed the anti-Semitic campaign, and who popularized the term, "The international Jew." Liebold, who was reported to have said, "When we get through with the Jews there won't be one of them who will dare raise his head in public," had, according to one of his agents, "the most sickening nightmares" about Jews.[35] Boris Brasol, the Russian émigré officer who was active in spreading the Protocols (which became something of a Bible to the Ford staff), knew Liebold as early as 1919. Ford was said to have received the Protocols from a certain Bishop Patrick, a former Episcopalian priest who had entered the Russian Orthodox Church, but it was Brasol who was most influential on Liebold and the Ford entourage.

In order to gather anti-Semitic material, Liebold established a special office in New York City and employed private detectives and secret agents. The head of the New York office, although he denied it, was C. C. Daniels, a lawyer and brother of Josephus Daniels, Secretary of the Navy. Employing many operatives, this office investigated Jewish influence in such agencies as the War Shipping Board and the War Finance Corporation, and spent much time trying to find such absurdities as a private telephone wire from Justice Louis Brandeis's home to the White House over which the ailing Wilson supposedly received his orders. Ford agents were also active in Europe in attempting to obtain incriminating material on Jews. Sir Paul Dukes, former chief of British Intelligence in Russia, was approached in the vain hope of receiving damaging data on Jewish Bolsheviks.[36] Liebold's agents, despite occasional failures, were able to supply the Ford machine with sufficient information and misinformation to provide dozens of anti-Semitic articles.

When Ford Motor Company officials throughout the country displayed signs of confusion and indignation at the *Independent's* campaign, Liebold addressed a letter to them on behalf of Ford, attempting to explain the crusade and allay their fears:

> People ask you every day, perhaps, a question which runs like this, "Why is Henry Ford attacking the Jews?" The answer is, "There is no attack and no campaign against the Jews. The Jewish question, as every businessman knows, has been festering in silence and suspicion here in the United States for a long time and none has dared to discuss it because Jewish influence was strong enough to crush the man who attempted it. . . . Jewish leaders have gone from one excess to the other, until the time came for a protest or a surrender. . . ."

> You, as officials of the Ford Motor Company, may deny all Jewish explanations for this series of articles, namely, that Jews stung Ford in a business deal, that Jewish bankers refused to let Ford have a loan, and that Ford is a Jew-hater anyway.

> No Jew has succeeded in getting the better of Ford. No Jew had the chance to refuse him a loan. No Jew can say that he ever got anything but the squarest kind of a man-to-man deal from Mr. Ford as thousands of Jewish Ford employees can testify.[37]

To a Jewish subscriber who protested the *Dearborn Independent's* articles, Liebold replied that "that our present campaign against the international Jew is based on facts which we have gathered for some time past and is not based on prejudice." [38]

While Liebold organized the campaign, it was William Cameron, Pipp's erstwhile assistant, who wielded the pen. Cameron, whom Pipp regarded as one of the best reporters in the business, stepped into the editor's shoes and acceded to Ford's order for the publication of anti-Jewish material. He confessed to friends he despised himself for carrying out Ford's instructions. He dreaded writing the articles, but did it because he was "getting the jack." Although he ridiculed Ford's ideas and called the whole Dearborn institution "a mad house," he dutifully did his research and writing, using the Detroit Public Library, among other sources.[39]

Cameron eventually entered wholeheartedly into the enterprise. His proficiency became remarkable as he grew to understand Ford's idiosyncrasies. The chief personally visited Cameron's office almost daily, discussing the general line of the paper, including Ford's own page, which Cameron wrote. Thus, Cameron, who had written in defense of Leo Frank in 1914, and who admitted being impressed by the history of the Jews, became the willing and able author of the *Dearborn Independent's* articles.

Those who regarded Ford as too dull on non-mechanical matters to be capable of having his own prejudices, often thought of him as "mere clay in the hands of the potter." Marshall and other Jewish leaders suspected that Ford's opinions could be traced in part to his pacifist association with David Starr Jordan, former President of Stanford University. Although they did not publicize this suspicion, they felt that Jordan's book, *The Unseen Empire,* written shortly before the war, had been critical of the "international financiers," and that Ford had perhaps imbibed Jordan's views.

If Ford was subjected to malevolent influences from

friends and subordinates, he was urged in the opposite direction by his family. Mrs. Ford and Edsel Ford, it was reported, were not at all in sympathy with the elder Ford's anti-Semitic proclivities. Edsel, believing his father under Liebold's power in this matter, remonstrated with Ford on many occasions. Ford, however, was impervious to the wishes of his wife and only son, and remained obstinately, if not obsessively, anti-Semitic.

Propaganda Distribution

As the *Dearborn Independent's* series of anti-Jewish articles progressed, its readership mounted. The editors claimed that the Jewish series was "the most talked-of magazine feature in the country today." [40] Subscription figures indicated that Ford's sensational anti-Semitism aided the *Independent's* business success. At the end of 1919, with a circulation of 72,000, it had lost $284,000, but by 1922 it was up to almost 300,000 subscribers and reached a peak of 700,000 in 1924–25.

These statistics are deceptive because much of the circulation was based on semi-compulsory buying by the chain of Ford dealers, who were used as subscription agents for the *Independent*. When a dealer signed a contract for the following year's models, he was obliged to estimate the number of copies of the *Independent* he could handle during the year. The company often assigned quotas and required that periodic estimates of subscriptions be included in reports to the home office of car sales. In 1924, dealers were ordered to start contests in each county, with a Ford car as the prize for the person bringing in the largest number of subscriptions. Periodic circulars harangued the agents to solicit subscriptions for the *Dearborn Independent,* which was "just as much of a

Ford product as the car or tractor." If dealers neglected their manifest duty, a form letter was dispatched to them from Dearborn:

1. You have not sent in a single *Dearborn Independent* subscription this year.
2. You have disregarded our special requests to send in your estimated monthly subscriptions so we can remove your name from the non-producer list sent to the Home Office each month.
3. You signed a sales agreement to secure _____ subscriptions during 1925.
4. You are fully expected to live up to this agreement.[41]

Most dealers bowed to the pressure from Dearborn. Some paid for their assigned quotas of subscriptions themselves and sent them as gifts to local organizations; others merely sent in an occasional check with a random list of subscribers. Braver souls, who apparently were willing to risk the loss of their franchise, protested strongly, but without effect.

Despite the manufactured nature of its circulation, the *Dearborn Independent* managed to acquire a following, especially in the Midwest and Eastern rural areas. Louis Marshall's contention that "there are very few non-Jews who read the *Dearborn Independent* except an occasional farmer or persons having business relations with Ford" was wishful thinking.[42] Ford's machinery was in high gear, and no possible circulation booster was overlooked.*

The weekly *Dearborn Independent* was not the only means for the dissemination of Ford's anti-Jewish propaganda. In its issue of October 20, 1920, publication was announced of a 200 page booklet containing reprints of the first twenty articles on the Jews, available for the nominal cost of twenty-five cents. This was the first of four booklets titled *The International Jew*. The three subsequent ones were subtitled, respectively, *Jewish Activities in the United States, Jewish Influences in American Life,* and *Aspects of Jewish Power in*

---

* The AJC received complaints about stickers, "Are You Reading the *Dearborn Independent?*" that had been pasted to mailing wrappers of *Jewish Farmer* magazine.

the United States. In the early twenties, these pamphlets had an enormous distribution in the United States alone; Ford reprinted them in lots of 200,000 copies. For special friends and a key list of influential persons, a gift edition, bound in leather, was prepared. Flyers were inserted in the books that alerted readers to their importance: "This is only a *little* book —but it deals with a subject which, in the opinion of many, is the world's biggest problem."

Distributed gratis in large numbers to mailing lists of clergymen, editors, legislators, and other community leaders, *The International Jew* penetrated every corner of the nation. Faculty members at the University of Pittsburgh received free copies; teachers and officials in Utah were swamped; the Arkansas State House was sent a whole mail sack filled with the books. All this was in addition to the normal mailing of free *Dearborn Independent* subscriptions to public libraries, Y.M.C.A.'s, and fraternal and business groups. Reprints in mat form of the weekly articles were distributed free to country newspapers. The Ford Motor Company openly displayed and sold copies of *The International Jew* in its tent at the Michigan State Fair.

The International Jew found its way to the homeland of modern anti-Semitism—Europe. Sold in England, highly praised in Germany, it was soon translated and made available in the leading tongues of the world. German publication rights were held by the firm of Hammer-Verlag, run by Theodor Fritsch.* Dearborn spokesmen, however, denied rumors that Ford was subsidizing Hitler and the German anti-Semitic movement; the American Jewish Committee was unable to find confirming evidence.

The *Dearborn Independent* articles, replete with wild and unsubstantiated exaggerations, misrepresentations, half-truths and whole lies, were nevertheless cloaked in a veil of objectivity, if not intellectuality. Cameron was an able expounder of other men's ideas, and Liebold's secret service

* See Chapter 7 on the Ford-Fritsch relationship.

provided him with mountains of material to digest and feed to the presses.* The themes selected for exploitation revealed very little about Jews in the United States, but a great deal about Ford's mind and his insight into the malaise affecting many Americans in the small towns and farms where his journal was read.

These people were emotionally buffeted by the changes sweeping post-war America; they were hit economically by an agricultural depression. Unable to understand the forces destroying their precious values, they struck back blindly. Ford's international Jew, derived from the conspiratorial motifs of the older Populism and the newly imported Protocols, provided an outlet for the accumulated frustrations of these rural Americans. His elaboration of the nefarious workings of a Jewish subversive plot provided them, for the first time in America, with a relatively well-organized native source of anti-Semitic propaganda.

* Ford was later urged to turn over his collection of anti-Semitica to the Hebrew Union College for historical purposes, but he never did.

Chapter six

reaction
to the
ford
propaganda

The extensively propagated, sensational, anti-Jewish charges sponsored by Henry Ford caused considerable public comment in America. Ford's wealth and national image of folk hero guaranteed an outburst of popular interest, indignation, and apprehension. Jews were particularly disturbed by the dangerous attack of a man whose word was accepted by many Americans as gospel. Ford's agitation had potentially harmful consequences throughout his seven year campaign; however, it was readily apparent that American opinion- and policy-makers found his propaganda unpalatable.

Ford's onslaught met a negative reaction in the large urban areas. Agents of the *Dearborn Independent,* attempting to increase street sales in the cities, faced open violence and legal restrictions. In Toledo, the street sale of the *Independent* precipitated a riot in front of the Federal Building which blocked traffic and necessitated police reserves to disperse the mob. In Pittsburgh street violence also became riotous, leading, in one incident, to the arrest of nine participants. Many major communities, including Boston, Chicago, Cincinnati,

Cleveland, Columbus, Detroit, Pittsburgh, and St. Louis, rashly tried to prevent or discourage the sale of the *Independent* through police orders or special city ordinances.

Accusing the Jews of trying to suppress freedom of speech and press, the *Dearborn Independent* immediately dispatched members of the Ford legal staff to battle. Injunctions were granted by the courts of Pittsburgh, Cleveland, Chicago, and St. Louis restraining authorities from interfering with the sale of the *Independent*. The American Civil Liberties Union protested to the Mayor of Cincinnati against a new city ordinance banning the *Dearborn Independent*. When vendors who had been arrested in Pittsburgh, Detroit, and Cleveland were freed by Federal judges, it was clear that suppression by municipal action would not work.

More sophisticated legal coercion was attempted in Michigan. A bill was introduced in the state legislature defining a new crime, "general libel," aimed at the *Dearborn Independent's* anti-Jewish slurs. There was enough support to bring it safely through the House and the Senate. However, it was finally turned down by the upper chamber, which reversed itself after pressure had been put on it by Detroit newspapers who feared the bill might stifle legitimate criticism.

Public libraries, traditionally subject to the outraged cries of citizens, were quick to ban the *Dearborn Independent* from their reading rooms. The Carnegie Library of Pittsburgh refused to bar it, but many libraries were ordered to do so by mayors and boards of trustees.

The furor over the attempted sale of the *Dearborn Independent* indicated that American officialdom would not countenance Ford's anti-Semitic campaign. The American press, for the most part, also strongly opposed the Ford propaganda. Such papers as the *Philadelphia Ledger,* the *Albany Times-Union,* and the *Hartford Courant* spoke of Ford's "mean and narrow mental attitude" and condemned the "vulgar attacks" on the Jewish people. The *Rochester Post* assured its readers they need not worry that newspapers would be taken in by Ford's campaign.[1] The Hearst chain turned its back on Ford and printed exposés by Jewish writers and editorial critiques by Arthur Brisbane. The potent New York City press stood aghast, as did the relatively weak labor press of the nation. Most important, few newspapers reprinted the *Dearborn Independent's* articles.

Magazines were vociferous in denouncing Ford. Liberal journals, such as *The Nation,* were joined by middle-of-the-road magazines in refuting Ford's allegations. *Hearst's International,* edited by Norman Hapgood, was particularly forceful in exposing Ford's "Jew-mania." *Pipp's Weekly,* although not widely distributed, provided excellent ammunition for anti-Ford forces.

Contrarily, a few Midwestern papers echoed the Ford line. Marshall vigorously protested an article in the *Charleston, Ill. News* that called Otto Kahn's proposals on the foreign debt an "international Jew scheme." An occasional sour note appeared in the metropolitan journals of the eastern seaboard. Letters appeared in the *New York Globe* praising Ford and condemning the Jews as Orientals, but the *Globe* hastily printed an explanatory editorial after Marshall objected. Crackpot sheets, such as *The Anti-Bolsehvist* of Brooklyn, denounced Jews along with Ford, but when an article in the highly respected *Atlantic Monthly* spoke of "the pathological state of the Jewish mind," Jewish leaders were concerned. Herbert Adams Gibbons, whose *bête noire* was Zionism, wrote in the *Century Magazine* that

> . . . scarcely a day passes that some one does not write to me that the Jews are plotting to control the world. . . . The Ford campaign is symptomatic of a condition that is new in the United States. Mr. Ford did not create this condition. He has aggravated it, of course, but if the minds of the American people were not ready for what the Dearborn "Independent" has asserted, Mr. Ford's "international Jew" would have been laughed out of existence in the same way Mr. Ford's peace ship was.[2]

Mr. Gibbons took Ford seriously, but his was a minority opinion in the flurry of magazine articles then appearing.

Most of them decried Fordianism and very few displayed open hostility to Jews.

A mounting chorus of non-Jewish Americans openly condemned Ford's attack. From clergymen to Congressmen, professors to ex-Presidents of the United States, these men made it clear that Ford as an anti-Semite was *persona non grata* in the respectable, opinion-molding sectors of American life. Nicholas Murray Butler contributed a statement on the desirability of avoiding racial and religious schisms to the *American Hebrew*. President W. H. P. Faunce of Brown University said, at a ceremony marking the 300th anniversary of the landing at Plymouth, that the descendants of the Pilgrims and Puritans would reject Ford's propaganda. The dean at Syracuse University who publicly endorsed Ford's doctrine that Jewish control of the movies was degrading America was rare in academic circles.[3]

Politicians, including such men as William G. McAdoo, William Jennings Bryan, and even Tom Watson, contributed their denunciations of the Ford doctrines (although Jews were adverse to Watson's friendship because of his earlier activities in the Leo Frank case).[4] The former Governor of Massachusetts, Samuel W. McCall, wrote an informative book called *The Patriotism of the American Jew* as an answer to Ford and the Protocols; ex-President Charles W. Eliot of Harvard added a foreword. William Howard Taft, whom the Ford scribes called a gentile front for the Jews, was especially active in flaying the new anti-Semitism. In a speech before the Anti-Defamation League in Chicago, he equated the Protocols with the tales of Baron Munchausen; in Brooklyn he hopefully observed, "We are too enlightened for such a recession to the Dark Ages." [5]

A very important influence on American opinion in the 1920's was the Christian clergy, and most of its members were outspokenly anti-Ford. A Baltimore pastor called anti-Semitism treason to America; a San Francisco preacher referred to Ford as a moral coward; a Baptist minister in Brooklyn claimed Ford did not represent Christian sentiment in America; a Presbyterian leader in Rochester called on Christians to combat anti-Jewish hatred; and the Rev. John Haynes Holmes in New York said that Jews were among the noblest peoples in the world. Roman Catholic Bishop Bonaventure F. Broderick joined eminent Catholic laymen in open denunciations. In Utah the president of the Mormon Church proclaimed to his flock:

> There appears to be a good deal of agitation against the Jewish people. We should hold no ill-will against them. . . . We believe that they will yet come into the fold of the gospel. Let no Latter-Day Saint have any part in any agitation or movement against the Jewish people.[6]

Apparently, the anticipated conversion of the Jews, still a dream of many church leaders, helped turn some of them against Ford.

There is little direct evidence that Protestant, fundamentalist preachers in the hinterlands of America were propagating Ford's ideas, but even in large urban areas, clerical minds were not immune. In Seattle, the pastor of the largest and most influential Presbyterian congregation vouchsafed the truth of the Ford dogma; Rev. John Roach Straton, well-known fundamentalist leader of the Calvary Baptist Church of New York, asserted that Jews would eventually dominate the world.

> There is no denying many of the facts that Mr. Ford gives. From the standpoint of numbers the Jewish race is insignificant. Despite this there is the phenomenon of their world-wide power, not only in money making, but in the field of statesmanship and letters.

He qualified his agreement with Ford, however, by revealing that Jewish success was not the result of a conspiracy, but rather a part of the providential plan for universal redemption.[7]

Louis Marshall received a particularly bitter letter from a Methodist minister, Rev. A. E. Potter of Belleville, a small town in upper New York:

Bolshevism is Jewish and is anti-Christian. . . . The Jew is seeking political power more than any other race in America. . . . You are as bitter Christ-rejectors, as a race, as you were 1900 years ago. . . . The Jew is the wealthiest person in New York. . . . Of all my Jewish acquaintances not one volunteered for the great war. . . . It is too true that the modern Jew is so accurately represented by Shylock. . . . If ever Satan possessed a race, as a whole, I believe he does the Jew. . . . The Jew in America has added nothing whatever to its real progress. His wealth came not so much from toil as from exploitation. . . . I believe firmly in the "Independent's" theory of the Protocols. . . . I deem the Jew of today a moral degenerate. . . . I deem the Jew the most criminal element in our land at the present time. . . . I have written strongly, but I express the thoughts of every real patriot whose eyes are open to our country's dangers. God speed the *Dearborn Independent* which has courage to tell the truth, and success to Henry Ford who dares face Jewish capital.[8]

To this epistle, Marshall wrathfully replied:

There is not an epithet that can be invented by the most filthy mind that you have not employed in your references to the Jews. Whenever you mention them you foam at the mouth like a dog stricken with hydrophobia. Every line of what you have written drips with falsehood and runs over with hatred, malice, and all uncharitableness. . . . It ill becomes one who is capable of harboring such thoughts as you have expressed and who thus rejects the Sermon on the Mount, to speak of Christ-rejectors. Apparently your reading of the Bible has not benefitted you. . . . All that I might say could not penetrate through the hide of a pachyderm. Nor would it be useful for me to suggest that you look into your own heart and soul in order that you may ponder whether all is well there. I sign myself, with utter contempt, Louis Marshall.[9]

Marshall's anger at the ravings of such small-town preachers was matched only by the satisfaction of Jewish leaders at the positive action taken by the Federal Council of Churches of Christ in America. At its quadrennial convention in Boston, December, 1920, the Federal Council, representing the major Protestant denominations, expressed disapproval of the Ford propaganda in a strongly worded resolution. Jewish organizations had been prepared to lobby for passage of such a resolution, but the Council acted on its own initiative and pressure was not necessary. Marshall believed that the Council's action would take the sting out of Ford's venom and was convinced that "the best way to fight this anti-Semite movement is through the Christian clergy." [10] The generally unfavorable response of the clergy to Ford's challenge, together with similar reactions of other leaders, was creating a climate of opinion antithetic to the *Dearborn Independent*.

The *coup de grâce* which destroyed any hopes Ford may have had for attracting high level support was delivered by the publication, on January 17, 1921, of a manifesto called "The Peril of Racial Prejudice"; it was signed by a group of 119 distinguished Americans, headed by President Woodrow Wilson and the only living ex-President, William H. Taft. The petition was originated by John Spargo. Spargo, a socialist, was absolutely convinced it was the duty of all progressive gentiles to stand up against the anti-Semitic propaganda emanating from Dearborn. Regarding it not so much of a danger to Jews as a danger to American democracy and Christian civilization, he believed that Ford's anti-Semitism was part of an international reactionary campaign.

Acting on his own, he drafted a petition of protest against racial prejudice and submitted it to over 200 prominent Americans for signature. The task of correspondence was arduous and cost Spargo more than two months of labor and considerable financial expense (for which he later refused payment from Jews). It was only after the work had begun that Marshall and the American Jewish Committee learned of it. Marshall, who did not meet Spargo until after the publication of the manifesto, was enthusiastic because he considered him to be like E. G. Pipp—not a "subsidized warrior," but one who spoke from the heart. When Spargo informed him that he lacked the signature of distinguished Catholic prelates, Marshall obtained them through an influential Catholic lawyer. Writing to his friend, the Chancellor of Syracuse University, Marshall urged him to sign, assuring him that "although Mr. Spargo is a Socialist he has been making the most able and clean-cut campaign against Bolshevism." [11]

Spargo later admitted he had been unable to secure the

adherence of many influential figures. Charles Evans Hughes, Herbert Hoover, and Josephus Daniels did not reply to his invitations. Presidents A. Lawrence Lowell of Harvard and Arthur T. Hadley of Yale refused to sign on the grounds that anti-Semitism had not really taken root in this country and therefore should not be taken seriously; former President Charles W. Eliot declined to sign a petition prepared by a Socialist. More serious was the unwillingness of President-Elect Harding to lend his signature to the petition despite repeated appeals from Spargo. Harding finally replied to Spargo in a letter that explained his attitude:

> I am sure you can understand why, at the present time, I am seeking the avoidance of undue publicity and reluctant to make public statements relating to any of our pending problems. I am no less sure that you already know, and that the American people already believe, that I come giving no sanction to anything so narrow, so intolerant or so un-American as the antisemitic movement.[12]

Marshall and Spargo accepted Harding's excuse that the etiquette problem prevented his signing before taking office. Although the absence of his signature might be construed as a weakness, they believed that the letter, later published, strengthened the manifesto.

The petition itself, as released to the press without mentioning the name of Ford, called on gentile Americans to rise up against the dangers of racial propaganda:

> The undersigned citizens of Gentile birth and Christian faith, view with profound regret and disapproval the appearance in this country of what is apparently an organized campaign of anti-Semitism, conducted in close conformity to and co-operation with similar campaigns in Europe. . . . We protest against this organized campaign of prejudice and hatred not only because of its manifest injustice to those against whom it is directed, but also, and especially, because we are convinced that it is wholly incompatible with loyal and intelligent American citizenship. . . . We believe it should not be left to men and women of Jewish faith to fight this evil, but that it is in a very special sense the duty of citizens who are not Jews by ancestry or faith. We therefore make earnest protest against this vicious propaganda, and call upon our fellow citizens of Gentile birth and Christian

faith to unite their efforts to ours, to the end that it may be crushed. In particular, we call upon all who are molders of public opinion— the clergy and ministers of all Christian churches, publicists, teachers, editors, and statesmen—to strike at this un-American and un-Christian agitation.[13]

The signatures to the manifesto consisted of a lengthy roster of the "molders of public opinion." William Cardinal O'-Connell, Jane Addams, Newton D. Baker, Charles A. Beard, William Jennings Bryan, George Creel, Clarence Darrow, Robert Frost, John Haynes Holmes, Robert Lansing, Samuel Seabury, Ida M. Tarbell, David Starr Jordan, Lyman Abbott, Paul Kellogg, Hamilton Holt, and dozens of others equally prominent, were listed. Among the signers were the heads of Columbia, Syracuse, Williams, Oberlin, Dartmouth, Princeton, Cornell, Catholic, and Brown Universities.

Leading politicians, newspapers, magazines, educators, and clergymen refused to accept Ford's propaganda attack and the Spargo manifesto confirmed this. Still, the *Dearborn Independent* persisted in its efforts, claiming the Spargo manifesto was a mere technique of the Jews who were resorting to the use of gentile fronts. American-Jewish leaders were heartened by the reaction of responsible Christians, but a sense of crisis remained.

Official Jewish Reaction

In its lead editorial of June 11, 1920, the *American Hebrew* gave vent to the outrage and shock many Jews felt on learning of the inauguration of the Ford series:

International anti-Semitism has struck the United States. No American in the whole of our history has perpetrated so shocking an attack, so dastardly a crime, against the Jews as has Henry Ford. . . . Mr. Ford deserves to be deprived of his American citizenship, to be tarred and feathered.

Henry Ford soon became prominent in conversations among Jews on the streets and in the cafes of the crowded Jewish sections of the great cities. In Chicago, 5,000 Jews came to hear John Spargo denounce Ford and the Protocols; and, in the same city, a near riot was touched off at a masked ball when a foolhardy guest came dressed as Ford. Stephen Wise and other rabbis accused Ford of libeling the Jews. From Europe came reports that Ford's propaganda was constantly discussed among Jews of England and France.

The first reaction of the Jewish socialists of the East Side, preoccupied with pogroms in Europe and with the Red Scare and union problems in America, was to see the anti-Semitism of the *Dearborn Independent* as incidental to Ford's hatred of bankers and Wall Street. However, they soon realized the grave implications of the articles, and B. Charney Vladeck, Managing Editor of the *Forward,* confessed he was "deeply worried."

Although the greatest immediate sensitivity to the Ford campaign was displayed by the more Americanized Jewish community, almost all Jews were alarmed when the persistence of Ford's attacks became obvious. Louis Marshall, in a moment of pessimism, considered Ford's campaign "the most serious episode in the history of American Jewry." [14] Familiar with European anti-Semitic movements and aware of the relatively limited forms anti-Semitism had previously taken in the United States, some Jewish leaders feared they were witnessing the first attempt "to foist a definite, organized consciously directed anti-Semitic movement upon these shores." [15] Coming on the heels of the publication of the Protocols in America, the Ford attack made the threat of such a development seem very real.

The question now was, "What shall be the response of the Jew to the thrown gauntlet of anti-Semitism? How shall we meet it?" [16] American-Jewish leaders were faced with delicate decisions. Should the Ford attack be met head-on with a vigorous counter-offensive, or should it be ignored? On the upper levels of American-Jewish society, opinion was divided. Jacob Schiff, the most powerful member of the American Jewish Committee (then near death), counseled caution, and was seconded by such men as Albert D. Lasker. Cyrus Adler agreed with them: "Nothing we can do can help this situation and I continue to feel the quieter we remain, the better it will likely be in the end." [17] The majority opinion among the leaders, however, corresponded more closely with that of the masses: hit back and hit hard. Louis Marshall insisted, at least in the early months of the Ford campaign, on the importance of waging an aggressive fight, and he had the strong backing of Jewish leaders in Ford's own city, Detroit. The initial reaction, therefore, was that Ford should not be suffered in silence, despite the possible risk of publicizing him.

Marshall was not aware of the *Dearborn Independent's* series until Julius Rosenwald informed him of the publication of the first two articles. Incredulous, Marshall, on June 3, 1920, sent a telegram to Henry Ford, hoping to squelch the campaign immediately, or at least to determine if it actually had Ford's approval:

> . . . On behalf of my brethren I ask you from whom we had believed that justice might be expected whether these offensive articles have your sanction, whether further publications of this nature are to be continued, and whether you shall remain silent when your failure to disavow them will be regarded as an endorsement of them by the general public. Three million of deeply wounded Americans are awaiting your answer.[18]

Marshall was not kept in suspense for long. On June 5, 1920, a blunt, telegraphed reply, signed by the Dearborn Publishing Company, was received:

> . . . Your rhetoric is that of a Bolshevik orator . . . you cruelly overwork your most useful term which is antizamitism [sic]. These articles shall continue and we hope you will continue to read them. . . .[19]

Marshall then knew that Ford was authorizing and sanctioning the Dearborn articles, and believing that Ford's action placed him among the international anti-Semites, he called for vigorous action by the American Jewish Committee.[20]

When Marshall's correspondence with Ford became known, however, a squabble occurred. Reform rabbis said that the use by Marshall of "intemperate invective" in the telegram to Ford had harmed the Jewish cause. Detroit's leading rabbi (and a warm personal friend of Ford), Leo M. Franklin, became the center of the storm, claiming that Ford was not an anti-Semite, but had been victimized by evil advice. Franklin said that Ford had been on the verge of retracting the Dearborn charges when Marshall's telegram arrived, angering him and resulting in the renewal of the attack. Adolf Kraus, national President of the B'nai B'rith, supported Franklin's belief that Ford had been amenable to friendly Jewish intercession until Marshall charged in.[21]

To Marshall, this reasoning was rank nonsense. "Without flattering myself I may say that I am not a novice and that I have been engaged in a hundred battles with men of infinitely greater ability than Ford and have succeeded in most of my controversies in protecting the honor of the Jews." [22] Franklin, who was willing to credit Ford with humanitarian impulses and who suspected that he was aiming his attacks mostly at Bolsheviks, was warned by Marshall that Ford was not simply against the Jews as Bolsheviks, but against the Jews as Jews. Ford was an "ignoramus," but his attacks were dangerous because of his unlimited wealth. Above all, Marshall advised, it would be extremely unwise to allow Ford to believe that some Jews excused his attacks.

Franklin, feeling that "these times are too critical for any of us to indulge in petty personalities," apologized to Marshall privately and later repeated his apology publicly at a meeting of Jewish leaders.[23] Nevertheless, he persisted in his idea that a more tactful approach would have stopped Ford at the beginning of his campaign. His stubbornness on this point provoked Marshall:

> . . . Do you believe that it would have been appropriate for us to have grovelled or crawled on our bellies before Ford, or to have prayed that he should be illuminated by the light of truth, or to have

humored him, or to have acted as toadies, or to have sent him
religious tracts? [24]

Despite the qualms of men like Franklin, Marshall and his
friends went ahead with consideration of counter-measures.
Restraining himself at first out of deference to Schiff, who
opposed any more public statements in defense of the Jews,
Marshall moved slowly. After Schiff's death in September,
1920, however, his tempo was more rapid.

At the October 10, 1920 meeting of the AJC's Executive
Committee, the Ford issue in its relationship to other forms
of anti-Semitic propaganda was exhaustively discussed. A subcommittee, consisting of Marshall, Cyrus Adler, and Oscar
Straus was appointed to study the matter, and, with the aid of
Judges Irving Lehman and Abram I. Elkus, proposed a plan
of action: a public statement would be issued emphatically
denying Jews were Bolsheviks and declaring the Protocols a
forgery; and a book would be prepared to provide an extended treatment of these subjects. In order to coordinate
Jewish actions on Ford and the Protocols, representatives of
all major organizations would be invited to attend the Annual Meeting of the American Jewish Committee on November 14, 1920.

On that day, a special conference convened at the Hotel
Astor in New York. It required some effort, but Marshall
swallowed his pride and resentment, and agreed to the presence of his critics, Kraus and Franklin. They represented,
respectively, the B'nai B'rith, and the Central Conference of
American Rabbis. Delegates from the United Synagogue of
America (Conservative) included Louis Ginzberg and Alexander Marx; the American Jewish Congress, rival of the Committee, was also represented. As Marshall told Kraus, "If there
ever was a time when there should be united action by
American Jewry, that time has arrived." [25]

The main item on the agenda was the reading and discussion of a lengthy document, written by Marshall, which attempted to destroy the Jewish-Bolshevik myth and to demonstrate the falsity of the Protocols. Marshall obtained the

agreement of all the organizations to his strategy of issuing this document as the united statement of the Jews of America in answer to the flood of anti-Semitic propaganda then emerging from Dearborn and other sources. Although some Jewish leaders had reservations about the wisdom of issuing any public reply to anti-Semitic allegations, and others felt that the language was "somewhat too aggressive," the statement was approved.[26]

On December 1, 1920, "The 'Protocols,' Bolshevism, and the Jews; An Address to Their Fellow-Citizens by American Jewish Organizations," was released to the press. Signed by the American Jewish Committee, the American Jewish Congress, the Zionist Organization of America, the B'nai B'rith, and all of the major rabbinical and congregational groups, Marshall called the address "the most important document that has ever been issued by the Jews of America." [27]

The emphasis in the address was on proving that "the Protocols are a base forgery" and that the alleged Jewish-Bolshevik nexus was "absurd in theory and absolutely untrue in fact." Marshall and other Jewish leaders felt that it was really essential to explain away the Jewish-Bolshevik charge because of its particular danger in the prevalent Red Scare atmosphere. After tracing the sordid history of the Protocols, the address stated that the number of Bolshevist Jews in Russia was greatly exaggerated, that most Jews were in non-Bolshevist parties, and that a man like Trotsky had "never in the slightest degree concerned himself with Judaism or the welfare of the Jews." The majority of Russian Jews, it was emphasized, had been ruined by the coercive measures of the Soviet government.

Ford's charges, although they were the stimulus to publication of the address, were not given a thorough analysis:

> We have refrained from commenting on the libels contained in the *Dearborn Independent*. Ford, in the fullness of his knowledge, unqualifiedly declares The Protocols to be genuine, and argues that practically every Jew is a Bolshevist. We have dealt sufficiently with both of these falsehoods. It is useless in a serious document to analyze

the puerile and venomous drivel that he has derived from the concoctions of professional agitators. He is merely a dupe.

The statement concluded with an analysis of the cause of the current anti-Semitic wave: "It is the motive that again and again has actuated autocracy and its adroit supporters—that of seeking a scapegoat for their own sins, so that they may be enabled under the cover of a false issue to deceive the public."

The address was well-constructed and carefully reasoned counter-propaganda. Its purpose was to place on the record the official Jewish answer to Ford and his cohorts. It might not turn a convinced anti-Semite from his ways, but it would provide those who were willing to understand with arguments against intolerance.

Released to the press on December 1, the statement was printed in almost all major newspapers in the country, sometimes with the encouragement of local Jewish leaders. From Atlanta, Boston, Baltimore, Chicago, San Francisco, and Pittsburgh, reports of the publication flowed in to Marshall, who had already seen it through the New York press.[28] Editorial comment was generally favorable, with many newspapers, including the *New York Times,* regretting the fact that Jewish organizations should have thought it necessary to issue such a document. The *Chicago Tribune,* on the other hand, received the address coolly: "We do not think anti-Semitism will make headway in this country, unless the Jews themselves should organize Semitism and attempt thus to influence public policy for special causes or for particular Jewish interests." [29] But the *Tribune* was in the minority, and even the Beckwith Company, one of the American publishers of the Protocols, reprinted the statement in pamphlet form to provide owners of the Beckwith edition with "an important reference."

The public reaction to the document among individual Jews and non-Jews varied. A Masonic leader in an Arkansas town congratulated Marshall, "I shall see that all the brethren are fully informed and put on guard against this insidious effort of the Jesuit to discredit Jews and Freemasons." [30] This, of course, was not exactly the reaction Marshall anticipated or approved, and neither was he pleased at the objection of a Catholic college instructor who disliked the use of the phrase, "recrudescence of mediaeval bigotry and stupidity," because it reflected adversely on the Church. Openly hostile individuals, such as a clergyman in Minnesota who called the statement "surprisingly weak," could not be convinced.

Marshall and top echelon Jewish leadership were, however, quite satisfied with their handiwork. They had hesitated before answering ridiculous falsehoods, but, as Marshall remarked, "The world has lost its sense of humor in these terrible days," and it was feared that critics might point to the absence of a reply as a tacit admission of guilt. The American Jewish Committee, pleased with what it considered a heartening public response, appropriated $10,000 to print the address, and distributed 250,000 copies of the pamphlet to legislators, educators, and other influential men.

Shortly after the release of the Jewish address came the resolution of the Federal Council of Churches, decrying the racial propaganda. At the same time, Marshall was assisting Spargo in the collection of signatures for the manifesto of distinguished Americans. In the eyes of some Jewish leaders, the tide of public opinion had turned against the attacks on the Jews. Further defense action, therefore, would have to be carefully limited in order not to exacerbate conditions unnecessarily. There was really no further need for apologetic statements, thought Marshall: "We are too sensitive and too ready to regard ourselves under an obligation to answer every lie that is uttered against us." [31]

Jewish Counter-Measures

Yet, there remained a strong undercurrent of feeling in the American-Jewish community that not enough had been done by its leaders, that anti-Semitism "runs deeper than we think," and that the official statement of the Jewish organizations left the issue unresolved and the Jews on the defensive.[32] During the years of Ford's anti-Semitism, there were recurrent suggestions or demands for positive and vigorous action. Marshall and his associates may have regarded the Ford affair as dead, especially after the *Dearborn Independent's* attacks became more sporadic in 1922, but many others remained unsatisfied. A Jewish explanatory statement and affidavits from gentiles were not enough for them. What was desired, ultimately, was that Ford, despite his "moribund mind," should cry *"peccavi."* [33]

One of the most persistent calls was for a dramatization of the Jewish-Ford controversy by open debate or by instituting some sort of impartial jury or investigatory body. Lester Markel, a Jewish newspaperman, called for the appointment of a commission of eminent historians that would call both Ford and outstanding Jewish scholars before it for expert testimony and then issue an impartial verdict. Two Jewish congregations in Detroit, including Rabbi Leo Franklin's, demanded that Ford allow an inquiry of his charges by government secret service agents to be selected by him and paid for by the Jews.[34] As late as 1926, Nathan Straus issued a well-publicized challenge to Ford to allow the appointment of a committee of ten eminent Christians, eight to be named by Ford and two by the Jews, to pass judgment on Ford's propaganda.*

* The *Dearborn Independent* shrugged off the Straus challenge in its issue of December 25, 1926.

To Marshall, all of these calls for public debates, juries, proofs, and disputations were ridiculous. He felt that Ford's charges were so insane that they were not worthy of direct reply. By participating in a disputation of the kind suggested, Jews would lose dignity and self-respect, and more important, they would tacitly recognize what Ford wished to create and what the Jewish leaders denied, the existence of a Jewish Question in the United States.

The investigation proposal that drew the greatest publicity, and the strongest wrath from Marshall, was the challenge to Ford published by the *American Hebrew* in its issue of November 12, 1920. Isaac Landman, the editor, claiming that "the time for equivocating has passed," bluntly challenged Ford to permit an investigation of his charges by a corps of detectives to be named by Ford with the approval of the chief of the U. S. Secret Service. If the charges proved accurate, the *American Hebrew* would publish the results in 100 major newspapers, and if proved false, Ford would officially retract his allegations in the *Dearborn Independent*. The magazine called upon its readers to be prepared to pay the cost of detectives, if necessary. The naive proposal of the *American Hebrew* met with a favorable response. The *New York Sun* said that "it put the whole wild Fordian fancy about where it belongs." [35]

Marshall, however, was seriously alarmed. Landman's challenge occurred at the very time that the American Jewish Committee, in conjunction with other Jewish organizations, was preparing to issue the statement on the Protocols and Bolshevism. His concern mounted as reports came in that highly regarded individuals were impressed with the *American Hebrew* challenge.[36] Marshall denounced the proposal to his friends as a "cheap, vulgar, and yellow" journalist's trick. He argued that the Landman challenge implicitly recognized there might be a foundation of fact to the odious charges and urged him not to play a lone hand in view of the concerted action under way. Landman, however, defended his idea by pointing to the many requests he had received from readers for action. In the *American Hebrew,* he replied more aggressively: "If you want anti-Semitism stopped in its tracks, do something. Stop playing the ostrich. Take your head out of the sand of self-complacency." [37]

In the early days of the Ford campaign, there was considerable activity among Jews to choke it by coercive tactics. Local Jewish leaders frequently supported and encouraged abortive actions by municipalities and police to ban street sales of the *Dearborn Independent.* Occasionally, direct pressure was used to ban the *Independent* from libraries. Attempts were made to get the Postmaster-General to ban the *Dearborn Independent* from the mails and, when that failed, to introduce legislation in Congress for the same purpose.

Marshall and the American Jewish Committee opposed all such attempts. "We, of all people," he wrote, "cannot afford to rest under the imputation that we are prepared to proceed with a policy of suppression." [38] Preferring to rely on what he called "the sense of justice of the American people," he argued cogently that coercive actions would be regarded as interference with freedom of speech and press, would be ineffective, and would only provide Ford with publicity. On the other hand, he recommended privately to Judge Samuel Greenbaum, one of the trustees of the New York Public Library, that anti-Semitic publications should not be allowed to circulate, but should be kept in a "chamber of horrors."

Jewish organizations also tried to secure the passage of amendments to state libel laws, which would cover such publications as the *Dearborn Independent.* Lawyers of the Anti-Defamation League of the B'nai B'rith drafted bills and influential Jewish politicians propagandized for them. At first, Marshall was inclined to favor this legal approach and he urged Governor Nathan L. Miller of New York to support an amendment to the libel law providing for punishment of malicious publications defaming a particular race or religion. Charging that Ford's campaign, "for mendacity, violence and indecency," was without parallel in America, he pointed out that Catholics had also been subjected to similar sustained attacks.[39] However, efforts at changing the libel laws fizzled out, and before long Marshall changed his mind on their efficacy. Still, it disturbed him that a man of immense wealth could hide behind a corporation he had created and with impunity spread whatever propaganda he wished.

The American Jewish Committee was urged to call for a Congressional investigation of the Ford campaign. Because of the improbable investigation by Senator David I. Walsh of Irish persecution by England (then under way in Washington), it was argued that the Jews should try the same technique. Jewish leaders considered the idea carefully and Oscar Straus spoke to Congressman Julius Kahn of California on the possibility. Kahn was amenable, but suggested that the proposed investigation include anti-Catholic propaganda. Marshall and his associates finally decided, however, that a full-scale Congressional investigation might do more harm than good by dragging anti-Semitism into politics.

Despite the decision of the American Jewish Committee, the idea of a Congressional investigation or resolution did not die. Marshall ridiculed these suggestions as "the use of a Big Bertha to demolish a fly," but many believed there would be great value in exposing Ford before the nation. It would be pleasant, thought street-corner strategists, to have Ford answer some charges against him, including his alleged tax-evasion and the much discussed draft-dodging of his son, Edsel. In December, 1926, Congressman Sol Bloom of New York introduced a resolution in the House of Representatives calling for a select committee to investigate Ford's claim that the Jews controlled the financial system of the United States, including the Federal Reserve Bank. Nothing came of it, but it illustrated the ferment still going on in Jewish minds.

Another significant form of agitation was the frequent proposal that a libel suit against Ford under existing statutes be brought on behalf of the Jews of America. If Paul Warburg, for example, were to bring a $20,000,000 libel action against Ford, and if enough leading Jews did likewise, would not Ford be discouraged or even stopped? The idea was discussed in the upper ranks of Jewish leadership, but was turned down. Marshall, as a lawyer, knew that an individual could not sue because the class or group to which he belonged had been made the subject of libelous remarks. He thought that the technical difficulties of trying such a case would be enormous, the expense prohibitive, and if the case were dismissed, the effect most unfortunate.

Three major lawsuits were, however, brought against Ford by individual Jews, the last of them leading to the dénouement of the whole Ford assault.* The first of these was the work of Morris Gest, a well-known theatrical producer of the day, and son-in-law of David Belasco. In February, 1921, he filed a $5,000,000 damage suit against Ford, claiming injury by an article in the *Dearborn Independent* that had attacked his control of theaters, his production of "salacious" spectacles, and his "neglect" of aged parents in Russia. Gest said, "I'll make that peace ship Henry pay dearly for what he has said and more, too, I'll make him eat his own words." Ford's private secretary icily replied, "Mr. Gest will be ignored." [40] Gest's lawsuit was not taken seriously and never came to trial.

More important was the suit brought against Ford by Herman Bernstein, the Jewish editor who had written a book exposing the Protocols and who, aside from Mme. Schwimmer, had been the only Jew aboard Ford's Peace Ship. Bernstein sued in 1923 for $200,000 damages because of an article in the *Independent* that had called him a spy for international Jewry, and also because Ford had publicly stated that a Jew on the Peace Ship told him all about the Jewish conspiracy to rule the world and foment wars.[41] Marshall advised Bernstein against filing the suit and refused to undertake its prosecution as lawyer. He also advised against the engagement of Sam Untermyer, his partner, as lawyer, urging that a first-rate, non-Jewish lawyer might be better. Nevertheless, the suit was brought by Bernstein, with Untermyer as his

* See Chapter 7.

lawyer. The action was met by immense difficulties. Ford could not be caught in the jurisdiction of New York so that he could be brought into court. According to Untermyer, Ford kept out of the state except for rare occasions when he sneaked in and out on weekends; efforts to serve him were fruitless.[42] The case could not be brought to trial, but Bernstein had the minor satisfaction of tying up $115,000 of Ford's money in a New York bank on court order. Although this order was vacated in 1924, Bernstein reopened the proceedings and secured another order attaching $65,000. The case then languished until the third major suit against Ford, brought by Aaron Sapiro, reached its conclusion in 1927.

Thus, it appeared that not only was Ford immune to Congressional investigations and calls to submit evidence to impartial bodies, but that he could not even be reached by court proceedings. Under the circumstances, it was not surprising that American Jews persistently regarded the boycott as one of the best weapons against Ford since he could not avoid it and it hurt him most directly. Early suggestions that Jewish organizations consider a formal boycott of Ford products were rejected as inexpedient by the American Jewish Committee. The idea, however, was a natural and immediate reaction of many Jews, and the English-language Jewish press in particular advocated it. "Next time you ride in a Ford car, think of what Ford said about you," advised one journal.[43] To Marshall, this appeal was regrettable. He opposed open boycott, but hinted that self-respecting Jews would know what to do when it came to purchasing an automobile, without having to be told. A publicly avowed boycott campaign, he feared, might turn into a two-edged sword, with Ford urging retaliation against the Jews; while he would not encourage a *sub rosa* boycott, he did not object to it.

Marshall strongly urged Yiddish newspapers not to accept advertisements from the Ford Motor Company, but because of self-respect rather than financial pressure on Ford. When the *Foward* did print a Ford advertisement, his anger was intense at what he regarded as a sacrifice of dignity for Ford's "dirty money."

The imagination of American Jewry, stimulated by the Ford attack, was moved to invent a multitude of projects and schemes for countering the Dearborn charges. A distinguished lawyer, Max Kohler, seriously advised Marshall to secure written denials from the remaining delegates to the First Zionist Congress that any such meeting of the "Elders of Zion" as was charged in the Protocols ever took place. Judge Harry M. Fisher in Chicago envisaged the creation of a Jewish Information Bureau that would issue periodic press releases on such topics as the suffering of the Jews under the Bolsheviks, thereby countering Fordian propaganda. Boris Fingerhood suggested sending copies of the Protocols to the governors of all forty-eight states and other top leaders with a request that they submit appropriate comments; this, he thought, would provide excellent press publicity. The Vice-Commander of the Jewish Valor Legion proposed that a delegation of five highly decorated Jewish veterans be dispatched to Ford to expose his lies about Jewish patriotism. To all of these proposals, Marshall's response was negative.

Satire, ridicule, and invective were other weapons hurled at Henry Ford by American Jews. Carl Laemmle, noted Hollywood producer, commented on Ford's charge that the movies were being used for Jewish propaganda: "By preventing a showing of all pictures favorable to gentiles in moving picture theatres, we hope to drive all gentiles out of our audiences, in this way leaving none but Jews. . . . I used to think a good deal of Henry, but I guess he rattles a bit now when he goes into high." [44] Writing of a Jew who was suspected of endorsing Ford's candidacy for the Presidency, Marshall hesitated, "I do not wish to express my opinion with regard to him in a letter, otherwise the Government might seize it on the score that it constitutes obscene literature." [45] Marshall was a master of vigorous language, but Samuel Untermyer, his partner, was less inhibited in public:

> One's first impulse on reading this medley of stupidity, asininity, and medieval bigotry, is to doubt the evidence of sense and to wonder whether we really are living in the twentieth century. . . . I have long leaned to the charitable point of view that Ford's great money success

had driven him crazy, but I never believed that even an inflamed mind
could harbor such a combination of unbounded egotism, ignorance,
bigotry, and impudence.[46]

The *American Hebrew* struck back at Ford in a parody of the
Dearborn Independent conspiracy theme: "Henry Ford Ac-
quires Railroads, Coal Fields, and Timber Lands of Vast
Quantity and Wealth. Aims at Great Power. Flivver King's
Interests Stretch Out to Control America's Natural Re-
sources. Ford's Desire to Become President Considered a
Menace to Nation." [47]

The Ford attacks were also the occasion for a considerable
amount of soul-searching among Jews who preferred to ex-
amine their shortcomings. Marshall admitted privately that
the percentage of Jews engaged in illegitimate bootlegging,
including quite a number of rabbis, was shamefully large,
and reflected discredit on the Jews.[48] A man of German-
Jewish extraction, Albert Hoefeld, argued that East European Jews had traditionally taken advantage of their gentile
neighbors in European farming communities and therefore
had to be educated to a higher standard by American-Jewish
leaders. A Jewish weekly called on Marshall to lead a campaign to clean house within American Jewry. Cyrus Adler,
attacking Jewish nationalists, said that the Jews themselves
were somewhat to blame for the anti-Semitic attacks:

> We have made a noise in the world of recent years in America and
> England, far out of proportion to our numbers. We have demonstrated
> and shouted and paraded and congressed and waved flags to an extent
> which was bound to focus upon the Jew the attention of the world
> and having got this attention, we could hardly expect that it would
> all be favorable.[49]

Religious leaders took advantage of this opportunity to call
for a back-to-the-synagogue movement in the hope that more
Jewish education and the leading of righteous lives would
provide the best answer to anti-Semitism.

Marshall sympathized with the motives of those who recommended looking into the house of American Jewry. He
also used this as an argument in favor of exercising self-

restraint in relations with non-Jews and in combatting Ford. Although he thought of himself as the champion of the Jews in the struggle for the vindication of their rights, and was so regarded by many contemporaries, he believed that the fight against Ford would not be won by what he considered strident publicity stunts. Throughout the years of the Ford propaganda, Marshall was strongly for containing Jewish agitation and against a vigorous, public anti-Ford campaign. Especially after the address on the Protocols and the manifesto of the 119 distinguished Americans were issued, Marshall's general policy was to avoid a direct confrontation with Ford.

He was aware, however, of the gravity of the situation and was more willing to speak openly than some of his colleagues in upper Jewish society. To Cyrus Adler, he complained, "There is no doubt that some of our friends who are afraid to talk above a whisper and believe that the proper policy is to ignore the anti-Semitic propaganda, are living in a fool's paradise." [50] Between the hesitancy of some of his associates and the pressure from below for action, Marshall pursued a moderate policy that he hoped would be eventually more effective.

Having placed on record the dignified official answer of American Jewry, and aware of the non-acceptance of Ford's ideas in respectable circles, Marshall felt there was little to be gained from constant public reiteration of denials and apologies. Ford, he confidently believed, was becoming a negligible factor and would soon exhaust himself. What hurt Ford most, he contended, was non-action and non-response of Jews. Ford was seeking publicity more than anything else and to play into his hands would be folly. "The intelligent American public understands him. He is recognized as an ignoramus and a vulgarian." [51] Having done what we thought best, he affirmed,

Time will do the rest. We have been accustomed to be maligned for twenty centuries. We cannot prevent sporadic recurrences by standing on our heads and by getting unduly excited. We have better uses for our heads, after all.[52]

Marshall modified his premise that silence was the best policy in the Ford affair when opportunity appeared for behind-the-scenes political maneuvering, but, ordinarily, he believed the best treatment for anti-Semites was "silent contempt. This is gall and wormwood to them." Pointing to the inability of Ford to gain the support of the American press for his anti-Jewish crusade, Marshall claimed that his policy of non-response was frustrating Ford's plans. As evidence that Ford had been hurt, he offered the *Dearborn Independent* comment that Marshall had ordered the Jews to keep silent out of fear of the truth of the charges.

Marshall's efforts were thus bent on keeping his fellow-Jews from doing things he thought would upset the apple cart. Fraternal orders were urged to avoid action on the Ford matter and not to issue statements. Rabbis and other public speakers who discussed Ford were usually "strident, vituperative, and stupid," and worse, they were aiding the enemy. Jewish journalists who persisted in publicizing the Ford affair were acting like "neurotic fishwives."

Marshall saw the specter of Ford publicity in all sorts of situations. A call by East Side groups for demonstrations at the Polish consulate and on Wall Street against pogroms in Poland was viewed with alarm because of "the joy it would bring to the heart of Henry Ford," and a call for a world congress of Jewish leaders was opposed because it would supply Ford with ammunition on "Jewish internationalism." In fact, Jewish hysteria was largely responsible, Marshall claimed, for the rise in the circulation of the *Dearborn Independent.*

Marshall was pleased when he saw his strategy put into effect at the Buffalo convention of the Union of American Hebrew Congregations (Reform) in 1921. Ford was not mentioned by the delegates, at least for the public record, and, instead, a resolution was passed praising the American press, clergy, and people for resisting attempts to stir up prejudice. But this tactic was unusual, for, despite all his influence and despite the possible wisdom of his tactics, Marshall could not silence all Jewish voices nor restrain all open interest in the Ford case. As E. G. Pipp, a non-Jew, remarked, "The Jews are too much in the habit of thinking for themselves." [53]

Marshall and his American Jewish Committee colleagues did approve of answering anti-Semitic charges by Ford and others through the medium of apologetic books, preferably written by non-Jews. John Spargo's *The Jew and American Ideals,* a well-written analysis of the calumnies of Ford and the Protocols-inspired Bolshevik charge, was called a noble work by Marshall.[54] "I can assure you," he wrote Spargo, "that the memory of your deed will be perpetually enshrined in the grateful hearts of your Jewish fellow-citizens." [55] This sentiment was concretely supported when the American Jewish Committee purchased 2,000 copies (Julius Rosenwald bought another 1,500) and distributed them to libraries throughout the country. When rumors circulated that Ford was planning to publish an anti-Semitic translation of the Talmud, Marshall personally ordered several hundred copies of Josef Bloch's *Israel und die Völker,* a work that refuted anti-Semitic interpretations of the Talmud, and had them shipped to all major university libraries. This activity was admirable; however, its effectiveness in combatting Fordian anti-Semitism was doubtful.

Temporary Halt to Ford's Campaign

Although Marshall was cautiously selective in endorsing propagandistic approaches, he was not at all reluctant in quietly using his substantial political influence whenever he thought it useful. At the very time that he was discouraging Jews from public displays of emotion on the Ford issue, he was seizing an opportunity for the discreet application of pressure on President Harding, a fellow Republican. In the summer of 1921, Marshall learned from the newspapers that Harding, together with Edison and Harvey Firestone, had accepted an invitation to join Ford on a camping trip near Washington. It shocked him that the Chief Executive would consent to be a guest of the man who was conducting a bitter campaign against the Jews, but this feeling passed as he saw a chance to use the incident to advantage. He wrote to Harding, appealing to him to use his personal influence to persuade Ford to drop the attack that was damaging to so many Americans.[56] Confidently expecting a prompt and affirmative reply, as he customarily received from Washington, he was disappointed when weeks and months passed without an answer. In the meantime, Marshall wrote to Albert D. Lasker, head of the U.S. Shipping Board and probably the Jew closest to Harding, to see to it that the letter received the President's personal attention.[57] Lasker did this, but still no reply came. Finally, Marshall went to Washington and personally saw Harding.

"I shall never forget the charm of his wonderful personality and the impression of his genuine goodness and humanity," he later recalled of his interview with the President.[58] Harding told Marshall that after receiving the letter, he had sent Judd to Detroit, to urge Ford to discontinue his anti-Semitic publications. Judd, it turned out, was Judson C. Welliver, a journalist friend of the President's, who had recently interviewed Ford for the *Review of Reviews*. Welliver did go to see Ford and gently passed on the President's message.

Remarkably, shortly after Welliver's visit, the *Dearborn Independent*, in its issues of January 7 and 14, 1921, announced the conclusion of the original series of anti-Jewish articles. It appeared to Marshall that Harding's influence had worked and that his one initiative had been most wise. But did this fully explain Ford's behavior, or were there other reasons involved?

Ford himself supplied part of the answer in press interviews explaining the switch in the *Dearborn Independent's* line.[59] He was calling off the attacks on the Jews, Ford asserted, not because he lacked sufficient material to keep at them. As a matter of fact, he had five years' worth of information that might be used. The reason for the change was that the campaign against Jews had led naturally into the question of money and he now wanted to hammer away at that issue. As the Jews were the founders of the present financial system, he hoped they might be willing to aid him in constructing a badly needed new one. Certain Wall Street influences, he hinted, were bringing pressure on him to maintain the Jewish campaign, and leave money alone, but he would not bow to them. As for the Jews, he retracted nothing and boasted that his campaign had been helpful.

The left-handed compliment that Ford paid the Jews did not hide his monumental gall and in no way indicated a real softening in his attitude. The ostensible desire for Jewish assistance in propagandizing on the money issue masked complex motives. Ford was not completely immune to the feelings of men such as Harding, Thomas A. Edison, Arthur Brisbane, and his own son, Edsel. The quiet Jewish boycott of Ford products, while not a determining factor, was felt by Ford. More important, Ford had other interests that diverted his attention from the Jewish issue. His drive for control of the Muscle Shoals power complex was under way, and behind that lay his ambition to secure political power.

Ford, who had a natural rapport with the prejudices of small-town America, may have at first considered that criticizing Jews would win him potential votes. But with more political experience, it probably dawned on Ford that no one could hope to win the large urbanized states by such tactics and that the support of these areas would be essential. The bitter opposition of Jewish voters could be expected to provide a substantial obstacle in his road to a presidential nomination, even by a third party. Although he was not yet willing to retract his charges against the Jews, Ford thought it expedient to focus more attention on the gold standard. Perhaps he was naive enough to believe that Jews would flock to his standard on this issue; more likely, he thought he could propagate a milder form of anti-Semitism under the cloak of the cheap money agitation. Ford displayed some concern that his anti-Jewish campaign might get out of hand. In January, 1922, he told Allan Benson, "There is too much anti-Semitic feeling. I can feel it around here. If we were to keep this up, something might happen to the Jews. I do not want any harm to come to them." [60]

In any case, the impression was given by Ford that henceforth the *Dearborn Independent* would be muzzled on the subject of Jews. The American Jewish Committee's annual report for 1922 confidently saw the collapse of anti-Semitic agitation in the United States. Privately, however, Louis Marshall was not entirely convinced that Ford's suspension of the articles was cause for satisfaction or comfort. "He has simply rolled in vileness until he has tired or until, with his eye to the main chance, he regards it to be politic to cease his vilification." [61] Marshall's inner suspicion was justified, for Ford had not basically changed his views on the Jews. His conversations with friends were still sprinkled with uncomplimentary references to Jews. In an interview in Boston, in October, 1922, he let his confused emotions get the best of him:

> I curry favor with no man, but when I do say that I have no hatred in my heart for the Jew, I mean it. In fact, I do not blame the Jew moneylender for bunking humanity just as long as humanity lets him get away with it. . . . However, that does not wipe out the fact that the Jew, who is a victim of the false money system, is the very foundation of the world's greatest curse today—war. He is the cause of all abnormality in our daily life because he is the money maniac.[62]

The respite from anti-Semitism in the *Dearborn Independent* was very short-lived. Although there was no resumption of the systematic, potentially explosive, anti-Jewish attack characteristic of 1920-1921, Ford's inclinations apparently could not allow the Jewish issue to vanish completely. Articles began to appear again on Jewish moviemakers, armsmakers, bootleggers, and criminals, and by late 1923 and early 1924, the anti-Jewish theme was assuming significant proportions. Such articles as "Negroes of Harlem Exploited By Jews," "A Christian Church in the Ghetto of New York— St. Augustine's Engulfed in the Flood of Degraded Alien Influence," and "Cabal May Govern World's Gold," again pointed an accusing finger at the Jew.[63]

Rosenbluth Case

Most grievous in the eyes of Marshall and other Jewish leaders was the attempt by the *Dearborn Independent* to create a *cause célèbre* in the United States that might have become a facsimile of the Dreyfus case. The issue at stake was the case of Robert Rosenbluth, a graduate of the Yale School of Forestry who had worked in the New York State civil service and for the Joint Distribution Committee. During the war, he served at Ft. Lewis, Washington as captain in a regiment of engineers. In October, 1918, Rosenbluth, his commanding officer, Major Alexander Cronkhite, and a Sergeant Pothier, had been amusing themselves by target practice when Cronkhite was shot and died. Cleared by an Army investigation that decided Cronkhite had killed himself accidentally, Rosenbluth and Pothier were later arrested for murder at the insistence of the dead man's father, Major-General Adelbert Cronkhite. In the trial which followed, Pothier was tried first and acquitted, whereupon Rosenbluth was discharged at the request of the prosecution.

During the course of the tortuous legal proceedings and maneuvers, involving technical questions of jurisdiction and extradition, the *Dearborn Independent* maintained a continual barrage aimed at implying that the Jews were engaged in a conspiracy to protect Rosenbluth and thereby cheat American justice. Jewish leaders were indeed concerned that the *Dearborn Independent* be prevented from hounding an innocent man and from charging that his defense implicated the Jews in a conspiracy. Marshall was active in legal efforts on Rosenbluth's behalf, and Felix Warburg, together with Herbert H. Lehman, stood his bond; all three were attacked from Dearborn.[64] The affair aroused Marshall to the extent that he disregarded his normal public caution in a sharply worded letter to the *New York Times* after Rosenbluth had been finally released:

> There lives in Michigan one Henry Ford, who for several years past has been amusing himself by publishing a personal organ known as the *Dearborn Independent* which likewise bears the caption "The Ford International Weekly." Being a great litterateur, his name adorns the editorial page as president. Learning that Rosenbluth is a Jew, that damning fact was enough to serve the malign purposes of the ignorant fanatic to embark on one of his characteristic crusades to compass the destruction, nay the judicial murder, if possible, of a fellow-being. For weeks and months his columns reeked with vile falsehoods, wicked and insane imaginings, cunningly contrived appeals to passion and prejudice. . . . It is interesting to speculate as to what this intellectual brother of the Ku Klux Klan and the inspirer of Hitler and Ludendorff and other Swastika heroes, whose text-book is his "International Jew," will do now. . . .[65]

But not even Rosenbluth's discharge by the courts satisfied the Ford paper which hinted that "shameful interference of racial organizations" had prevented justice from being done for Cronkhite.[66]

The Rosenbluth case indicated that the Ford machine was still intent on creating damaging propaganda. A remedy that would force Ford's hand was not yet found, and Marshall continued to exert himself in the hope that renewed political pressure from Washington might be the answer. He wrote Charles D. Hilles of the Republican National Committee during the 1924 Presidential campaign that Ford was ready to stand at the side of the Ku Klux Klan and "exterminate the Jews if an opportunity presents itself." [67] After Coolidge's election, hoping perhaps that Harding's cooperation would be repeated, he urged the President to use his power to "abate this iniquity." [68] There was no evident result from either of these appeals.

Though thousands of Jews continued to express their concern at mass meetings and elsewhere, it appeared questionable whether Ford would ever be stopped.[69] True, the Ford presidential bubble had burst and there was no longer any danger he might one day occupy the White House. It was clear also that American opinion leaders were basically opposed to the vulgarities emanating from Dearborn and that there was no actual threat of pogroms. Yet Ford's attack, associated with other anti-Semitic manifestations, remained a thorn in the side of American Jewry. The relatively cautious strategy of American-Jewish leaders, while partially successful in containing the Ford threat, had been unable to eliminate it. It remained for someone outside the inner circle to take the initiative and, with the aid of favorable circumstances, to precipitate the final scenes of the Ford drama.

Chapter seven

decline
of the
independent

The last major attack on the Jews by the *Dearborn Independent* began April 12, 1924. Significantly, the subject for the new series was agriculture. With the establishment of industrial prosperity in the mid-1920's farming remained the chief area of weakness in the American economy. As such, it may have appeared to Ford, with his persistent interest in the old American yeoman, to offer possibilities for scapegoating.

Entitled "Jewish Exploitation of Farmer Organization," the series of twenty articles ran for about a year, under the byline of Robert Morgan, a former Hearst newspaperman.[1] The major target of the campaign was Aaron Sapiro, a distinguished and successful Chicago lawyer whose specialty was agricultural economics and whose major activity was the organization of farmers' marketing cooperatives. The key theme of the articles was that Sapiro, with leading Jews, like Albert D. Lasker, Bernard Baruch, Eugene Meyer and Otto Kahn, was engaged in a plot to use the farmers' cooperatives as an instrument for seizing "control of the agricultural and horticultural resources and production of America." [2] This charge, expounded in detail and with many variations, was illustrated by such devices as a picture of a celery field with the caption, "Every stalk of celery shown in this corner of a large field pays direct tribute to Jewish domination of the co-operative marketing system in this section of the United States." [3]

Who was Sapiro and how did Ford happen to seize upon him? [4] Born in San Francisco in 1884, Aaron Sapiro was orphaned at an early age. The "one-time street gamin and orphanage waif," however, went on to study for the rabbinate, switched to law, and became active in organizing farmers' cooperatives in California. Advocating a standard form of binding legal contract among cooperating farmers, he spread the cooperative gospel with evangelical vehemence throughout the United States and Canada. By the time of Ford's attack, there was no one in the farm cooperative movement better known than he. Fruitgrowers in California, wheat farmers in Western Canada and the Middle West, tobacco and cotton planters in the South, potato growers in Maine—all were organized by Sapiro. Because of the post-war decline in agriculture, farmers were ready for intensive promotion of cooperative organization, and Sapiro's performance was, according to E. C. Lindeman, "the most spectacular event in American agriculture since the days of Populism."

By 1923, Sapiro was attorney for sixty farm cooperatives, half of which he organized personally, and he had been retained by the American Farm Bureau Federation as legal adviser of its department of cooperative marketing. However, intense controversy within the Farm Bureau over Sapiro's approach to cooperatives led to his resignation. In addition, he aroused personal enmity because of his undoubted messianic complex and hot temper. The *Dearborn Independent,* opposed to Sapiro's plans for cooperative organization, and sensing his vulnerability, apparently decided he would make an excellent target, enabling it to champion the farmer at the same time as it denounced Jews.

Aaron Sapiro was not a man to sit idly by, fuming, while his name was dragged into the mud. In January, 1925, he sent a formal demand to Ford and Liebold for the retraction of the *Dearborn Independent* articles. When this was not done by April, he initiated a suit, in the Federal District Court of Detroit, for $1,000,000 damages against Ford and the Dearborn Publishing Company.[5]

Marshall, who learned of Sapiro's libel action through the newspapers, had never spoken to him or seen him or had any correspondence with him. In his opinion, Sapiro had ample justification for a libel suit, but the action was unwise because it gave Ford publicity. Marshall was growing more confident as the dust of the Rosenbluth case settled, and as it appeared that the *Dearborn Independent* was tapering off its attacks. In an interview with the Yiddish press on his seventieth birthday in 1926, he optimistically stated that Ford's anti-Semitism was "a played-out song." Nathan Straus was charged by Marshall with making a great mistake in reviving a dead issue when he challenged Ford in 1926 to allow an impartial investigation of the anti-Jewish charges. Now, possibly offended at Sapiro's independent action, Marshall confessed he did not feel that the libel suit was a subject for excitement. Classifying it "an ordinary action for libel," he asserted that Sapiro could not act as a representative of the Jews, that it was a personal action and "nobody else's business." [6] Marshall, therefore, played no role at first in the drama unfolding in Detroit.

Other observers, less legalistically minded, saw in the Ford-Sapiro contest a battle of David & Goliath proportions; here was a relatively obscure individual Jew challenging the wealthiest man in America. When the trial began, it was fully covered by the press and was front-page news for weeks in papers such as the *New York Times* and the Yiddish *Forward*. The trial had been scheduled originally for March, 1926, but a series of postponements delayed it until March 15, 1927. Meanwhile, both sides were collecting depositions from farmers in all parts of the country where cooperatives had been organized by Sapiro. A corps of Ford investigators and lawyers scoured the land, sparing no expense, in an effort to prepare damaging affidavits and gather defense witnesses. It was estimated that the Ford defense cost more than a million dollars. Rejecting a final offer by Sapiro to have the case submitted to arbitration by a committee of the Detroit Board of Commerce, the Ford forces confidently awaited the courtroom battle.

When the trial opened, under Judge Fred M. Raymond, Ford was represented by a cast of high-priced lawyers, headed by Senator James A. Reed, of Missouri. He was assisted by half a dozen Detroit attorneys as well as the regular Ford legal staff. Opposing him was Sapiro himself and William Henry Gallagher, a Detroit lawyer assisted by Robert S. Marx, a former Cincinnati judge. Gallagher, a Roman Catholic who called himself "first-cousin to a Jew," performed valiantly, as did Reed, who was brilliant in cross-examination. Some viewers were surprised to find Reed, who in 1921 referred to Ford as "the most contemptible character in public life today," suddenly arrayed on his side. The fact that Sapiro was defended by a Detroit Catholic and not a New York Jew came as a shock to Ford, who used to say afterwards that Catholics were tools of the Jews.

After the selection of the jury, from which the plaintiffs rejected ex-Klansmen, while the defense excluded Jews, argument began. A basic controversy soon developed, centering on Gallagher's insistence that the *Dearborn Independent* had libeled not only Sapiro as an individual, but Sapiro as a member of the Jewish group, and that Ford's anti-Semitism was therefore germane to the trial. Reed's counter-argument was that Sapiro could not legally sue on behalf of his people and then collect damages as an individual. Judge Raymond agreed with Reed on the technical argument and barred the Jewish issue from the case. Gallagher, however, continued to insist on its importance and raised it frequently in spite of adverse rulings.

When William J. Cameron, editor of the *Dearborn Independent*, testified as chief defense witness, the major question was Ford's responsibility for the allegedly libellous material printed in the magazine. Despite rigorous examination by Gallagher, Cameron steadfastly refused to implicate Ford. "I run the paper," he flatly stated, thereby taking full responsibility for its contents.[7] The best Gallagher could get from him was an admission that "Mr. Ford used to drop in occasionally and chat quite frequently." [8] Cameron was plainly shielding Ford from the consequences of his own actions, for, as everyone knew and as Liebold once proudly proclaimed, "The *Dearborn Independent* is Henry Ford's own paper and he authorizes every statement occurring therein." [9]

Sapiro himself then took the witness stand and, despite a few flare-ups, successfully resisted Reed's hammering. The Ford counsel's main points were that Sapiro had exploited farmers by charging excessive fees for legal services and that many of the cooperatives he organized later died. Sapiro refused to concede the validity of these arguments during thirteen gruelling days of sharp questioning. Although he admitted charging large fees, he claimed that they were not excessive because he had employed many legal assistants. Far from exploiting farmers, Sapiro asserted that his cooperatives had benefited them tremendously and that growers had made millions because of his services.

While Sapiro testified, attention turned to the long-heralded appearance of the main defendant. After six months of tireless efforts by process-servers, Ford had finally been handed a subpoena in an unguarded moment at the Ford Airport. Sapiro thought so little of Ford's courtroom prowess that he had him subpoenaed as a witness for the prosecution, although, as such, Ford could not be discredited in cross-examination. Ford, however, never appeared in the courtroom of the old Detroit Federal Building. On the evening prior to his scheduled testimony, he was involved in a mysterious car accident. Riding along Michigan Avenue in Dearborn, his automobile had been forced off the road near a bridge by hit-run drivers and Ford had been taken to the Ford Hospital where his condition was reported as not serious. Whether the accident was staged or merely a lucky coincidence is still not known. Allan Nevins believes that Ford's injuries were real, but Harry Bennett, his detective chief, reported that Ford told him, "Harry, I wasn't in that car when it went down into the river." [10] In Sapiro's eyes, the accident was undoubtedly faked, and Nathan Straus called Ford "a contemptible coward." [11]

As bulletins of Ford's progress came from the hospital during April, his long-awaited appearance at the trial once more became a strong possibility. In the meantime, Liebold had also been served with a subpoena by a process-server after a mad chase by car and on foot. At this crucial juncture, Ford counsel suddenly moved for and obtained a mistrial, thus bringing the court proceedings to a premature end.[12]

The grounds for this startling turn of events had been well prepared through the efforts of dozens of Ford detectives who had packed the corridors of the courthouse, snooping for information. One of the women jurors, it was charged by Ford's lawyers, had told a relative, who in turn had told a Ford detective, that she would never vote for Ford. It was also charged that she had negotiated with one Kid Miller, a Detroit real-estate dealer, for a bribe, and that her husband ran a speakeasy and was not the plumbing contractor she had sworn he was. When the infuriated lady indiscreetly gave an interview to a Detroit newspaper reporter, denying the Ford allegations, the judge had no alternative but to declare a mistrial. Exonerating the juror and Sapiro from the charge of collusion, Judge Raymond placed the blame for the mistrial on the misguided enthusiasm of the press.

The trial was over, but most observers concluded that Sapiro had emerged vindicated while Ford had apparently been afraid to take the stand. After the dismissal of the jury, one of its members declared that it had been almost unanimous in the belief that Ford's defense had collapsed by the time of mistrial. Aaron Sapiro, still pressing his case, announced that he would insist on a resumption of the trial; September 12, 1927 was the tentative retrial date.

Shortly after the anti-climactic end of the trial, the *New*

York Times editorially called on Henry Ford to disregard legal aspects and speak openly and honestly on the so-called Jewish conspiracy. Whether or not Ford read this challenge, he had already committed himself to end his seven-year war against the Jews. According to Joseph A. Palma, an intimate friend of Harry Bennett and head of the New York office of the U.S. Secret Service, Ford told him in the spring of 1927 that he had been studying the *Dearborn Independent's* articles on the Jews and had been shocked at some of the statements. Ford informed Palma that he was prepared to help undo the damage and that the latter should consider himself authorized to attempt a settlement with the Jews.

The widespread interest in Sapiro's suit brought home to Ford the strength of public disapproval of his anti-Semitic campaign. In addition, he seemed frightened at the unpleasant prospect of appearing on the witness stand if the Sapiro case was retried. He was also not oblivious to the advice of friends and family. Arthur Brisbane had opposed the anti-Jewish propaganda from the start, regarding it as the one great defect of Ford's career. On a visit to Dearborn in May, 1927, Brisbane opened the subject again and was relieved to learn that Ford had made up his mind to permanently discontinue the attacks. Edsel Ford had likewise persistently opposed his father's policy. It was said in Detroit that Edsel had offered to invest $1,000,000 in Palestine economic development, but had been turned down by the Zionists because of his father's unsavory activities.

The cumulative effects of the underground boycott of his automobiles may also finally have had some impact on Ford. Not only individual Jews, but Jewish firms and gentile firms with Jewish trade were not buying Ford products. A car dealer in the Southwest reported that wealthy Jews in New Orleans, San Antonio, Houston, Dallas, Kansas City, and Memphis had not bought a single Lincoln in years. When Ford agents investigated a decline in sales in Missouri, they were told by Jewish businessmen that Fords would not be used if they were given away. Ford had difficulties within his organization about this. Gaston Plantiff, New York area sales chief, as well as other Ford dealers, tried to convince Ford that his anti-Jewish campaign was hurting sales. A Ford sales director in Europe quit, charging that the European market was suffering because of the *Dearborn Independent,* and one of Ford's chief legal advisers fell into disfavor for speaking out against anti-Semitism.

It was hardly in keeping with Ford's character to recant solely because his opinions somewhat decreased car sales. More significant was that the spring of 1927 marked the demise of Ford's Model T and the start of the switch to the Model A, the first major shift in two decades. The Model T had been in trouble for several years, with dealers and the public criticizing its many mechanical and stylistic shortcomings. Ford had stubbornly supported it, despite indications that competitors, such as Chevrolet, were absorbing a larger share of the market. When Ford registrations fell by almost half a million cars in the first eight months of 1927 as compared with 1926, it was clear that a change could not be avoided.

The discontinuance of the Model T seemed to dampen Ford's enthusiasm for political causes, for never again did he embark on grand crusades. The birth of the Model A, also, was a time of feverish and anxious activity at Ford headquarters. Distractions such as the *Dearborn Independent* were no longer important, and the continued risk of a prolonged boycott might unnecessarily injure the chances for success of the new car. These practical considerations, added to the fear of renewed legal entanglements, and the pressure of trusted friends, led to Ford's decision for peace with the Jews.*

It was Palma's task, together with Earl J. Davis, a former U.S. assistant Attorney-General, to negotiate the settlement; the man they approached was Louis Marshall. Palma and

---

* Nevins believes that Ford was innately decent and discontinued the campaign when its damaging aspects were brought home to him (Nevins and Hill, *Ford: Expansion and Challenge,* p. 322). It is strange, however, that Ford's decency took seven years to manifest itself.

Davis first conferred, in June, 1927, with a Jewish friend of theirs, George C. Nordlinger of the Internal Revenue Service in New York. Seeking a recognized Jewish representative with whom they could deal, Nordlinger referred them to Nathan D. Perlman, Vice-President of the American Jewish Congress. Stephen Wise, head of the Congress, was then in Europe, and Perlman, aware of the significance of the Palma-Davis visit, in turn referred them to Marshall as the only person who could handle the matter.*

The Ford negotiators stated that Ford now realized he had been deceived by Cameron and others, that he knew nothing of the published articles and wished to put an end to them. Marshall, for the sake of accuracy, rebutted that Ford undoubtedly knew of the articles and their contents. Finally, Palma and Davis asked for peace terms and Marshall laid down the conditions: An unqualified retraction of the charges against the Jews, together with a complete apology to be written by Marshall and signed by Ford; cessation of all publication of anti-Jewish articles and withdrawal of *The International Jew* from circulation; and severance of Ford's relations with Liebold and Cameron. About the Aaron Sapiro and Herman Bernstein suits, although he had nothing to do with them, Marshall was sure that if Ford signed the statement he would prepare, and in addition, made satisfactory separate retractions to Sapiro and Bernstein and reimbursed them for expenses, their litigation would come to an end. Palma then told Marshall that the terms were "entirely in accord with what was in mind," that they would report to Ford and inform Marshall if he agreed. Ford acquiesced and Palma soon returned with a request that Marshall prepare the statement of apology. At the same time, negotiations were begun between the Ford and Sapiro lawyers, looking toward an out-of-court settlement. Marshall took an interest in these negotiations, keeping informed through Lewis L. Strauss, a

* This sequence of events became the subject of bitter controversy between Marshall and Perlman, with overtones of the rivalry between the American Jewish Committee and the American Jewish Congress.

friend of Sapiro's, and through associates in Detroit. Marshall then dictated a letter of retraction and apology which Ford was to sign and send back. Palma took the letter to Detroit, showed it to Ford and warned him, "Mr. Ford, this is pretty strong and I suggest you read it over carefully before you sign it." Ford replied, according to Palma, "Joe, no matter how strong it is, it could not be too strong. Let the Jews judge me by my acts in the future." [13]

Ford obtained Marshall's consent, through Palma, to the public release of the retraction. On July 7, Arthur Brisbane released to the press Ford's signed letter of apology, without a change in Marshall's phraseology:

> For some time past I have given consideration to the series of articles concerning Jews which since 1920 have appeared in the *Dearborn Independent*. Some of them have been reprinted in pamphlet form under the title "The International Jew." Although both publications are my property, it goes without saying that in the multitude of my activities it has been impossible for me to devote personal attention to their management or to keep informed as to their contents. . . . To my great regret I have learned that Jews generally, and particularly those of this country, not only resent these publications as promoting anti-Semitism, but regard me as their enemy. . . . This has led me to direct my personal attention to this subject, in order to ascertain the exact nature of these articles. As a result of this survey I confess that I am deeply mortified. . . . Had I appreciated the general nature, to say nothing of the details, of these utterances, I would have forbidden their circulation without a moment's hesitation. . . .
>
> I deem it to be my duty as an honorable man to make amends for the wrong done to the Jews as fellow-men and brothers, by asking their forgiveness for the harm that I have unintentionally committed, by retracting so far as lies within my power the offensive charges laid at their door by these publications, and by giving them the unqualified assurance that henceforth they may look to me for friendship and good will. . . .
>
> Finally, let me add that this statement is made on my own initiative and wholly in the interest of right and justice and in accordance with what I regard as my solemn duty as a man and a citizen.[14]

The apology thus allowed Ford to plead ignorance, although Marshall was fully aware of his active involvement. But

Palma had hinted originally to Marshall that Ford would apologize on this basis, and Marshall was statesmanlike enough to realize that even this would be humiliating, without rubbing Ford's face in the dirt.

To Ford's extraordinary statement, Marshall replied in a moving letter made public at the same time as the recantation:

> . . . For twenty centuries we Jews have been accustomed to forgive insults and injuries, persecution and intolerance, hoping that we might behold the day when brotherhood and goodwill would be universal. We had fondly hoped that in this blessed republic, with its glorious Constitutions and its just laws, it would be impossible to encounter the hatred and rancor to which our brethren have been and still are subjected in other lands. We could not at first credit the information that the *Dearborn Independent* had permitted itself . . . to introduce the exotic growth of anti-Semitism. Happily such excrescences could not flourish on American soil. Happily the enlightened press of this country treated them with contempt and as unworthy of notice. But we Jews none the less suffered the anguish of tortured memories, the nightmares of a horrible past, and the sorrow that, in spite of the progress of civilization, there were those who stood ready to misunderstand us.[15]

Concluding with the "sincere hope that never again shall such a recrudescence of ancient superstition manifest itself upon our horizon," Marshall promised to exert his influence to secure for Ford the pardon he requested.

Privately, Marshall expressed surprise that Ford had been willing to sign the retraction without any changes. "If I had his money I would not have made such a humiliating statement for one hundred million dollars." Ford's plea of ignorance, Marshall said, showed the world the mentality of a man who was "willing to indulge in a series of disgraceful and criminal attacks upon a whole people and capable at the same time to resort to the most infantile of excuses. It tended to prick the popular myth that he is a genius and what not, and to show him in all his intellectual nakedness." As for pardoning Ford, "I said that I would use my influence to induce the Jews to forgive. I said nothing about forgetting." [16]

Among the American public, Ford's apology, after initial surprise, caused enthusiastic expressions of relief, tempered by amused skepticism. None was more staggered than William Cameron, who, on learning of the retraction, could only protest, "It is all news to me and I cannot believe it is true." [17] Ford had conducted the entire negotiation on his own and had not consulted anyone on the *Independent,* or even his family and lawyers. While editorial opinion generally applauded Ford's action, many found it hard to take at face value.[18] E. G. Pipp, Ford's ex-editor, reserved comment on whether his former chief was sincere. Clarence Darrow thought it strangely coincidental that Ford's change of heart came so near the announcement of his new automobile; Norman Thomas remarked that "Ford's backdown is good evidence of what a consumer's boycott and a lawyer's million dollar libel suit can do in the way of educating a man who has heretofore been impervious to history"; and Hendrik Willem Van Loon summed it up, "Well, he has gone to Canossa or his lawyers have gone to Canossa for him. The *Dearborn Independent* will cease to conduct paper pogroms. But cheer up, some other idiot will continue the good work." [19]

An editorial in the *Outlook* (July 20, 1927) seemed to give some weight to Van Loon's pessimism; it commented that attacks on the Jews would not cease as long as Jewish leaders did not denounce "offensive Jewish traits" as vigorously as they did criticism of Jews. Despite a good dose of cynicism, interest in the Ford apology was widespread. A New York radio station devoted a program to a symposium on it, and the Astrologers' Guild of New York advanced an astrological explanation of the forces behind Ford's reversal.

Among Jews, skepticism took second place to a feeling of welcome relief. This was the moment many had anticipated for so long, and the sweetness of it overcame doubts of its validity. Marshall, joined by other leaders, confidently hailed the Ford retraction as "a staggering blow to the anti-Semites, especially those of Europe." [20] He brusquely dismissed cynics who pointed to the material motives behind Ford's apology, saying that motives were unimportant in this matter and, besides, "automobiles do not concern me to the slightest degree—I have never owned one and probably never shall." [21] Some influential Jews in Detroit were irritated that Ford had settled with Marshall in New York rather than with them, but the overwhelming sentiment among Jews of all classes, from the lower East Side to Fifth Avenue, was one of intense satisfaction. Stephen Wise, despite reservations, lauded the retraction and asked Ford to show his sincerity by paying for a commission to make a survey of the rise and development of anti-Semitism; Adolph S. Ochs, publisher of the *New York Times,* said: "Mr. Ford has shown superb moral courage in his wholehearted recantation, and has gained the respect and admiration of his fellow men"; Jonah J. Goldstein, New York communal leader, exclaimed enthusiastically, "I clasp the extended hand of Mr. Ford and congratulate him for his outstanding basic Americanism." [22] The joy was such that the President of the East Side Chamber of Commerce was moved to congratulate Ford and invite him to a tribute dinner at which he would share the honors with Mayor James J. Walker as toastmaster and Louis Marshall and Nathan Straus as principal speakers.

Marshall deplored this hysteria among Jews and did his best to prevent various manifestations of public exultation. Decrying the peculiar reaction that had turned Ford from the Haman of last week to the Mordecai of this one, he sought to maintain calm and balanced appraisal of the situation in the Jewish community. Still, he regarded the affair as one of historic importance, and the American Jewish Committee distributed the Ford apology together with Marshall's reply in a pamphlet edition of 50,000 copies. Content with his achievement, Marshall proudly stated, "My great and outstanding objective has been accomplished with universal approval. Today the Jews stand vindicated and absolved." [23]

Yet, one cannot help wondering whether the Ford retraction, acclaimed by the Jewish press as "another span in the erection of the bridge of better understanding and good-will," was as meaningful as Marshall and some of his con-temporaries professed to believe.[24] Marshall conceded that the Ford apology could hardly put an end to anti-Semitism, and, in many hearts, Ford remained despite public acclama-tion, "the inexplicable colossus of jackasses." [25]

While the bells were ringing in celebration of Ford's apology, negotiations were quietly proceeding between Ford and his two suitors, Sapiro and Bernstein. Sapiro announced that he would not insist on punitive damages, but would set-tle for expenses alone. On July 17, 1927, the settlement of the Ford-Sapiro suit was reported and a special letter of apology from Ford to Sapiro was published. It was ru-mored that the financial settlement amounted to $140,000 for expenses, but this may have been exaggerated. As part of the agreement, the *Dearborn Independent* printed Ford's apology to Sapiro in its issue of July 30, 1927. Bernstein, through his lawyer, Samuel Untermyer, settled at about the same time, receiving a smaller monetary payment and a sepa-rate letter of apology. When Herman Bernstein visited Dear-born in the fall of 1927, he saw Ford personally and later re-ported that he received a most cordial welcome and enjoyed a delightful conversation with him. Ford assured Bernstein that he had made his retractions and apologies without "any mental reservations whatsoever." [26]

Although Marshall had been the recipient of the Ford let-ter of retraction to the Jews, popular interest and adulation centered on Aaron Sapiro. "His deed, his bravery, his courage should be a shining light to the Jewish youth of today," wrote one Jewish newspaper. The *New York Times* commended Sapiro for having stood up for his rights against a powerful adversary. Sapiro himself was not at all reluctant to accept a hero's role. To record crowds in New York and other cities, he spoke at length on what he called "my fight with Henry Ford." An unprecedented burst of homage poured forth from all shades of Jewish opinion—from the Yiddish East Side to the heights of Reform.

A discordant note, however, was apparent. Stephen S. Wise, implying he had disagreed with Marshall's silent approach to Ford, spoke out strongly:

> It is not comforting to recall that Aaron Sapiro derived a minimum of aid or comfort from his fellow Jews. . . . On the contrary, the private managers of the affairs of American Israel, while they did not openly obstruct or thwart Aaron Sapiro's course, looked upon him from the heights of their impeccable, withal futile, leadership as if he were some wanton vandal invader of the holy of holies who had not even asked the sanction of them that sit in the seats of the mighty.[27]

Sapiro sarcastically referred to the "King of the Jews" who "hurt me rather than helped." [28] In his speeches, he said that the Ford repudiation of anti-Semitism was a direct result of the libel suit and that Marshall had little right to claim credit for it. Indiscreetly, he revealed that Marshall had written the Ford apology and that Ford had signed it without having read it. In general, Sapiro charged that he had been the only one to stand up effectively against Ford.

Marshall did not reply directly to remarks such as Wise's, nor did he comment publicly on Sapiro's behavior, but he was disturbed. Exaggerating in his turn, he claimed that the Sapiro case had nothing to do with the Ford apology, but that the retraction had contributed largely to the settlement of Sapiro's suit. Sapiro's public statement that Marshall had dictated the text of Ford's apology, although it was not generally noted by contemporaries, was regarded as a blunder, for it would allow anti-Semites to charge that it had been secured by coercion. Marshall resented the fairly widespread feeling that he and the American Jewish Committee had refrained from giving Sapiro just recognition. The charge that only Sapiro had fought Ford was answered by Marshall through his friend Herman Bernstein in a sharp editorial in the *Jewish Tribune*.[29] As for Sapiro personally, Marshall wrote, "I deem it beneath my dignity to have anything to do with him. . . . Sapiro never had the grace to say a word to me in recognition of what I had done and of the way in which I had treated him and helped him. . . ." [30] Even if Sapiro sought to see him and apologize, Marshall stubbornly vowed he would not receive him.

Marshall's annoyance was calmed somewhat by Henry Ford's pre-arranged visit in New York in early January, 1928. Ford told Marshall he felt better now that his mind was relieved of the burden of the great mistake and blunder he had made. Marshall reported that Ford appeared repentant and was determined to undo the wrong he had committed. He asked Marshall to keep in touch with him and assured him that he would do whatever advised. As a parting gesture, Ford offered Marshall any of his products. Marshall respectfully declined, informing Ford of his "devotion to pedestrian locomotion." After the meeting, Marshall assured reporters that he thought Mr. Ford was entirely sincere in his declarations.

Convinced of Ford's desire to restore himself to the good graces of American Jews, Marshall was amused at the great confidence Ford was now placing in him after all the bitter attacks the *Independent* had made against him. Ford's apparent sincerity, if not his possible motive, was tangibly demonstrated when, in December, 1927, he placed $156,000 of advertising in the Jewish press, the only ethnic press medium so honored. [31]

A surface accord now existed between Marshall and Ford, but the former was greatly concerned over Ford's tardy fulfillment of the specific commitments he had undertaken when the apology was made. Especially important, in Marshall's opinion, was the very urgent matter of the circulation of *The International Jew* in areas of Europe where anti-Semitism was a pressing danger. Translated into many languages and all the more vicious because it bore the imprimatur of a man of great wealth reputed to be a leader of twentieth-century civilization, *The International Jew* was particularly threatening to Jewish leaders. Not long after the retraction, Ford burned five truckloads of the American edition, but overseas circulation presented a more difficult problem.

Publication rights for the continent of Europe had been granted by Ford to the firm of Hammer-Verlag, Leipzig. It was run by the notorious anti-Semite, Theodor Fritsch, who now refused to cooperate, claiming that Ford had not specifically withdrawn his authorization.[32] As a matter of fact, Fritsch was advertising a new Spanish edition of the work. Jewish agitation rose and Marshall engaged in a lengthy correspondence with Ford and his associates, pressing them to complete the withdrawing of all anti-Semitic publications. Finally, in November, 1927, Ford officially notified Fritsch of the withdrawal of publication rights. Fritsch, however, refused to comply, demanding a compensation payment of 40,000 marks. Marshall counselled Ford against such blackmail, warning that it would lead to similar demands from other anti-Semitic publishers, including those in Latin America. Instead, he urged Ford to publish his retraction statement as an advertisement in all major German newspapers.

Marshall's suggestion was not adopted, despite Ford's personal assurance to both Marshall and Bernstein that he would follow their advice. Fritsch continued to publish *The International Jew* and after the assumption of power by the Nazis, there was no longer any possibility of preventing him.[33] The Ford apology and efforts by Marshall to publicize it were almost entirely fruitless in halting overseas distribution of *The International Jew*. In England, an ultranationalist group, The Britons, refused Marshall's demand that it cease circulating the disavowed Ford work.[34] A new English edition contained the entire Ford-Marshall correspondence together with the editorial note that Ford had not specifically denied the truth of the charges and that, in any event, the apology merely demonstrated once again the overwhelming power of the Jews.[35]

The attempted overseas suppression of dated Ford propaganda did not go well, but what of the United States? The *Dearborn Independent,* whose anti-Semitic articles had disappeared after the Sapiro series, now disappeared itself. In July, 1927, Ford dealers were ordered not to take any more subscriptions, and in December it was announced that the magazine would cease publication by the end of the year.

Marshall had told Ford's friends that the sincerity of the recantation would be questioned unless Ford severed all relations with Cameron and Liebold. Ford removed Liebold from his duties as general manager of the *Dearborn Independent* and told Marshall when he visited him that Cameron had been fired. It developed later, however, that Cameron and Liebold remained on the Ford payroll long after the collapse of the *Independent*.[36]

In fact, there was something of a resurgence of Ford's anti-Semitism during the 1930's. Cameron resumed his racism as president of the anti-Semitic Anglo-Saxon Federation, Harry Bennett used Rabbi Leo Franklin as a pawn in shady maneuvers with Father Coughlin, and in 1938 Ford accepted the Grand Cross of the German Eagle from Adolf Hitler.[37] The record clearly belies Ford's assertion in 1933, "I have never contributed a cent, directly or indirectly or any other way, to anti-Semitism anywhere." His anti-Semitic campaign of the 1920's alone constitutes a permanent stain on the career of the Dearborn automobileer.

The editors of the *Dearborn Independent* recognized the difficulty of spreading anti-Jewish doctrines in America. A strong current of nativism containing such doctrines attained great influence following World War I, but the nation as a whole, and even advocates of Anglo-Saxon racism, were not prepared to accept forthright anti-Semitic propaganda. Although the Ford writers seemed to be groping towards a conscious and thoroughgoing anti-Semitic ideology on the European model, there was always a crackpot naiveté about the *Dearborn Independent*. The association with Ford's name added financial strength and organizational drive, but, in the minds of influential Americans, his link with too many discredited, if not hare-brained, schemes militated against the serious reception of his anti-Semitism. In addition, the American tradition of religious freedom and racial peace, while dangerously strained, was never completely broken. As economic prosperity and normalization succeeded the confusion of the immediate post-war years, the material basis which might have fostered the acceptance of Fordian anti-Semitism declined.

Jewish leaders, especially Louis Marshall, were gratified; he wrote that the outcome of the Ford episode had given him "more happiness than any action in which I have ever been engaged." [38] On the other hand, the record of Jewish leadership during the long years of the Ford campaign was not altogether flawless. Hampered by hesitation, inconsistency, internal power struggles, and personality clashes, the official fight against Ford was weakened. The struggle derived its final effectiveness less from organizational unity and strength than from the activities of independent individuals aided by a fortunate combination of circumstances which determined the behavior of Henry Ford and the nation at large.

Ford's anti-Semitic campaign of the 1920's collapsed, but its impact should not be underestimated. With the aid of the Protocols, the stereotype of the international Jew, equally threatening as banker or revolutionary, had been superimposed on the earlier stereotypes of anti-Christ, Shylock, and Rothschild. During the 1930's, social and economic problems converted this Jew into an even more sinister figure. Ford's scriptures were again reprinted, this time by such groups as the revived Ku Klux Klan.[39] As late as 1954, the appearance of a Swedish version of *The International Jew* testified that the usefulness of Ford's work was still recognized by anti-Semites throughout the world.[40]

americanism
of the
twenties:
the k. k. k.,
immigration restriction

Henry Ford's campaign against the international Jew was a particularly dramatic manifestation of anti-Semitism during the 1920's; its true significance lies, however, within the related activities and movements that threatened to put up barriers between Jews and non-Jews in America. The national post-war mood in America provided fertile soil for ideologies opposing change or non-conformity. Responding to deep emotional needs aggravated by the pent-up hatreds of the war and the rapidity of social change, many Americans aggressively asserted their identity by defining certain groups as outsiders.

Jews were not the sole, nor even the major, victims of the psychology of the tribal twenties, but their historical experiences and traditional scapegoat role made them potentially vulnerable and peculiarly sensitive. Louis Marshall, although he consistently denied the existence of a basic Jewish question, was nevertheless obliged, as an outstanding American Jewish leader, to deal with these disturbing, peculiarly American phenomena.

The Klan

The most spectacular mass movement of the 1920's, and possibly its most characteristic, was the Ku Klux Klan.[1] The modern Klan was founded in 1915 by William J. Simmons of Atlanta, Georgia. For several years, it grew slowly and by 1920 had only 5,000 members. By 1924, however, aided by the promotional talents of Edward Y. Clarke, Klan membership, it is estimated, attained the astonishing figure of over 4,000,000.[2] Especially strong in the Southwest, Midwest, and Far West, it had invaded all parts of the country and penetrated even the New York metropolitan area. This amazing response of Americans to the Klan has been attributed by historians to both the immediate historical circumstances and long standing habits of mind. The high idealism and emotional tone of the war to save democracy had given way to post-war disillusionment which found one outlet in the Klan's xenophobia and bigotry. At the same time, the Klan offered its members a moralistic feeling of participating in a movement to cleanse America of the evils that, seemingly, thwarted their aspirations. Encroachments by foreigners and threats to the status quo had to be resisted, if necessary by sadistic violence and terror. Sheer ennui, just pure and simple boredom, propelled many small-town Americans into the exciting ranks of the Klan.

The central proposition of the Klan was the defense of what it called "one hundred per cent Americanism." This quality could not, by definition, be shared by Catholics, Jews, "niggers," or foreigners. In fact, these groups were regarded as the chief obstacles to the maintenance of the real America. Although the Klan successfully dabbled in politics and dominated the capitals of several states for a time, its major emphasis was not so much political or economic as it was cultural or ethnological. Nonconformity in race, religion, or customs was the enemy of the Klan, and politics was used as one weapon in the struggle against this distressing disease.

In the Klan's ideology of the early 1920's, anti-Catholicism played a role parallel to anti-Semitism in the Nazi ideology. Keeping the Negro in his place was a major object of the Klan, but as the movement's strength spread to areas outside the Old South, anti-Catholicism became more important. A canvass of the expressed motives of members in joining the Klan revealed fear and hatred of the Catholic Church. The demonology dominating the outlook of Klansmen, particularly outside the South, had its own hierarchy: "Pope, Catholic, foreigner, nigger, and Jew." [3]

But even ranking last was a danger to the Jews of America. For the Klan, despite its protestations in favor of religious toleration, was the first substantial, organized movement in the United States to use anti-Semitism. According to a renegade Klan organizer, anti-Jewish propaganda conducted by members and officers was carried on "as viciously as against the Catholics." [4] To the Klan's predominantly rural and small-town membership, the Jew symbolized the evils of a changing, urban America.

The kind of Americanism propagated by the Klan was immediately apparent from its membership restrictions. Only "native-born, white, gentile, Protestant American citizens of good moral character" were eligible.[5] One of the questions asked Klan applicants was, "Do you believe in the tenets of the Christian religion?" Klan leaders defended their exclusionist policy by pointing to restricted Catholic and Jewish fraternal orders, forgetting that the purpose of the Klan's restriction was to foster action against the excluded groups. Edward Y. Clarke, Imperial Giant of the Klan, expressed this attitude clearly:

> The Ku Klux Klan stands primarily for the principles of Jesus Christ and that explains why it is impossible for us to take the Jews in. . . . Now the Christian white men are about to band themselves into one great Klan and give the Jews some of their own medicine.[6]

Col. Simmons, the founder of the Klan, testified in 1921 before a Congressional investigating committee that his organization was not anti-Semitic.

> . . . They say we are anti-Jew. No; we are not. I can count my Jewish friends by the score. We are not any more anti-Jew than they are anti-me in their own particular orders. If there is any Jew that can subscribe to the tenets of the Christian religion we will gladly welcome him in the faith.[7]

Speaking more frankly at a Klan Koncilium in Dallas, attended by 75,000 Klansmen, Imperial Wizard Hiram W. Evans accused the Jews of a "racial and religious antipathy unrelenting and unabating since the cross of Calvary." [8]

The old folk-myth of Jews as Christ-killers thus provided part of the essential background of Klan prejudice. The major attacks on the Jews, however, as in the case of the *Dearborn Independent*, emphasized contemporary cultural, political, and economic themes. Klan newspapers printed Ford-like exposés of Jewish radicalism, accusing Jews of not only causing the Bolshevik Revolution, but of plotting the same in the United States. A typical anti-Semitic letter, signed "American," which appeared in the *Searchlight* (July 30, 1921), accused the Jew of "creating war between blacks and whites and working to overthrow all the gentile governments of the world." The *Fellowship Forum* (Jan, 26, 1924), a "national Masonic and patriotic weekly" published in Washington, spoke unofficially for the Klan when it carried such headlines as, "Jews and Catholics Maintain Strong Invisible Government in U.S.—Senator Hensley of Oklahoma State Legislature Reveals Yiddish Have Powerful Clan and Jews of World Flock to New York not Palestine in Conspiracy to Internationalize America." According to this journal, the invisible government of the Jews was located in New York and was known as the "Ke-hil-lah" [*sic*]. The Klan, it claimed, was merely a defensive device to protect Americans against this threat.

In addition to the radical-international Jewish threat, Klan propaganda claimed that Jews were unassimilable, unpatriotic, urban-dwelling, economic parasites who practiced a selfish clannishness at the expense of real Americans. Writing on the "Attitude of the Klan Toward the Jew," Dr. Evans, the Dallas dentist who succeeded Col. Simmons as Imperial Wizard, denied that hostility to the Jew was fostered by the organization. The K.K.K., he wrote, was not the enemy of any man "who so commits himself to his country that nothing is reserved." Jews, like Catholics, were not in this patriotic category. They did not explore, navigate, cultivate, mine, or colonize America, but came here only after the continent had been won by Christians. Now, nearly all Jews lived in large cities ("this violates a fundamental law of our social life," commented Dr. Evans) maintaining their distinctiveness and exclusiveness, and engaging in money-lending and petty trade.

> The Jew produces nothing anywhere on the face of the earth. He does not till the soil. He does not create or manufacture anything for common use. He adds nothing to the sum of human welfare. Everywhere he stands between the producer and the consumer and sweats the toil of the one and the necessity of the other for his gains.

Finally, the Jew, by nature and custom, could not participate in the American nation:

> By deliberate election, he is unassimilable. He rejects intermarriage. His religious and social rites and customs are inflexibly segregative. Law-abiding, healthy, moral, mentally alert, energetic, loyal and reverent in his home life, the Jew is yet by primal instinct a Jew, indelibly marked by persecution, with no deep national attachment, a stranger to the emotion of patriotism as the Anglo-Saxon feels it.[9]

While not neglecting Jews, Klan leaders emphasized that their principal enemy was the Roman Catholic Church. "The Jew the Klan considers a far smaller problem. For one thing, he is confined to a few cities, and is no problem at all to most of the country." [10] The Klan sometimes issued statements indicating that Catholics would be attacked exclusively and the Jews let alone. But temporary shifts in tactics and verbal excuses did not obscure the fact that the Klan was still basically hostile to Jews. Dr. Evans admitted that Jews were allied with Catholics because, as he phrased it, "the Jew in America sees in the rise and extension of Klannishness an arrest placed upon his activities in money getting." [11]

In terms of political action, the Klan's attitude toward Jews and Catholics coincided with and reinforced the postwar upsurge of immigration restrictionism. If the United States were to be saved from becoming a "Jewish-Roman nation," immigration had to be stopped. The native-born, white, Protestant American had all he could digest or assimilate, and the Klan believed that the best remedy was complete cessation of immigration for a decade or two. Although the Klan never dominated the federal legislature, its immigration program suited the prevailing American spirit and its support made restrictionism easier to put across.

Local actions aimed specifically at Jews, while never approaching pogrom proportions, did occur. The anti-Semitism of the Klan was probably strongest in the North, but the small Jewish communities of the South and West were most vulnerable to direct annoyances. As a Southern Jewish leader remarked privately to Louis Marshall, the Jews of his city, Little Rock, were in a difficult situation; they were a "hopeless minority" in an area "cursed with a half-baked, illiterate, Protestant pulpit." [12]

In Arkansas, Alabama, Texas, and elsewhere, the Klan boycotted Jewish merchants in its campaign against foreign elements. Confronted with accusations of Klan-inspired boycotts, leaders of the movement lamely asserted that they were not officially sanctioned: "I don't mean to deny that individual members might have organized a boycott among themselves in several instances, but no Klan assembled in its Klavern in regular session would ever vote a boycott." [13] Regardless of the manner of organization, boycotts did take place. In Indianapolis, for example, the Klan started its own department store, named the One Hundred Per Cent American Store, in order to drive Jewish merchants out of business.

Equally disturbing was additional Klan-related anti-Semitism. A circular distributed in Montgomery, Alabama during a primary election warned voters to make a proper choice between the candidates:

> Vote the Gunter ticket and help swell the ranks of the Catholics, the bootleggers, the immoral men and women, the Jews, the theater owners, gamblers and Un-Americans. Vote the Bob Jones ticket and help swell the ranks of loyal Americans, real citizens, moral men and women who are trying to raise children in a decent town. Judge a man by the company he keeps. Who are Bob Jones friends. They are the Pastors of our Protestant churches and their congregations. Who are Gunter's friends. They are the libertine Catholic priest and the whiskey-swilling, card-playing pro-German Jews.

From Houston, Texas came messages urgently calling the attention of Jewish leaders to a wave of anti-Semitism which seemed to be sweeping that part of the country. A Ft. Worth, Texas lawyer wrote that juries in his city were usually made up of "brothers of the Klan" and added that he was sure that "a Kike Jew wouldn't stand much shot before such a jury." [14] In Pocatello, Idaho, a Jewish dentist received an ultimatum from the local Klan leader: "You are being watched. If you appear on the streets of Pocatello in ten days from this date, God Help Your Soul. We are going to rid this beautiful City of all Catholics, Jews, Greeks, and Bootleggers." [15]

Even the New York metropolitan area was not exempt from the Klan. An informed estimate placed the number of Klansmen within twenty-five miles of City Hall at over 75,000, and the Exalted Cyclops of the Yonkers Klan claimed that 15,000 of these were in Westchester County. These figures were probably inflated, but the Klan was active in New York and New Jersey. A former Klan organizer testified that he was instructed to start in New York City by "giving the Jews the dickens. . . . Their idea was this . . . that the Jew patronizes the Jew, if possible; therefore, we as klansmen, the only real 100 per cent Americans, will only patronize klansmen." [16] A letter from a New York Klansman to a state legislator summed up the feelings of his fellows by promising that a "torrential flood" of Protestant, Anglo-Saxon Americanism "shall sweep away every disloyal and

Christ-hating Jew from the face of our beloved land, washing it clean and pure as a fit habitation for Christ and his followers." [17]

Reaction to the Klan

Marshall and other Jewish leaders were faced with an organized, mass movement, that, while not primarily anti-Semitic, contained dangerous elements in its ideology and practice. However, the basic policy of Marshall and the American Jewish Committee toward the Klan was watchful inaction. Jews, Marshall believed, need not take the Klan too seriously, but should regard it with patience and a sense of proportion. "If matters are permitted to be worked out in a normal way, the Ku Klux Klan will die of inanition and of ridicule and of contempt in a very short time." [18]

This confidence in the sanity of the American people was ultimately justified when the Klan disintegrated in the later 1920's, but there were times when it seemed particularly threatening. One of these occasions was the election campaign of 1924, when the Klan was thrust into politics. Marshall tried to convince Republican leaders that forthright denunciation of the Klan was necessary, not only for political reasons, but because the possible success of the Klan might mean "the murder or exile of all Catholics, all Jews, and all Negroes in this country." [19] Only once did Marshall issue a public statement on the Klan, and that was in reply to the Dallas speech of Imperial Wizard Evans in October, 1923, when the Klan leader affirmed the impossibility of Jews being true Americans. Marshall retorted that it was now apparent that only Anglo-Saxon Protestants would be allowed to live in America if the Klan had its way, thus excluding Negroes, Italians, French, Irish, as well as Jews. This, said

Marshall, was distinctly unconstitutional, and the Klan, therefore, not the Jews, was unpatriotic. The Klan, he asserted, was an insult to the American people who would undoubtedly react negatively. In this confidence, he concluded, he would resume his "former attitude of indifference toward the Ku Klux Klan and its works." [20]

The disdain Marshall expressed for the Klan was combined with the feeling that Jews should not inject themselves into public anti-Klan activities. It was "beneath our dignity" to discuss the Klan in terms of a movement directed against Jews. Repeatedly, Marshall insisted that the Klan was a danger to America and that it could be fought most effectively through the Protestant churches.

> The only way to fight the Ku Klux Klan is in the open, and that fighting should be done . . . by the Protestant Church, at whose door lies this iniquity, because, besides masquerading in sheets and pillow slips, it is seeking to make it appear that it is the protagonist of Protestantism.[21]

Marshall also feared Catholic and Jewish attacks on the Klan might exacerbate the problem by adding "thousands of weak minded persons" to its ranks.

Possibly as a precaution, Marshall preferred to work through a man like Major Henry P. Fry in exposing the Klan's machinations. Fry was the son of a Confederate officer and had joined the Klan in Tennessee; he had been an organizer for a brief period, and then resigned. He later contributed to the series of articles on the Klan that appeared in the New York World in September, 1921. Fry then established an independent press bureau specializing in Klan news and in this activity he received encouragement and, perhaps, financial support from Marshall and his friends.[22]

Marshall's attitude toward Protestantism was shared by other Jewish leaders, including Rabbi Stephen Wise. The rabbi of Temple Emanu-El, Marshall's congregation, likewise expressed the belief that the Klan would be destroyed if every Protestant minister denounced it from the pulpit. The Federal Council of Churches of Christ did denounce the Klan and, in 1925, issued a joint condemnation with the Central Conference of American Rabbis, but Marshall's hopes that Protestant Church action would kill the Klan were only partially fulfilled.

As the Klan persisted in its growth and power, American Jews were disturbed and were generally more willing to take a stronger anti-Klan position than Marshall approved. Stephen Wise, agreeing with Marshall that the burden of the fight against the Klan should be borne by non-Jews, added that "there are other sides to the question which cannot be left out of account." [23] His organization, the American Jewish Congress, publicly adopted an anti-Klan resolution. Similar resolutions were adopted by Jewish fraternal groups, one of whose leaders urged united action by all anti-Klan groups, including Jews, in a great non-sectarian movement to kill the Klan.[24] The Independent Order of B'rith Sholom called on President Harding and Congress "to use, if necessary, the armed forces of our Government and all its agencies to exterminate without delay this vicious and unhealthy organization." [25] Rabbis denounced the Klan as a menace to America, and the Reform Union of American Hebrew Congregations, over the opposition of those who felt it would play into the hands of the enemy, also adopted an anti-K.K.K. resolution. The socialist *Forward* explained to its Yiddish readers that the Klan was similar to the Czarist Black Hundreds and that it was, in essence, a capitalist tool which the workers must oppose. In California a Jewish leader called upon Pacific Coast Jews to raise a $200,000 fund to fight the Klan in the West.

Marshall and the American Jewish Committee attempted to restrain their fellow-Jews from taking precipitate anti-Klan action. Influential Jews, leaders of organizations, editors of newspapers and magazines—all were urged to refrain from making a Jewish issue out of the Klan. Marshall thought it unwise for Jewish fraternal groups, such as the B'nai B'rith that were themselves secret orders, to condemn another secret order. In any case, Jewish attacks would only intensify the conflict and bring additional recruits to the Klan.

Particularly deplorable, in Marshall's opinion, were efforts by Jews to bring the Klan issue into politics through pressing for anti-Klan resolutions by political parties. Although he modified his stand in the latter stages of the 1924 Presidential campaign, Marshall did so reluctantly. He opposed the effort to insert an anti-Klan plank in the Republican state platform in Missouri in the spring of that year. Writing to Louis Aloe, Jewish Republican leader in St. Louis, Marshall hoped that his courage and backbone would not be questioned, but "there are times when one must not follow impulse, but should exercise diplomacy." A Jewish or Catholic attack on the Klan, he warned, might be interpreted as an attack on Protestantism. Aloe refused to accept Marshall's reasoning, and replied that "the Protestant ministers of America will not act unless tremendous and overwhelming public sentiment is aroused." In the end, the Missouri Republicans did pass an anti-Klan resolution; similar action was taken by the state's Democratic Party, also with Jewish backing.

Marshall refused to provide financial aid or encouragement to anti-Klan candidates in Southern states. When Texas Republican leaders who were seeking funds for their candidate against the Klan-backed Democratic Senatorial nominee were referred in 1922 to Marshall, he refused to lend his support, asserting that it might lead to charges of Wall Street Jews interfering in the sovereign state of Texas. An appeal for assistance to Ex-Governor James C. Walton of Oklahoma, who had been ousted by a Klan-dominated legislature, was likewise met by no response from Marshall.

Marshall's attitude was not merely negative, however, as was shown by his voluntary participation in a crucial test case involving the Klan in Oregon. In this normally Republican state, the Klan demonstrated surprising power by electing a Democratic Governor, Walter Pierce, with the largest majority in the history of the state. Shortly after, in 1922, a Klan-backed law compelling attendance of all children at public schools only was carried under the initiative system by a majority of the state's voters.

Marshall became involved in this situation through a dispute with one of Portland, Oregon's Jewish leaders; he was Jesse Winburn, an ardent supporter of Governor Pierce. Winburn and his family had come from Syracuse where Marshall had known them. Since he could not understand how any sane Jew could get enmeshed in the Klan cause, Marshall's only explanation was that Winburn was obstinate, not very clever, and had fallen prey to flatterers. Acting on the appeal of embarrassed Portland Jewish leaders, Marshall urged Winburn in strong terms to withdraw from Klan entanglements and, in particular, not to back the public school law. Otherwise, Marshall warned, Winburn's acts would contribute to the eventual "annihilation of your own people and of all other minorities." [26] After receiving Marshall's complaints, Winburn denounced the public school law, but continued to endorse Governor Pierce.

The Oregon statute at issue was the result of the Klan's anti-Catholic agitation and was aimed principally at Catholic parochial schools. No Jewish interests were directly involved and there were only a few Protestant schools in Oregon. The Catholic group, therefore, took the initiative in appealing to the state's courts against the law. After the failure of these appeals, William D. Guthrie, well-known Catholic lawyer and a friend of Marshall's, brought the case to the Supreme Court. Guthrie realized that Jewish help was essential:

> It was important to emphasize before the Court and in the forum of public opinion that the principle involved was of vital importance and the precedent, if upheld, a direct menace to all religions, and not alone to the Roman Catholics. I appealed to Marshall for help, and he gave it unstintingly.[27]

Acting on behalf of the American Jewish Committee and, as he said, "representing the parents of Jewish children and the teachers who maintain private schools for the education of Jewish children in the country," Marshall responded to Guthrie's appeal by filing a classic brief with the Supreme Court as *amicus curiae*.[28] Marshall's argument was that the Oregon law, by compelling attendance at public schools only and thereby, in effect, outlawing private, parochial schools, was destructive of liberty and property and therefore unconstitutional. Granting the great merits of the public school system, he argued that it was unthinkable for compulsion to be used to give it a monopoly of all education. To do so would result in a nation of "mechanical robots and standardized Babbitts." On the same theory, state legislators might compel all to read the same newspaper or attend the same church. Defending the quality of private school education, he concluded by asserting that it was the right of parents, not the state, to control the education of their children. In a unanimous decision written by Mr. Justice McReynolds, which followed Marshall's arguments very closely, the Oregon statute was declared unconstitutional by the Court. Marshall, naturally, was overjoyed: "I do not think the importance of this decision can be exaggerated. It will prove a landmark in our history." [29]

By the time of the Oregon decision, the Klan was already disintegrating as a major force in American life. In part, this was due to internal difficulties that beset and discredited the Klan organization, as well as to the return of general prosperity. But also responsible for the decline of the Klan were the leaders of the nation who could not countenance its tactics nor support its wilder aspects. Despite unofficial support from fundamentalists, the Klan was never approved by most American Protestant churches, and was indeed condemned by important church leadership and the press. Even members of the Klan were sometimes distressed by the activities of their colleagues, feeling guilty, for example, at "picking on the Jews whom they had known as good neighbors all their lives."

Marshall was at least partly correct in his assumption that the Klan need not be taken too seriously and that the "unfailing sense of fairness and of decency of the American people as a whole" would sooner or later triumph. As he humorously remarked to the Golden Jubilee Convention of the Union of American Hebrew Congregations, "We have had a long line of enemies who have been bent on our destruction, from Balak to Belloc, not to mention the vast hordes of bullocks that have bellowed and bullied in the interval. All their efforts have been, and will continue to be, futile." [30] Nevertheless, although the Klan never formulated or consummated an explicit political program directed at Jews, its use of anti-Jewish stereotypes and propaganda indicated that anti-Semitism was still potent in the minds of many Americans. Temporary boycotts of Jewish merchants were insignificant in themselves, but they revealed the existence of a substratum of nativistic hate. Most important, the Klan spirit included an anti-alienism which was shared, less outspokenly, by the great majority of Americans after the war. As Marshall recognized, it was this spirit which was linked with and partly responsible for the successful culmination of the immigration restriction movement in discriminatory quota legislation.

Post-War Immigration Restriction

The Immigration Act of 1917, in which the literacy test had been included, had not satisfied immigration restrictionists. For one thing, the resumption of large-scale immigration after the war indicated that the flow of newcomers would not be reduced sharply enough by the provisions of the existing law. In the last half of 1920, net arrivals averaged 52,000 monthly and, in 1921, over 800,000 immigrants entered the United States. Jewish immigration, which had dwindled to a trickle during the war years, spurted to 120,000 in 1921, or more than 21 per cent of the net immigration. Significantly, whereas Jewish immigration was about 10 per cent of the gross total from 1908 to 1914, it rose to almost 15 per cent of the total in 1921, reflecting the chaotic situation in Eastern Europe.[31]

Even before this upsurge, however, the post-war restrictionist campaign had begun. An outcome of the intense nationalism of 1917 and 1918, it was much more drastic than its pre-war counterpart. Among native Americans, as John Higham has noted, "the issue after the armistice no longer concerned the desirability of restriction but simply the proper degree and kind." [32] The restrictionists now aimed for a more definitive and explicit exclusion of certain immigrants; many would have liked to stop immigration completely.

By 1921, open and deliberate restriction of immigration was law, and in 1924 the same principle was further codified. Behind the successful imposition of this legislation lay the nationalistic spirit of the war years. Associated with fear and suspicion of hyphenates, this mood was heightened by the Red Scare, with its distorted emphasis on dangerous alien radicals. As Louis Marshall noted, immigration and Bolshevism came to be regarded as "convertible terms."

When immigrants began once more to flock to America in 1920–1921, the old fear of an ethnic transformation merged into horror at an anticipated alien indigestion. The economic uncertainty of the immediate post-war years intensified doubts as to the absorptive capacity of the American economy. Businessmen who opposed restriction in the early 1920's gradually retreated as prosperity returned and increasing mechanization made cheap European labor less essential. Even native-born progressives and certain Northern European immigrant groups joined the restrictionist stampede. Foremost in the ranks of the proponents of restriction were the new super-patriotic groups, including the American Legion and the Ku Klux Klan. The organized labor movement, represented by the American Federation of Labor, continued its support of restriction, and did so on racial-national, as well as economic, grounds.

The racist theories of the pre-war period, propagated and elaborated during and after the war, now found wide acceptance among both educated and uneducated Americans. In fact, the distinction between old and new immigrants came to be taken almost for granted, and to the framers of the quota laws, this probably assumed even greater importance than restriction itself. Although the fear of an alien flood was important as a cause of the Immigration Act of 1921, racism and ethnic prejudice were the major factors behind the Act of 1924.

The wide acceptance of restrictionism by the American people, with the exception of a few immigrant groups, indicated that it was a nationalist phenomenon accurately reflecting the sentiments of the era. The impetus for restriction in the 1920's did not derive from anti-Semitism. Still, it did not require much effort to notice an anti-Semitic strain which occasionally came to the surface in restrictionist arguments. It was this, as much as restriction itself, which disturbed American Jews. The attack on immigration carried with it implications concerning the alleged inability of Jews and other immigrants to become capable American citizens. An editorial in the *Minneapolis Journal* (May 26, 1919) inquired, "Are Russians and Russian and German Jews and others besides psychologically unfit to be citizens of an Anglo-Saxon state or country?" A similar point of view was expressed by a lady who wrote to Marshall that Southern Europeans and Jews were "spiritually inferior" and had to be kept out of America:

> We are populated enough now, and do not want the low refuse that Europe is sending us. Of course the Nordic race is superior. He has settled this country, gave us law, religion, decency, and is not on a soap box trying to overturn the Government after he is here six weeks.[33]

A Methodist minister expressed similar thoughts with greater vehemence:

For a real American to visit Ellis Island and there look upon the Jewish hordes, ignorant of all true patriotism, filthy, vermin infested, stealthy and furtive in manner, too lazy to enter into real labor, too cowardly to face frontier life, too lazy to work as every American farmer has to work, too filthy to adopt ideals of cleanliness from the start, too bigoted to surrender any racial traditions or to absorb any true Americanism, for a real American to see those items of a filthy, greedy, never patriotic stream flowing in to pollute all that has made America as good as she is—is to awaken in his thoughtful mind desires to check and lessen this source of pollution.[34]

Even those regarded as friendly to Jews spoke up against the "extremely lower classes of foreign Jews who have been permitted to come indiscriminately to American shores, people who are ignorant of real Americanism and unwilling to learn." [35] A Maine newspaper editorial called for complete cessation of immigration, which had been fine twenty-five years ago when land was still plentiful and cheap, but not any more. It suggested also that Jewish immigrants be sent to Palestine, their "natural home." As for the editors of the *Chicago Tribune,* Marshall called their attitude "pestilential":

They have deliberately tried to make it appear that all of the Jews of Russia and Poland are seeking to come to this country. This gives Main Street the creeps and the Ku Kluxers go gibbering through the graveyards.[36]

Respected molders of American public opinion participated in the post-war restrictionist campaign, often emphasizing the Jewish aspects of immigration. One of the most widely publicized attacks on the Jews during the 1920's was Burton J. Hendrick's book, *The Jews in America* (New York, 1923), which stressed the undesirability of further Jewish immigration. The author, a well-known journalist with experience in the muckraking school, published this work originally as a series of articles in *World's Work* during 1922 and 1923.[37] Hendrick disclaimed any personal anti-Semitic feeling: "I have no animus against the Jew myself, though I do believe that certain phases of his activities in this country are unfortunate. . . ." [38] In his articles, which were polite and scholarly in tone, Hendrick distinguished between the major waves of Jewish immigration to the United States— Spanish, German, and Russo-Polish. Creating a dichotomy analogous to the distinction made by restrictionists between old and new immigrants, Hendrick asserted that older Spanish and German Jews were fairly easily assimilated, but the real problem came with the mass transfer of millions of Polish Jews. This latter group Hendrick traced back to the Khazars of the Crimea, thus enabling him to claim that East European Jews had a considerable element of Asiatic blood in their ancestry. Hendrick implied that this might explain their stubborn, religious orthodoxy and peculiar mentality.

In America, these Jews huddled together in New York: "Any race fifty per cent of whose people live in one city, and the remaining fifty per cent in other large American cities, can hardly be regarded as having become flesh of the flesh of the American body." [39] Economically, they concentrated in businesses allowing a maximum of individualistic capitalist aggressiveness and a minimum of money. As for politics, most Polish Jews were socialistic and pacifistic, and had brought forth a new type of radical labor unionism. Generally, they were not good patriots, and this was attributed by Hendrick to "a deep lying racial trait" rather than historical experience with persecution in Europe.

Hendrick's solution for the Jewish problem was to prevent further immigration:

> There is only one way in which the United States can be protected from the anti-Semitism which so grievously afflicts the eastern sections of Europe. That is by putting up the bars against these immigrants until the day comes when those already here are absorbed. This country has too many racial and social problems and too many tasks of economic regeneration to add unnecessarily to them. Happily this conviction has at last become a fixed one in the popular mind.[40]

In fact, Hendrick rejoiced, referring to the Immigration Act of 1921, "Congress has passed and the President has signed an immigration law chiefly intended—it is just as well to be frank about the matter—to restrict the entrance of Jews from eastern Europe." [41]

The Hendrick articles in *World's Work* were widely advertised in the New York press, under such titles as, "Is the Polish Jew a Menace?" A magazine advertisement asked some personal questions, under the heading, "Your Job and the Jews":

> Is there anything in this "universal control" by Jews? Are Jews officers or directors of your business? If not, do they control the business by lending it money? Would you be dismissed if known to be unsympathetic to the Jews? Would you be promoted if actively pro-Jew? [42]

Circulars along these lines were distributed by Doubleday, Page and Company, publishers of *World's Work*. When the articles appeared in book form, a prefatory note advised the reader that it was published "in compliance with a great public demand." [43] The book's jacket enticed readers with lurid questions:

> Do Jews Make Good Americans? Do Jews Dominate American Finance? Is There a Menace in the Polish Jew? . . . The great Jewish families in America are of Western stock. What of the unassimilable Polish Jews who comprise the bulk of the 3,000,000 Jews in this country? With their un-American creed, will they ever be absorbed into the American commonwealth? [44]

Louis Marshall, believing that Hendrick's attack on Polish Jews was in reality an attack on all American Jews as well as a plea for immigration restriction, protested bitterly to Frank N. Doubleday, Hendrick's publisher.[45] Condemning the anti-Semitic tone and commercialism of Doubleday's advertising campaign, Marshall defended Orthodox Judaism and the East European Jewish immigrants. Especially disturbing to Marshall was Hendrick's statement that the Immigration Act of 1921 was directed primarily at Jews, for this carried with it the implication that only Jews ought to be concerned in resisting immigration restriction. Doubleday and Hendrick, however, refused to respond, and Marshall finally wrote, "We can pray even for such as you. May the Almighty in His great mercy forgive you!" [46] At the same time, Marshall released his letters to the press.[47]

Jews and liberals were, naturally, antagonistic to Hendrick's work. One reviewer termed it an "excellent postscript to Mr. Henry Ford's anti-Semitic vagaries. . . ." [48] On the other hand, a scholarly journal contained a review which called it "an illuminating contribution . . . a book with no racial bias." [49]

Very influential in spreading racial propaganda was a book based on articles written for the *Saturday Evening Post* by a young reporter who later became a popular novelist, Kenneth Roberts.[50] The message of *Why Europe Leaves Home* could be inferred immediately from its frontispiece, a photograph of the crowded U.S. visa office in Warsaw, captioned, "Ninety per cent of these people are Jews." The basic theme was that pre-war immigration was small compared with "the serried ranks and the teeming multitudes which today are anxiously awaiting the opportunity to break all surging records between Europe and America." [51] Most of these would-be immigrants, according to Roberts, were Polish Jews who sought to escape Europe, not because of religious oppression or economic distress (they were accustomed to hardship, he asserted), but because America had been advertised as a land where the streets were paved with gold, and because Jewish immigration organizations had stimulated their desire to come to America.

The Jews of Poland, Roberts claimed, were

> human parasites, living on one another and on their neighbors of other races by means which too often are underhanded. . . . they continue to exist in the same way after coming to America . . . they are therefore highly undesirable as immigrants.[52]

The picture presented was of millions of pauper Jews battering on the doors of America, people who were "unassimilable, undesirable, and incapable of grasping American ideals." [53] The solution, said Roberts, was to close those doors tightly and see that the Jews went elsewhere. Emphasiz-

ing the disastrous racial consequences which could be expected if these non-Nordic aliens were not kept out, Roberts
forecast that "promiscuous crossbreeding" might result in the
mongrelization of America." [54] Even restriction based on
nationality quotas was not safe enough for Roberts, who
warned that ruthless Jews would still be able to get in. He
called for a racial quota and strongly implied that Polish
Jews, because of their "Mongoloid" origin, might be barred
completely as Asiatics.[55] As for those misguided people who
still did not see the light, Roberts had only contempt: "The
hazy dreams of sentimentalists and the partisan desires of
alien societies are poor substitutes for straight thinking and
the inflexible rules of biology." [56]

Robert's work, which attracted considerable notice when
it appeared in the *Saturday Evening Post* in 1920–1921 and as
a book in 1922, was recognized by Marshall and Jewish leaders
as extremely prejudicial to Jews. Beyond calling it "a shallow
concoction of vicious insinuations, distortions and fabrications," and publicly denying specific charges made by Roberts,
there was little that could be done.[57]

That the tide of anti-immigration feeling was irresistibly
growing seemed clear when even a prominent son of Italian
immigrants, and a man who had served with Marshall in the
New York State Immigration Commission before the war,
began to issue pronouncements on immigration's danger to
Anglo-Saxon America. In a series of articles appearing in
1923–1924 in *World's Work,* Gino Speranza claimed that
American civilization was fundamentally Protestant, Anglo-
Saxon, and Nordic, that foreign immigrants constituted an
unabsorbable mass, and that they were "alienizing" America.[58] "Something is wrong" in America, he claimed, and
aliens, "broadly speaking," were responsible.[59]

As for the "self-assertive" Jews, Speranza warned that they
were aggressively attempting to impose *"their* views and *their*
principles and *their* interpretations and *their* standards upon
the historic American majority." [60] In an obvious reference
to Louis Marshall, he questioned the right of "one of the

leading constitutional lawyers of American Jewry to tell us that . . . ours is *not* a Christian government." [61] "Is it bigotry," Speranza asked, "for the American people to be disquieted at the fact that the Jews of New York City spend yearly over $2,000,000 on *Yiddish* newspapers in that metropolis? That they maintained in that city in 1918, by their own count, 3,637 societies of their own wherein none but Jews may enter?" [62] Although he attacked Catholic parochial schools, Speranza granted that Roman Catholicism was modifying itself in America. But the clannish Jews were another matter: "Hardest of all, and perhaps impossible, will be the spiritual assimilation of Israel." [63] Speranza concluded with a clarion call for a "ceaseless effort at *complete* cultural conformity." [64]

Marshall, who knew Speranza, contemptuously referred to him as "a renegade Italian who for some years past has befouled his own nest." [65] Speranza's articles were regarded as in some respects more vicious than Hendrick's and were followed closely by Jewish leaders, but no direct counter-efforts similar to those made in the Hendrick case were attempted.

Feeling against Jewish immigrants was prominent not only among certain journalists during those years. Especially distasteful to Marshall and his associates were the words and actions of American officials associated with the State Department. American Jews were convinced that visa officials overseas showed "clear and unmistakable prejudice against the Jewish immigrant." [66] In 1921, the head of the U.S. consular service submitted a series of reports dealing with immigration from European consuls to Congressional committees considering legislation. These reports, printed as part of the Senate hearing on immigration, contained the usual accusations against Polish Jews and supported the alleged necessity for tightening immigration restrictions:

> The great mass of aliens passing through Rotterdam at the present time are Russian Poles or Polish Jews of the usual ghetto type. Most of them are more or less directly and frankly getting out of Poland to avoid war conditions. They are filthy, un-American, and often dan-

Americanism of the Twenties

gerous in their habits. . . . Eighty-five to ninety per cent lack any
conception of patriotic or national spirit, and the majority of this
percentage is mentally incapable of acquiring it. . . . The unassimil-
ability of these classes politically is a fact too often proved in the past
to bear any argument. . . . The increase of immigration from Poland
raises two important questions for the United States—first, public
health, and second, public safety. Many bolshevik sympathizers are in
Poland. It is difficult through visé control to keep out the unde-
sirables.[67]

Marshall wrote to Secretary of State Charles E. Hughes, protesting these "opprobrious references," and noting that the
director of the consular service was well-known as an anti-
Semite who had practically forced all Jews out of his department. There was no indication of any corrective action by
Hughes.

In keeping with the general line which concentrated on
attempting to demonstrate the racial and cultural inferiority
of Southern and Eastern Europeans, the attacks on Jewish
immigration singled out the Polish Jews for particular attention. Some Jews may have assured themselves that only East
Europeans were under fire, but Marshall was clearsighted
enough to realize that the distinction was trivial and that
attacks on Polish Jews had to be resisted. When the *Encyclopedia Britannica,* for example, in its article on Poland, included a section on "The Jewish Question" replete with
inaccuracies and innuendoes, Marshall publicly demanded a
retraction.

Marshall did his best to deride the racist concepts underlying immigration restriction:

I regard the Nordic as the figment of that useless part of our population who imagine themselves to be the cream of creation. . . .[68]

The right of immigration should not be dependent upon arbitrary
classification according to ethnological concepts. Character or ability
or usefulness is not dependent on any scientific or pseudo-scientific
classification of the human race . . .[69]

It is only pseudo-anthropologists who recognize that there ever was
any such race as the Nordic . . . the whole idea is a myth.[70]

Marshall knew the power of racial propaganda in stimulating the immigration restriction movement. If legislation were drawn not only restricting immigration, but doing so on racialist assumptions, he was convinced that a caste spirit and misunderstanding would be created and that the position of American Jews might deteriorate. This fear of the deleterious effects of immigration restriction both on America and on its Jewish citizens was the major motive for his fight against quota legislation.

Quota Laws

Marshall used a variety of techniques in his campaign to halt or delay the passage of restrictive immigration legislation. The application of direct political pressure, principally through the Republican Party, was one approach. Appearing before Congressional committees, filing briefs, writing lengthy letters to Senators, Marshall pressed his views vigorously. In addition, he cooperated with non-Jewish groups that also opposed immigration restriction. Marshall was legal adviser to the Inter-Racial Council, an organization of prominent businessmen who were active in the early 1920's in fighting quota legislation. He made overtures to Catholic leaders, suggesting that since the new immigration bills were aimed at Jewish and Catholic immigrants primarily, these groups should collaborate. In the end, all of these efforts were unavailing, for the progressive elaboration of a thoroughgoing restrictionist system was almost inevitable under the conditions then existing.

The restrictionist legislative campaign opened very soon after the Armistice with the drastic Burnett bill. This act would have prohibited all immigration for a period of four years and then restricted it severely by a quota system based on the nationality of naturalized immigrants. Marshall was incredulous: "Is it possible that, at this time, when we have been carrying on a conflict for the cause of humanity, we shall become an insular people and slam our doors in the faces of those who seek to bring to us their strength and their helpful devotion?" [71] In a letter to the House Committee on Immigration, he expressed strong moral, legal, constitutional, and practical objections to the proposed law.

This prohibition idea was too drastic, although it did win the support of the House of Representatives. The quota proposal, which went back to a bill originally presented by Senator William Dillingham of Vermont in 1913, was more successful. The Emergency Quota Act of 1921, a turning point in American immigration policy, embodied the principle of restricting the new immigrants by a 3 per cent quota based on the number of people born in a given country and residing in the United States in 1910.

Marshall appeared before the Senate Committee on Immigration to oppose this bill and spoke movingly of the devotion and Americanism of the immigrants.[72] Questioned on whether he recognized any difference between the assimilability of old and new immigrants, Marshall replied that they were equally assimilable, that assimilation was not a matter of outward appearance, but of mind and heart, and that the best American he ever knew, his mother, could hardly speak English:

> It is ideas which control, not the words in which those ideas are couched. There is nothing sacrosanct about the English language. I believe that we should have an official language in every country, but this idea of opposing all languages but that one is such a kind of chauvinism that ten years from now every one will blush at the thought that there ever was an American who entertained the views now expressed towards foreigners and foreign languages.[73]

Marshall denied that there was a crisis requiring emergency legislation or that Polish Jews threatened to swamp America. He informed the Committee that, "The Jews of Poland feel that they have now an interest and a stake in Poland, that they have equal rights there. . . . They were born there. They love their country. Their ancestors died there. They . . . have no desire to leave Poland." [74] This, of course, was an exaggeration, but it was intended to allay the fears of the Senators.

Later, during the same hearings, Senator Thomas Sterling of South Dakota questioned Congressman Isaac Siegel of New York on the disposition of foreign elements to settle in New York and other large cities. Siegel replied that this was only temporary and that many Jews were moving to Sullivan County where they practiced farming. "Well," said Senator Sterling, "something over a year ago I walked in one of the streets of New York for a mile and a half or perhaps two miles, and it seemed to me as though I was in a foreign country." [75]

The attempts of Marshall, Siegel, and others, to reassure the Congressmen were ineffective. There was, at bottom, a firm suspicion that the old America was threatened. It was clear, also, as was evident from the testimony of another witness at these hearings, that exclusion, not assimilation, was the real issue:

> There is a dilemma. If these Hebrew colonies assimilate with the rest of the population by intermarriage, the result would probably be bad, owing not only to the low physical standards of most of these immigrants but also to the great differences of an ethnic nature. If assimilation does not take place in the racial sense then the objection is political, i.e., we have an alien element which is singularly tenacious of its racial and cultural habits of life and institutions, which in many respects are anti-pathetical to American life and institutions. [76]

Thus, Jews were dangerous if they did not assimilate, but were equally dangerous if they did.

After the passage of the 3 per cent quota bill by both houses of Congress, the measure went to President Harding for signature. Marshall, in a final try, urged him to veto it. He argued that there was no emergency, that the quota system was arbitary and unworkable, that it was designed "not only to discriminate against Southern and Eastern Europe, but to shut off immigration altogether."

> This measure casts an undeserved slur upon our foreign-born citizens. It tells them that they are men and women of inferior race, that they are not assimilable, that they are undesirable, that even though they are citizens and have performed the duties of citizenship they are not wanted. This is an unfortunate manifestation of a spirit of arrogance and of racial prejudice that bodes ill for the future. . . .[77]

Marshall was unable to convince Harding to exercise the veto, but even if he had, a veto would have been overridden. As Marshall saw, in analyzing the situation afterwards, "There has been so much agitation, based on false premises and on prejudice, that it was impossible to overcome the impetus of the restrictionists. . . . Even the manufacturers who depend on immigration for their labor supply have been cowed into silence."[78]

After the Act of 1921 became law, the restrictionists concentrated still more sharply on racial arguments. New legislation was proposed which would change the quota from 3 per cent to 2 per cent, shift the basis of calculating it from the 1910 to the 1890 census, and finally, in 1927, establish a permanent limit of 150,000 immigrants annually, to be divided by the relative proportion of all Americans of the various national origins as reported in the census of 1920. The object of this proposal was, first, to further reduce the number of Southern and Eastern European immigrants, and, second, to increase the eligibility of immigrants from the British Isles.

By this time, Marshall knew that it was impossible to reverse the tide by eliminating all restrictions, and he therefore tried to save the status quo. Appearing again before the Senate Committee on Immigration, he requested the appointment of an immigration commission to study the situation, and, in the meantime, urged the retention of the 1910 quota base.[79] His major object was to prevent the 1890 date from being adopted: "When I hear reference to the census of 1890, the first thing that comes to my mind is why not make

227

it 1790, or 1492. It is ridiculous." [80] To Marshall, there was "no appreciable difference between the pronouncement of the Imperial Wizard, who opposes all who are not white, Protestant and Anglo-Saxon, and that which, in less honest form, is to be found in the Johnson-Lodge Bill." [81] The measure had to be fought with vigor, and Marshall was now more direct in using political arguments. He informed the Senate Committee,

> If you place on your statute books a law which, in effect, says to us: You are inferior, you are not a first-class American, but a second class American; what shall we think of it? Shall we sit by without protesting in the only way in which an American can protest? [82]

To Congressmen Fiorello H. LaGuardia and Nicholas Longworth, Marshall wrote letters warning that Republican sponsorship and support of this legislation would result in serious political losses, especially in the urban Northeast, where immigrants were most numerous.

Again, the efforts of restriction's opponents were unsuccessful. By overwhelming margins, 323-71 in the House and 62-6 in the Senate, Congress sent the measure to President Coolidge. Marshall, as he had done in 1921 with President Harding, wrote to Coolidge requesting a veto. The law, he asserted, was unworkable, stimulated "racial, national and religious hatreds," and encouraged "one part of our population to arrogate to itself a sense of superiority, and to classify another as one of inferiority." [83] He was not surprised, however, when Coolidge signed the measure for he knew that a veto would have been overruled. In any case, Marshall suspected that Coolidge himself had "the New England idea" that restrictive immigration laws were desirable.[84]

If Coolidge indeed felt this way, he merely reflected the spirit of the nation, as did the Congressional vote on the 1924 law. A sectional analysis of that vote indicated that negative ballots had been cast, generally, only by those representing constituencies with large blocs of Southeastern European residents. Even in the Northeast, the dissent was not unanimous. Marshall regarded Senator David Reed of Pennsylvania, who had introduced the national origins provision, as the "evil genius" behind the law. His remonstrances to Reed that he was creating resentment against the Republican Party, and pointing to the phenomenal success of Al Smith in New York ("naturally a Republican state"), were not heeded.

Marshall was understandably disappointed at the outcome of the fight against restriction. Referring to the "narrow-minded" supporters of restriction, he placed them principally in the South, Far West, and Middle West, "where they don't know an immigrant when they see one and think he wears horns. . . . Where there has been no immigration you will find the most backward communities." [85] As for Congressmen, he declared, "There is very little of the milk of human kindness in the average member of the House of Representatives, and practically none in the average Senator." [86]

Jewish Attitudes on Restriction

Marshall need not have been shocked at the attitude of Congressmen, for within the Jewish group itself opinion on the immigration question was divided. As he admitted to Israel Zangwill, "a very large precentage of the Jewish citizens have permitted their prejudices to get the better of their judgment and of their hearts and have favored this restrictionist policy." [87] The tactics of the restrictionists, with their emphasis on the undesirability of further Polish-Jewish immigration, apparently softened the resistance of some Americanized Jews, particularly those of German background. Writing to a leader of the uptown community, Marshall confessed that many of "our very good friends" were in favor of restriction.

Marshall, of course, would not join this group and criticized them strongly. When Jews advocated restricted immigration, he prophesied, "it would be a sorry day in our history." [88] A Reform rabbi who had written to the Secretary of State in approval of policies implying restrictionism received a bitter letter from Marshall, and the same treatment was accorded those who argued that restriction might alleviate the problem of anti-Jewish propaganda. Cyrus Adler, Marshall's close associate in the American Jewish Committee, seemed to accept the restrictionist viewpoint when he placed at least part of the blame for the success of the new legislation on the recent immigrant groups themselves, because they had not merged quietly into the American way, but had publicly announced that they had cultures of their own which would enrich America. A Jewish newspaper called on Marshall to lead an energetic campaign to clean house within American Jewry, because Jewish bootleggers and radicals were aiding the restrictionist cause.

Most American Jews continued to oppose restriction; their efforts, however, created what Marshall considered serious obstacles to his own campaign. Marshall insisted that his opposition to restrictive laws was not due to his Jewishness, but rather to his Americanism; at Congressional hearings, he emphasized this. Time and again, Marshall sought to restrain Jews and their organizations from giving the contrary impression that restriction was a Jewish issue:

> The tendency of the Jews has been to put themselves too much in the forefront in these discussions. . . . We have many enemies who would like to make this legislation appear to be aimed at the Jews, and there is no use of disguising the fact that in various sections of the country that idea is quite prevalent.[89]

Appearances before Congressional committees by representatives of Jewish fraternal groups and "landsmanshaften" were discouraged by Marshall, who felt that most of them made "unfortunate presentations." It was unwise, Marshall believed, for Jewish members of Congress to seem to be overly concerned with pro-immigrant activities; on the other

side, when Jewish Congressmen voted for restrictive measures, Marshall advised against any public chastisement. For
all his efforts, Marshall could not eliminate the Jewish factor,
nor did he succeed in establishing himself as sole spokesman
for all Jewish organizations. When the 1924 law was finally
passed, he wrote to a rabbi that immigration

> . . . has been made a Jewish question, when it never should have
> been. In none of these arguments that I have presented before the
> Congressional Committees have I ever sought to deal with it otherwise
> than as an American question. But when every lodge and Chevra and
> association sends delegations to Washington, so that the Committee
> room looks like a synagogue on Yom Kippur, it is not to be wondered
> at that our enemies made the most of the situation and became ab-
> solutely heartless.[90]

In line with his desire to prevent Jews from exacerbating
Congressional feelings, Marshall urged that no possible opportunity be given to restrictionists to use the argument that
Jews were in any way trying to stimulate immigration to the
United States. He strongly opposed attempts to call Jewish
conferences on immigration, and termed a proposal to establish a Jewish steamship company for the purpose of transpor-
ting immigrants, "a death blow." When a Jewish journalist
rashly declared that if there were a ship large enough to
accommodate them, the 3,000,000 Jews of Poland would all
come to the United States, Marshall was beside himself; such
statements might induce Congress to adopt absolute prohibition, and, at least, contribute toward making immigration
laws more drastically restrictive. Similarly, Marshall warned
European Jews to keep hands off the immigration question in
the United States, for their intervention would antagonize the
American public and lead to further restrictions.

In Marshall's view, excessive Jewish agitation and talk
were considerably to blame for the success of restriction.
When a Rumanian rabbi, newly arrived in New York, indiscreetly remarked to reporters that half the Jews of Europe
would come to the United States if they could get visaed pass-

ports, Marshall wearily inquired, "Why cannot men like this rabbi exert some restraint upon themselves and learn the virtues of silence?" [91]

Marshall's struggle against the final imposition of the racially oriented quota system was in the nature of a rear-guard action: valiant but in vain. Those who battled to keep the doors of America open fought from a position of weakness in the early 1920's, for a large majority of the people favored restriction as a cultural, economic, and political necessity. Marshall was cognizant of this new climate of American public opinion:

> A change has occurred since the armistice. Chauvinistic nationalism is rampant. The hatred of everything that is foreign has become an obsession. The labor conditions accentuate this extraordinary phenomenon, and it requires unusual courage for a member of Congress to withstand the pressure that is brought to bear upon him to bring about a cessation of immigration. This has led to a virtual stampede.[92]

By 1922, Cyrus Adler had conceded that "with such modifications as we may be able to secure from time to time . . . the United States is forever closed as a field for immigration." [93]

Wartime nationalism, post-war disillusionment and isolation, the fear of subversion, and resistance to social change—all played roles in making Americans receptive to the message of the restrictionists. The amazing popular strength of the Ku Klux Klan, which specialized in searching out and condemning the alleged enemies of the nation who were already here, revealed the bigotry of American life that made the quota system possible.

Neither the restrictionists nor the Klan made anti-Semitism the primary ingredient of their ideologies, and Marshall was probably wise in resisting both movements on American rather than Jewish grounds. Still, both for restrictionists and the Klan, anti-Jewish propaganda was a useful campaign weapon, and Jewish leaders could not shut their eyes to it. In addition, the quota system, with its derogatory implications about American Jews, at the same time threatened concrete adverse effects on Jews throughout the world who were potential immigrants. It was natural, therefore, that Jews were in the forefront of the struggle against restriction. Marshall did not approve of Jewish actions which tended to exaggerate this fact, but it could not be avoided.

The Immigration Act of 1924 marked a dividing line in the history of the American Jewish community. Its most obvious result was a sharp and immediate decrease in Jewish immigration to the United States. In the five years preceding the First World War, 375,459 Jews entered the country, while in the five years after the passage of the 1924 law, only 57,507 Jewish immigrants arrived.[94] The stoppage of the influx of European Jewish workers contributed to the eventual transformation of American Jewry into an acculturated, middle class group, but the restrictionist prophecy that their policy would lead to thorough assimilation while reducing anti-Semitism was not fulfilled. The ethnic and religious ties of immigrant groups, including Jews, have been eroded, but, a generation later, they still possess considerable vitality.

The long-range effects of immigration restriction could not be foreseen completely in the 1920's. It appeared that the Jews of America, in common with other recent immigrant groups, had suffered a political defeat when the quota system became a feature of American life. Yet, however objectionable the new laws were, Marshall and other Jewish leaders believed that they could not prevent the continued development of Judaism in the United States.

social,
economic,
and
religious
discrimination

Social Discrimination

The anti-Jewish feelings of the Ku Klux Klan and the immigration restriction movement were exhibited simultaneously in the equally disturbing forms of social and economic discrimination. During the 1920's, Jews continued to be the most rapidly rising ethnic group in American society, and their upward mobility posed even greater challenges not only to the prestigious social elite but also to the white-collar middle-class. The pattern of social discrimination which had been worked out by World War I was therefore intensified and reached a climax in the college quota systems; at the same time, significant economic barriers began to appear.

To many American Jews, particularly those who were assimilated, educated, and wealthy, social disabilities were often more rankling than political ones. Heywood Broun reported a conversation with a famous Jewish leader:

I began by talking about employment, housing, education. He agreed
that these were the considerations to be stressed . . . and yet he
tended to stray from the point. Again and again he brought up the
fact that a certain New York club which supposedly is intended to
offer a meeting place for college graduates, was shut tight against
Jews. This seemed to be the ban which rankled most in his heart, and
I think it inevitably true that though sticks and stones can break no
bones, straws can accomplish that destruction.[1]

An individual Jew may have achieved a standard of conduct
and social level that entitled him to respect and equal treatment from his Christian fellows, but, as one of the latter put
it,

No effort of the individual can blot out his racial identification. . . .
However sincerely we may admire their fine racial traits, however
closely we may associate with individuals of the race, we cannot deny
that they constitute a separate body in our population in many respects.[2]

When a Christian minister, Dwight L. Cameron, writing a
thesis in sociology for a leading university, could attribute
part of the prejudice against "Hebrews" to the disgust felt at
their "quite different standard of table manners," it was apparent that social discrimination was deep-rooted and would
avail itself of almost any rationalization.

Marshall, in common with other Jewish leaders, usually minimized or discounted the psychological and economic
damage of social discrimination. When it was inflicted by
governmental or quasi-public institutions, Marshall opposed
it, but when it was what he considered private, there seemed
to him little cause for outcry. As a matter of fact, he was often
severely critical of Jewish social-climbing which helped
arouse discrimination:

There are some of them . . . of whom it may be said that first they
fawn and then they whine, first they flatter and then there is no limit
to their vituperation when things go amiss. They are ready to sell
their glorious heritage for a mess of pottage, and when they find that
they have not received what they bargained for, they speak of persecution and discrimination.[3]

I frequently rejoice at the fact that those who are actuated by social aspirations are occasionally rebuffed.[4]

Marshall refused to concede publicly that social discrimination resulted from undesirable traits displayed by some Jews, for if Jewish responsibility were granted, why expect anti-Semites to differentiate between the good and the bad Jews? The best way to meet social intolerance, Marshall advised, was to exercise patience and to demonstrate that Jews were good citizens broad-minded and free from bigotry. If this were accomplished, he suggested, "we may let the heathen rage."

But patience is a virtue rarely displayed by people unjustly restrained, and Marshall himself sometimes found it difficult to maintain his equanimity in the face of social discrimination. Complaints poured in to him, alleging discriminatory treatment of Jews by such diverse organizations as the Boy Rangers of America, the American Express Company, and the Mayo Clinic. Very annoying to many American Jews was discrimination by hotels and summer resorts. From the new hotels of Miami Beach to the inn which did not allow "persons of Hebrew nationality" to use its golf course, there were hundreds of establishments which could proudly boast, as one did, "We have never entertained Hebrews." [5] Jewish publications conducted polls of summer hotels to ascertain which accepted Jews, printed lists of such hotels, and advised Jews to shun the others.

Marshall, who had been instrumental in securing the adoption of a 1913 civil rights statute applying to hotels in New York, was aware of the problem, but felt that Jews should not try to force themselves by law into places they were not really welcome. Instead, he thought it might be eventually desirable to pass a federal statute on the use of the U. S. mails to carry discriminatory letters from hotels and other public places. In the meantime, he urged passage by other states of laws similar to that of New York, limited as it was.

Particularly galling to upper-class Jews was their exclusion from social clubs. As an anonymous Jew perplexedly wrote in the *Atlantic Monthly,* the reasons for this discrimination were almost incomprehensible:

> We are in no sense foreigners; my wife and I are both descended from generations of cultured people; I was educated at what is generally regarded as one of the most famous of American universities . . . and have occupied positions of trust and responsibility. We do not even have very pronounced Jewish names.[6]

This complaint might have seemed pathetic and the entire matter inconsequential but for the increasing business and social life of American communities being centered in the clubs.

Marshall was a member of the Lotos, Bankers, and Republican clubs in New York. While he did not feel he could object to exclusion from the more elite social clubs, he was angry at the attitude of the University Club which refused admittance to Jews even though, as college alumni, they were eligible. Marshall consistently refused to enter the University Club, as well as the Union League Club, even when invited to participate in professional or civic functions. When the University Club of Albany offered him the use of its house, he replied briefly:

> . . . that I thanked them for their courtesy, but apparently their invitation was sent under a mistake of fact and that therefore I could not accept it, first, because I was not a college graduate, and secondly, because I was a Jew; that while the possession of the honorary degree of LL.D. would probably permit the making of an exception as to the first point, the latter ground of objection was one that I could not and would not overcome.[7]

Marshall, who had a considerable collection of paintings, was once asked by the Union League Club to lend some of them for an exhibit at the Club. His reply was direct and incisive: "Under ordinary circumstances, I would be greatly pleased to do so; but I can scarcely reconcile myself to the incongruity of finding my property welcomed where I would be excluded." [8]

Ordinarily, Marshall maintained an attitude of noncha-

lance to the usual type of club exclusion. As he once remarked, he could not "aspire to association with the elect,"
and his pride did not allow him to make a public issue of it.[9]
In 1926, however, Marshall was thoroughly vexed by an
effort of a faction in the New York chapter of the Adirondack
Mountain Club to bar "objectionable" Jews from membership. Marshall, who was a member of the Club and had devoted almost as much time to the cause of the Adirondacks
and conservation as he had to Jewish affairs, was especially
bitter when a questionnaire was submitted to the members
requesting their views on the position which the chapter
should take on "people of the Hebrew race." If Jews were so
socially undesirable, Marshall asked the chairman, why not
assassinate all of them, as was done in the Ukraine? Although
he insisted that the matter was insignificant, his remarks on it
revealed the extent of his anger and disillusionment:

> The people of this country need considerable education in humane-
> ness and in common charity. . . . The step between civilization and
> bestiality is a very short one. . . . It is a pernicious state of mind on
> the part of bigots, fanatics, and uneducated and partly educated igno-
> ramuses, with which the Jews have been confronted for many cen-
> turies. . . . Even if they should apologize they would remain unre-
> generate and would be only looking for another opportunity to vent
> their spleen.[10]

Marshall was prophetic, for, not long afterwards, a dis-
gruntled member of the Adirondack Mountain Club circulated a letter to the membership calling Marshall "the presid-
ing genius of its invisible Sanhedrin" and objecting to the
naming of a peak in the Adirondacks after Marshall's sons,
who had explored it. Theodore Van Wyck Anthony was
quickly squelched, but Marshall was astonished that a presumably educated man could be so bigoted: "All of which
tends to show that the millennium is not yet at hand and that
there is still much to be done before we can speak with entire
satisfaction of our civilization." [11] To his son, Marshall was
franker, calling Anthony "a jackass, and an anti-Semite to
boot. In fact he would be a very fine object to boot." [12]
Discrimination by clubs directly affected a small propor-

tion of American Jews, but it symbolized to all Jews that acceptance by the non-Jewish community had limits they could not pass. Similarly, residential segregation, a fact of Jewish life before the war, became clearer during the 1920's, disturbing some Jews directly but many more psychologically. Most Jews who left the crowded immigrant quarters of the large cities, such as the lower East Side of New York, tended to move to primarily Jewish areas in outlying sections. This led some gentiles to conclude that ghettos were self-created, and in support of this Don C. Seitz offered the following tale:

> I recall one Jewish lady's reply to another, when asked if there were many Gentiles in Bensonhurst, a Jewish suburb of Brooklyn. "Not enough to be annoying," was the happy reply." [13]

This explanation of concentrated Jewish settlements contained an element of truth, but it overlooked the desire of many Jews to avoid risking the unpleasantness often associated with moving into gentile areas. The emotions felt by the writer who attributed his youthful dislike of Jews to the fact that they had "come in and broken up the community where I had lived all my life," were probably shared by many non-Jews.[14]

The most glaring residential discrimination during the twenties occurred, as with social clubs, to Jews with high incomes who were seeking the social conveniences normally associated with economic success. In New York City, for example, the major battlegrounds were the Fifth Avenue-Park Avenue section and the more expensive suburban areas. An advertisement on a Fifth Avenue bus for an apartment development in Jackson Heights announced as its major features, "Restrictions, Convenience, Service." The new cooperative system in East Side luxury apartment buildings was also used extensively as a device to keep Jews out, since new owners had to be approved by the co-owners.

The number of Jews active in real estate enterprises increased greatly during the 1920's, exciting the dismay of some old-line businessmen who felt the foreign element was a dis-

turbing feature of New York's economic life. But it was difficult to resist the trend of the times, as illustrated by the purchase of the Fifth Avenue château of W. K. Vanderbilt and
the home of Vincent Astor by a Jewish real estate specula-
tor.[15] Jewish ownership of apartment buildings did not automatically mean they did not discriminate against fellow
Jews. Louis Marshall received occasional complaints of such
malpractice, and to him it was "a crime against common decency. No Jew who will permit himself to profit from such
action is fit to be associated with. . . ." [16]

Opposition to Jewish residential integration was encountered outside of New York. In 1922, the Sharon, Conn.
Chamber of Commerce distributed a leaflet urging property
owners not to sell to Jews. Two years later, the Secretary of
the Chamber of Commerce of St. Petersburg, Florida, in a
speech before the local Kiwanis club, said that "the time has
come to draw the line against all foreigners and make this a
one hundred percent American and Gentile city." [17] Discrimination appears to have been practiced even by those
who reported that many of their most intimate friends were
"Hebrews."

Marshall's attitude toward residential discrimination was
seen in his reaction to the case of the Sea Island Company in
Georgia. This promotional venture, headed by a vice-president of the Hudson Motor Car Company, advertised that no
Jews would be permitted to buy property in its development.
Marshall immediately protested to the owners that their action was a "deadly insult" to men "who are your equals before the law and in the eyes of God." [18] Marshall wrote also
to the Georgia Jew who had informed him of the affair, tell-
ing him he was presently engaged in litigation to block restrictive housing covenants against Negroes in Washington,
D.C., "in the hope that it may incidentally benefit Jews and
non-Jews. . . ." [19] To Marshall, residential discrimination was evil, especially when publicly advertised or legally
enforced; it had to be fought in all cases, not just when Jews
were concerned. "I suppose," he wrote, "you of the South are

perfectly content to have such restrictions against Negroes, but when the enormity of the transaction comes home to you, you rebel against having Jews excluded." [20]

Some of the residential problems of urban Jews in later decades were foreshadowed in the 1920's. At that time, in New York City, Harlem was one of the most populous Jewish districts. As Southern Negroes and Puerto Ricans began increasingly to appear, the Jews, repeating the pattern of white gentiles, started to leave. Resentment and intergroup tension reached the point where serious violence was threatened. During one incident, several hundred Puerto Ricans and Jews fought a pitched battle in the streets with lead pipes, knives, and billiard cues.[21]

American Jews generally did not regard residential discrimination as serious. Upper-class Jews were inconvenienced, but most Jews found adequate housing without great difficulty. The discrimination which concerned Jews more directly was in higher education. To the Jewish elite, a good college education was a natural expectation, while to many working class Jews, college for the children was almost a *raison d'être*. Francis Russell remembered of Boston's Jews:

> Every Jewish junk-dealer from Chelsea, every shopkeeper or delicatessen proprietor in Dorchester, every tailor or fur-worker in Mattapan, above all else wanted his son to become a professional man. And because nearby Harvard was America's oldest and most illustrious university he wanted him to go there and to no lesser place. For this, any and every sacrifice was worth while, for this the first generation Jew would grub away his working hours.[22]

Boston Latin School, the best academic high school in the city, became a "brick intellectual sweatshop" in which the "frenetic driving ambition" of Jewish boys created a spirit of "fierce and gruelling competition." [23]

What was true of Boston was equally true of other urban centers of Jewish population. American Jews, in larger numbers and earlier than any other recent immigrants, believed higher education the key to economic independence and cultural status. As early as 1918–1919, a survey of enrollment in

106 major colleges showed Jews to be 9.7 per cent of the total student body, and almost 12 per cent of the male students.[24] Jews, who in 1918 constituted but 3.2 per cent of the nation's population, were sending their sons to college almost four times as frequently as the average American. Among the schools with a proportion of Jewish students greater than 10 per cent were City College, New York University, Hunter, Rutgers, Fordham, Columbia, Chicago, Tufts, Pennsylvania, Pittsburgh, Temple, Johns Hopkins and Harvard, all of which were located in or near large, metropolitan, Jewish centers.

The young Jews who entered these institutions were, for the most part, either themselves immigrants or the sons of recent immigrants. As such, many of them undoubtedly lacked American manners and background, and were externally uncouth, spoke English with an accent, wore shabby clothes, and had little interest in athletics, dancing, or extra-curricular activities. In contrast to the genteel social tradition of American colleges, these Jewish students tended to be determinedly intellectual and serious minded.

When Eastern colleges in particular were faced with the increasing post-war waves of prospective Jewish students clamoring for admission, more and more began to place restrictions on them. By the end of the decade, many private colleges had erected quota systems under a variety of guises. On the campuses, those Jewish students admitted often faced social aloofness and resistance to participation in the higher levels of student activities. Out of sixty-seven colleges surveyed in 1926, moderate to pronounced anti-Jewish feeling was reported in thirty-five.[25] Apparently, the pressure of second-generation Jewish youth threatened the prestige system built up in previous years by American colleges, and counter-measures were taken, especially in the Northeast.

Trouble first appeared at private institutions in the New York area; at New York University, where the proportion of Jewish students approached 40 per cent, matters came to a head in 1919. Ill-feeling between Jews and non-Jews resulted in the controversial expulsion of a Jewish student, the administration's voiding of the election of certain Jewish students as officers of the campus government, and the institution of selective admission procedures. At a private conference, representatives of the University informed Jewish leaders that "the best service you can perform is to tell Jewish students not to come in such numbers to the New York University, and to distribute themselves among other universities." "This is a Christian University," announced one of the N.Y.U. deans.[26]

Jewish communal leaders in New York were naturally concerned over the N.Y.U. problem, but there was some resistance to an open fight. Cyrus Adler advised Marshall that a technical victory in the case of the expelled Jewish student might be won in the courts, but it would be injurious to the other Jewish students. A Jewish professor at New York University discounted charges of religious prejudice and placed the blame on the personality of Jewish students:

> The concentration of so many—often 40 or 50 per cent—of a special type must cause friction. At the slightest ground for complaint, the cry of persecution is raised and a general appeal for sympathy made. . . . They want to rule faculty and the entire concern. They do not understand the virtue of reticence and reserve. They think they are surrounded by enemies. They are too much spoilt by their friends and their grievances are given historic value.[27]

Louis Marshall, while recognizing the injustices at New York University, likewise felt the matter should be handled delicately and that Jewish students were to some extent responsible:

> They are always looking for grievances and seem to relish the idea of being martyrized. . . . A little more of the American spirit of give and take and a little less politics and chutzpah would be my prescription for the epidemic from which they are suffering.[28]

No strong protests were made in the N.Y.U. affair and Percy S. Straus, the only Jewish member of the University's board of trustees, implicitly agreed to limiting the number of Jewish students. Dean Archibald Bouton frankly admitted in

1922 that the new policy was meant to keep a balance between major ethnic and religious groups. Those students who did gain admission to the university were still faced with strong social resistance. Marshall was consulted in 1923 when Jewish fraternities were excluded from the Junior Prom and signs were posted in the dormitories announcing that "scurvy kikes" and "strictly koshers" were not wanted at New York University. Again, a decision was taken to avoid militant efforts to secure social recognition; it was believed they would be futile and might aggravate anti-Jewish feeling.

At Columbia University, where the percentage of Jewish students was almost as high as at N.Y.U., psychological tests were introduced shortly after the war and the proportion of Jewish students was cut to about 20 per cent. Jewish students, although some denied it, were often unhappy about prejudice at Columbia. One Jewish parent reported that his son had gained admission to Columbia only through the intervention of a prominent Christian clergyman. Columbia's sister institution, Barnard College, was also faced with accusations of anti-Semitism in admission procedures. Dean Virginia Gildersleeve denied this, but she did admit that the ability to pass entrance examinations with high grades was no longer the sole criterion for admission: "We are particularly anxious to have Barnard a college where New York girls, of every class and creed, can meet girls from other parts of the country and from other nations." [29]

Syracuse University, with which Marshall was intimately connected both as donor and chairman of the trustees of the School of Forestry, also experienced anti-Semitic jolts. In February, 1923, a special committee of the Senior Council urged the college authorities to substantially reduce the Jews admitted. Marshall was greatly shocked and angrily wrote Chancellor Charles W. Flint that the Senior Council appeared to be joining the ranks of Ford, Hitler, and the Ku Klux Klan. The charge made by the students that Jews were not involved in athletics was immaterial, for scholarship alone, said Marshall, was the university's concern. At the same time, he urged the Jewish students at Syracuse to maintain a "dignified silence." Marshall was pleased when Chancellor Charles W. Flint took immediate action to quell the Senior Council, rebuking it and obtaining a complete retraction of its resolution.

Marshall was not so happy about the outcome of another case at Syracuse University involving the dismissal of two Jewish students from the medical school for alleged deficiencies. Believing that anti-Semitism was involved and that the students had a strong case, he tried to obtain a reversal. The University authorities, however, were adamant, and Marshall strongly contemplated resigning his post in the School of Forestry, but finally decided not to.

Educational discrimination against Jews, mostly the *sub rosa* kind, was increasingly practiced after the war, but it did not become a national issue until public reference was made to it by the administration of Harvard College in June, 1922. The percentage of Jews at Harvard had grown from 10 per cent immediately after the war to over 15 per cent by 1922, and reports circulated that some faculty members were alarmed at the prospect of an even greater Jewish enrollment. Prof. Albert B. Hart declared that in one Government course, 52 per cent of the men were "outside the element" from which the college had been "chiefly recruited for three hundred years." President A. Lawrence Lowell, who had been an early supporter of the Immigration Restriction League, and its Vice-President since 1912, was quite concerned over the influx of Jewish students.

On June 1, 1922, a statement was issued by Frederick L. Allen, Secretary of the Harvard Corporation, confirming that the subject was under consideration:

> The great increase which has recently taken place in the number of students at Harvard College, as at other colleges, has brought up forcibly the problem of the limitation of enrollment. . . . Before a large general policy can be formulated on this great question, it must

engage the attention of the governing boards and the Faculty, and it is likely to be discussed by alumni and under-graduates. It is natural that with a widespread discussion of this sort going on there should be talked about the proportion of Jews at the college. . . .[30]

The statement did not stress the Jewish question, but it implied that Jews might be the objects of restriction. When it was learned that a special meeting of Harvard's Board of Overseers had been called and that Judge Julian Mack, the Jewish member of the Board, was much exercised, suspicions deepened. At commencement, on June 22nd, President Lowell officially announced that the college had to face its problems and that a faculty committee had been appointed to consider a new admissions policy.

Most Harvard students approved President Lowell's sentiments. A Jewish student leader at Harvard reported that there was not so much a dislike of certain Jews as a feeling that, good or bad, there were too many Jews and, consequently, Harvard might turn into a New Jerusalem—a second City College. A survey of eighty-three upperclassmen in the Social Ethics course revealed that forty-one believed in the justice of restricted admissions based on race or religion, eight were on the fence, and thirty-four were opposed. The proponents of limitation were unanimous in their belief that the unprecedented increase of Jewish students threatened the Anglo-Saxon character of the college, that admission should be based on personality as well as scholarship, and that education was more than pure knowledge. Jews, they felt, did not assimilate, were selfish, and had no alumni loyalty.[31] Harvard students shared the desire of many adults of their social class for a continuation of a homogeneous society in which ethnic groups other than the old American would be kept in their place.

Outside the Harvard campus, reaction to the proposed anti-Semitic admissions policy was negative. Other New England colleges, including Yale, Tufts, and Bates, publicly denied any intentions of limiting classes by discriminatory measures. Chancellor Elmer Ellsworth Brown of New York

University denied the existence of discrimination at his institution, but President Nicholas Murray Butler of Columbia refused to comment. In Massachusetts, local politicians, perhaps relishing the opportunity to deliver a blow to Harvard, condemned the alleged discrimination. Representative George Webster of the Massachusetts legislature proposed a state investigating commission; Speaker B. L. Young summoned President Lowell to the State House for an explanation; the Boston City Council passed a resolution of censure; and Governor Channing H. Cox finally appointed a legislative committee to inquire into opportunities for higher education in the Commonwealth. The annual convention of the American Federation of Labor, then in session, ordered the Executive Council to take appropriate action against Harvard's proposals.

A minority defended Harvard's right to limit admissions as it saw fit. *World's Work,* the Doubleday publication, said that the problem concerned primarily urban Russian Jews rather than the aristocratic Spanish and German Jews, and that Harvard, if it did not deal frankly with the situation, would soon have a 40 per cent Jewish student body. President Faunce of Brown University claimed that restriction of admission was a necessity. "The idea that any shrewd boy that can by cramming 'get by' on written examinations must thereby be automatically admitted to college is anti-American." Faunce disclaimed discriminatory intentions, but if, he said, there were not enough places to go around, then, "Let us exclude the greedy and overbearing and inconsiderate and disloyal." [32]

Generally, American press opinion was critical of Harvard's actions. This was especially pronounced after it was learned that the new questionnaire for Harvard admission raised, for the first time, the question, "What change, if any, has been made since birth in your own name or that of your father?" [33] An article in the *Atlantic Monthly* called the policy of exclusion unwise, although the author pessimistically predicted that Eastern colleges, faced with the social problem of admitting Jews, or keeping them out and risking a storm of protest, would do the latter. The *Nation* disapproved of the trend toward discriminatory admissions policies and feared that Harvard might set a pattern for other institutions: "The very fact that Harvard is considering a Jewish 'problem' and taking steps that seem to look toward measures of exclusion will be reason enough for scores of lesser colleges more or less avowedly to put up the bars." [34]

Possibly more important than opposition from the general public were signs that some Harvard alumni could not reconcile their alma mater's new attitude with its professed position of leadership in the American intellectual community. As Roger S. Greene, class of 1901, said,

> Harvard is not meant to be a glorified private school for the socially eligible. . . . If elements previously strange to our community, elements which are not altogether popular, are beginning to appear at Cambridge in embarrassing numbers, it is because they are now important elements of the American people. We must accept the difficulties involved in our position as a national university or we shall sink to the grade of an insignificant parochial institution.[35]

Rev. Dr. Percy Stickney Grant called on Harvard to become more democratic and John Haynes Holmes expressed outrage that anti-Semitism was "rearing its ugly head in the sacred precincts of this great institution of learning." [36] The temper of Harvard alumni feeling was illustrated also by an incident at the meeting of the Associated Harvard Clubs in Boston. Dr. Clarence C. Little, the newly elected President of the University of Maine, and former Secretary of the Harvard Corporation, demanded an official retraction of reported plans for racial discrimination in admissions. President Emeritus Charles W. Eliot blunted the attack with a reassertion of Harvard's devotion to the principles of racial and religious equality. Eliot frankly admitted that some members of the faculty had become prematurely excited and that there had been a stir on the Jewish question. He advised the alumni to leave the matter in the hands of the faculty committee appointed by President Lowell.

In the meantime, Jewish public opinion had been greatly aroused by the news from Cambridge. Some Jews were satisfied that the national reaction to the Harvard proposals was a "tribute to the soundness of America," but many others agreed with the rabbi who characterized the situation as "the most disturbing manifestation of anti-Semitism in America up to date." [37] The shock was most apparent among the more Americanized Jews; Rabbi David Philipson's comment was revealing: "Had the thing not happened, we would have said with confidence that such a thing could not happen here. It would not have occurred to us in our wildest imaginings." [38] The implications of Harvard's proposals for the status of Jews in America were reinforced by the knowledge, as Rabbi Louis L. Newman wrote, that "If the Jew loses his fight to gain admission to the college campus, he is defeated in a far more significant battle, namely the right to entrance into the higher spheres of the professions and commerce." [39]

Outrage led to invective, and one Jew called Harvard an "intellectual Ku Klux Klan." The Harvard affair led also to the usual self-criticism, with a Jewish fraternity leader calling on his fellows to show the gentiles that Jews were not "ostentatious, greedy or materialistic." Horace Kallen, however, observed that it was not "the failure of the Jews to be assimilated into undergraduate society which troubles them. . . . What really troubles them is the completeness with which the Jews want to be and have been assimilated." [40]

Shortly after the Harvard proposals reached the press, A. A. Benesch—a Cleveland attorney and Harvard graduate, class of 1900—addressed a letter to President Lowell, protesting plans for discriminatory admissions. Lowell's reply offered an interesting explanation of the Harvard authorities' motivation. According to him, anti-Semitic feeling, imported from Europe, was on the rise in the United States. As the number of Jews on campus grew, anti-Semitic feeling grew in proportion, and if the percentage ever reached 40 per cent, feelings would be intense. Lowell concluded that limitation of the Jewish student body would "go a long way toward eliminating race feeling among the students." To this curious argument, Mr. Benesch retorted that anti-Semitic restriction of Jews in order to overcome anti-Semitism could logically be carried to the extent of getting rid of Jews completely. President Lowell, however, stood his ground, once more alluding to the inescapable "problem of race." [41]

Lowell further clarified his ideas in a letter of declination addressed to a sisterhood in St. Louis:

> To some of us it appears that the conditions are drifting in the direction that they have been in for centuries in central and eastern Europe. . . . Some of us here at Harvard feel that this prospect is real, and that something could be done to prevent, in part at least, that segregation of the Jewish race.[42]

He expressed disappointment that Jews had not approved of this worthy object by supporting his plan for restricted admissions.

The controversy grew more heated; a Jewish alumnus of Harvard reported that he had engaged Lowell in conversation during a train trip. According to him, Lowell spoke with great bitterness on the subject of Jews, predicting that in twenty years Jews would be treated as Negroes were in the South, and that the same conditions that existed in central Europe, with Jewish blood being spilled, might reach the United States. He was happy to see that Columbia and New York Universities were reducing their Jewish student quotas. As a way out, he suggested that Jews adopt complete assimilation, including religious conversion and intermarriage. Finally, he was quoted as having remarked that there was no need to complain about Harvard, because at some other colleges "the students duck the Jews in the river." [43] Lowell issued a denial that these views were accurate, but the alumnus vouched for them and offered to produce witnesses who participated in the conversation.

American Jews reacted negatively to Lowell and his ideas. The *American Hebrew* termed his proposal "probably the most humiliating suggestion regarding the Jews that has been made in America," while the *Jewish Tribune* asked for the resignation of Lowell and his staff and for their replacement by men whose Americanism had not been "clouded with Fordism or Ku Kluxism." [44]

Marshall was greatly concerned about the Harvard affair. He viewed discrimination by private preparatory schools as relatively insignificant, and in the N.Y.U. affair he had shown displeasure at the behavior of some Jewish students; but the Harvard case, to Marshall, appeared differently. Writing to his sister-in-law, he spoke of a serious outbreak of anti-Semitism in the United States, specifying that he meant Harvard, not Henry Ford. As for President Lowell,

> He has played with fire, and has given the sanction of his great office to what, after all, is a vulgar expression of Jew-baiting. . . . We must insist upon equality of right and of treatment. We cannot concede that there is any social aspect to the question. . . . The only tests that we can recognize are those of character and of scholarship. . . . If President Lowell wishes to . . . ally himself with the vilest of European politicians, let him do it. We shall not make the way easy for him to accomplish his disgraceful purpose.[45]

Marshall was informed of the Harvard situation long before it received public attention. His major informant was Judge Julian A. Mack, with whom he continued to work closely in behind-the-scenes maneuvering for a peaceful settlement. In this work, Marshall was fearful that some "Jewish snobs" might be willing to go along with Lowell's proposals. He was even more concerned about the tendency of each Jew to act as a spokesman for the entire people, rushing into print with platitudinous nonsense, intemperate speech, or unfortunate generalizations. When the *Forward* expressed disappointment that Marshall and the "wealthy west side Jews" were apathetic on the college question, Marshall defended himself by challenging the usefulness of public agitation. "Arguments and persuasion and an appeal to their sense of right and justice are more likely to prove successful." [46] Colonel Isaac Ullman, a leading American Jewish Committee member, remarked that brass bands were not needed.

Mack, Marshall, and the other Jewish leaders preferred to

concentrate on the Faculty Committee designated in June, 1922, by the Board of Overseers to investigate and report on "principles and methods for more effective sifting of candidates for admission to the university." [47] The committee consisted of thirteen professors, including three Jews—Paul J. Sachs, Harry A. Wolfson, and Milton Rosenau. It was charged with consulting alumni and prominent Jews throughout the country.[48] Professor Charles H. Grandgent, chairman of the committee, issued an opening statement that supported Lowell's position:

> The proportion of Jewish students at the university is greater than that of any other race. Consequently, the problem of restricting Jews, if it is necessary to restrict, is the greatest. The committee will devote a year to the investigation. . . . Today Jews are practically ostracized from social organizations. This prejudice is reflected in the college. If there were fewer Jews, this problem would not be so. I believe this is a racial rather than religious prejudice. . . . Just how to make a sifting of students seeking admittance to the college is most difficult. It seems plain that a college entrance examination would not solve the problem. The Jew is a remarkable student. He is intelligent. The Jewish race as a whole is intelligent. It is astounding the number of Jews from poor districts who enter Harvard and become remarkable students. They are very industrious.[49]

Grandgent's remarks were hardly encouraging, but the committee proceeded to its task with scrupulous fairness. On August 23, 1922, Marshall was visited at his home by members of the Harvard Faculty Committee, including Professor Sachs. Frankly, Marshall told them that if Harvard established a *numerus clausus* for Jews, it might be "responsible for a new group of pogroms and for stimulating anti-Semitism in the United States, as well as abroad, to an extent that can scarcely be estimated." The college had every right to apply scholarship and character tests for admission, but nothing else. If it excluded applicants on racial or religious grounds, the result would be "a calamity to the United States and a menace to the Jews of the world." [50] The impact of Marshall's warning is hard to measure, but he believed he made an impression on the committee. At the same time,

Marshall and his friends busily steered the committee members to other prominent Jews, including the Straus family.

On April 9, 1923, the Harvard Faculty Committee on Admissions presented its report to the Board of Overseers, which unanimously endorsed it. The Committee recommended that Harvard maintain its policy of "equal opportunity for all, regardless of race or religion," that admissions policies be continued free of all forms of discrimination, and that no "novel process of scrutiny" be adopted. The report was a sharp repudiation of the proposals originally made in June, 1922.[51]

The Harvard Committee's report was hailed by the press and most observers as a great moral victory. Defeated in its most blatant form, Lowell's restriction of Jewish enrollment nevertheless was accomplished indirectly through the use of differential standards on entrance examinations and other technical methods. Candidates attaining 75 per cent on Harvard's entrance examinations were admitted automatically, but those who scored between 60 and 75 per cent were admitted at the discretion of the admissions board. In 1926, Harvard announced a new admissions policy, limiting the freshman class to 1,000 and instituting careful screening procedures, including photographs, character testimonials, and personal interviews. The *Harvard Crimson*, while admitting that "Harvard's most precious quality" was its heterogeneity, editorially supported the new policy with a veiled reference to Jews: "If non-assimilable elements in the college tend to choke the freedom of the rest, their numbers should be reduced. Commuting students are an example of this class, racial groups another." [52] President Lowell refused to repudiate these new procedures, despite the intervention of Judge Mack.

Similar conditions prevailed at many other universities. Columbia was reported to have maintained its proportion of Jewish students at no more than 20 per cent. In 1927, commenting on the existence of considerable anti-Jewish prejudice among Cornell students, Marshall remarked, "these conditions exist quite generally in most Eastern colleges and universities." There was some prejudice in the Syracuse public schools when he was a boy, Marshall recalled, but it was a trifle compared to the college situation in the post-war years.[53]

Within colleges themselves, the problem of social exclusion continued to demand attention. Jewish students, for example, had experienced fraternity difficulties even before the war, and the problem was aggravated during the 1920's. In general, Marshall was strongly opposed to fraternities, for "booze and sex and their concomitants seem to constitute the be-all and end-all of their mental lucubration." [54] He was, therefore, not particularly disturbed by the fraternity question:

> College fraternities are a curse, and . . . more good men have been ruined by their association with these silly organizations than from any other one cause. While it is always unpleasant to be the subject or object of discrimination, I have entertained the belief that it has been rather fortunate that the Jews are not readily admitted to Fraternities. It will not injure their habits or their diligence or their scholarship if they are kept out. There is just one misfortune in this regard and that is that it has brought about the organization of Jewish fraternities which, so far as my observation goes, are even worse than those of the other creeds.[55]

Joining their own fraternities, however, seemed to many Jewish students the only effective answer to exclusion from other groups. The twenties, therefore, saw the formation of many new chapters of these segregated fraternities.

When President Faunce of Brown University refused to grant permission for the establishment of a Jewish fraternity because it might kindle racial antagonism, Marshall became quite incensed. His opinions of fraternities, in general, and the Jewish kind, in particular, had not changed, "but to have it declared from high places that the Jewish students shall not have the right to form their frats that has been accorded to non-Jewish students, is a doctrine which cannot be accepted by self-respecting men." [56] Marshall did not want to engage in a public campaign on this question, but he wrote to Faunce, asking him if Jewish fraternities were "dimming the light of learning, or muddying the stream of knowledge, or interfering with the flow of goodwill, by seeking a more limited brotherhood because a broader spirit of fraternity is denied to them." [57] Faunce, however, refused to be moved, even after Marshall spoke to him personally in Washington. Eventually, a compromise solution was worked out, allowing the formation of an unofficial Jewish fraternity.

One reaction to the Harvard affair and the increase of academic anti-Semitism was a renewal of appeals for the creation of a Jewish university in America. Rabbi Louis I. Newman, one of the foremost advocates of this idea, pointed to a growing intolerance in American life, and argued that a university would be no different from the segregated camps, clubs, and fraternities which already existed. Although he had some support, most Jews rejected the proposal as a cowardly surrender and a compromise of the principle of Jewish equality.

Marshall was greatly annoyed by talk of a separate Jewish university. A Jewish university, he predicted, would be an "unqualified misfortune"; it would be a glorified ghetto, eliminating the advantages of contact with the outside world, and would stimulate hostility to Jews and give an excuse for continued discrimination at other universities. Marshall was also opposed to the foundation of a Yeshiva College in New York, because it might convert the Jew into a "self-created alien," and would undoubtedly "do much to harm the best interests of the Jews in America." [58]

Marshall waged a losing battle to prevent the creation of separate Jewish social institutions. The social disabilities from which American Jews increasingly suffered in the 1920's inevitably stimulated a withdrawal into the group, reflected by the elaborate network of Jewish summer hotels, clubs, settlements, fraternities, and residential communities which multiplied as the years went by.

The defense against discrimination succeeded in averting the establishment of a precedent-setting, openly avowed *numerus clausus* system on the European model. More subtle forms of discrimination, however, persisted, and Marshall was unable and, often, reluctant to combat them systematically.

Economic Discrimination

Although satisfactory statistical data are unavailable, there is evidence that economic discrimination against Jews grew during the post-war decade. American-Jewish youth preferred not to enter the workshops where their parents labored, thus initiating during these years the steady decline in the percentage of Jewish workers employed in the clothing industry. Instead, many first-, and especially second-generation American Jews, equipped with high school or college diplomas, attempted to join the ranks of white-collar employees or the professions. In this upward movement, considerable resistance was encountered.

A survey was conducted in 1926 of employers whose advertisements in the New York press explicitly or implicitly indicated that applicants should be non-Jews. The results showed the existence of a mixture of the traditional anti-Jewish stereotypes and a fear of being overwhelmed by the Jewish upward drive. Half the argument against the Jews was that they adapted themselves too slowly, or not at all, to American life and manners, while the other half was that the trouble sprang from the much too rapid assimilation of the Jewish immigrant and his children.

Marshall and his associates were aware of anti-Jewish tendencies among some employers and in certain industries, but they could conceive of no constitutional manner of barring such discrimination. Marshall wrote to an aggrieved applicant:

> I fear that there is no way to require an employer to lay aside his prejudices, however unreasonable they may be. The spirit manifested

by these bigots is brutal and un-American, but one of the most difficult things in the world is to overcome age-long prejudice.[59]

In glaring instances, Marshall did not hesitate to comdemn prejudiced employers, but as he admitted in 1923, "All that I have thus far been able to do in the numerous cases . . . that have been brought to my attention has been to appeal to the sense of justice and fair play. . . ." [60]

This sporadic approach could not stem the mounting employment discrimination. During the 1920's, employment agencies had no compunctions about satisfying employers who specified gentile help, and, according to one Chicago agency, 67 per cent of its requests were of this character. Another agency estimated that it had found jobs for 44 per cent of all applicants over a ten year period, but that only 22 per cent of the Jewish applicants were placed. Help-wanted advertisements in the New York newspapers, including the Jewish-owned *New York Times,* showed, as Heywood Broun observed, a remarkable concern on the part of employers for the spiritual life of prospective employees, with such phrases as "state religion," or "Christian preferred." Especially disturbing to Marshall was a situation illustrated by a letter from the Director of Placements at a New York City high school:

> Approximately 90% of our graduates are Jewish boys. Never have we been able to place even a fraction of them with reputable houses. The discrimination against them apparently is not religious in character. Fully as many Jewish houses refuse to employ Jewish help as Christian houses.[61]

Discrimination by non-Jews was expected, but when Jews joined their ranks, Marshall was aghast.

Contributing to the difficulty was the refusal of Jewish youth to accept factory employment. Many found office positions or sales work with Jewish firms, but the demand for these jobs was always greater than the supply. Finding employment with the larger, non-Jewish corporations was not easy, and once hired there was always the risk of dismissal.

In banking and insurance, it was well known that Jews

could not find positions, except for a quota in those which were Jewish controlled. "South of Canal Street," as Marshall phrased it, the doors were shut. His protests, and even those of Jacob Schiff, met with a significant lack of response. The great public utilities corporations, despite denials, were among the worst offenders in discrimination against Jews. As Marshall told a disappointed Jewish employee of one of them, the difficulty was that the public utilities were really private.

To most Jewish parents, higher education for their children was the stepping stone to the liberal professions. The intense Jewish desire to achieve professional status had its roots in a long cultural tradition emphasizing the value of learning, but the professions were seen also as a means of achieving economic independence without resort to gentile-controlled businesses. Stephen Wise facetiously remarked, "The only profession I know of that does not bar Jews is the rabbinical profession." [62] This was an exaggeration, but Jews were subjected to many difficulties in the professional world.

Medicine, the most ardently desired profession, offered many obstacles to be overcome by Jewish students. For one thing, entrance into medical schools in the later 1920's became increasingly difficult for Jews as larger numbers of them passed through the colleges and applied for admission. City College of New York reported a steady decrease in the percentage of its Jewish graduates who were admitted to medical school—from 49.7 per cent in 1927 to 19.7 per cent in 1930.[63] In most cases, rejection of Jewish applicants was accomplished without open reference to religion, through the use of character tests, personal interviews, and geographical quotas. Occasionally, a medical school would openly announce, as did the University of West Virginia, that it accepted only a specified number of Jewish applicants. If not for these restrictions, the proportion of Jewish medical students, which was about 17 per cent in 1930, would probably have been more than twice as large.

Having entered medical school and having successfully graduated, the young Jewish doctor faced the more difficult hurdle of securing an adequate internship. It was estimated that there were three Jewish medical school graduates for every available internship at Class A Jewish hospitals. Non-Jewish hospitals often accepted only a token number of Jewish interns and even at public hospitals Jews faced unpleasantness. A notorious case concerned the hazing of three Jewish interns at Kings County Hospital in Brooklyn, resulting in an investigation by the Commissioner of Public Welfare and the expulsion of six fellow interns by Mayor James J. Walker.[64]

In their subsequent careers, Jewish physicians encountered prejudice in gaining positions on the staffs of non-Jewish hospitals. Out of 210 professorships, at the end of the decade, at Cornell, Bellevue, Physicians and Surgeons (Columbia), and Flower medical schools—all in New York City —only thirteen were held by Jews.

Law schools did not discriminate in the selection of students; Jewish law school graduates, however, were usually unable to enter a large, well-established, non-Jewish firm. Most Jewish lawyers, therefore, tended to work individually or in small partnerships with other Jews. The entrance of large numbers of Jews into the legal profession caused occasional adverse comments on their foreign background and unfamiliarity with American institutions.

George Gordon Battle, a leading New York lawyer, claimed that there was little prejudice in the New York Bar against Jews, but, he admitted, there were problems. Many Jews admitted to the Bar were without adequate education or training and often resorted to "unjustifiable and offensive methods of practice." He complained, also, of "the untiring Jewish ambition and will to succeed, coupled with the tendency to insist sometimes with too much vehemence upon their rights. . . ." [65] Marshall, who saw the situation differently, felt that discrimination was displayed by some members of the New York Bar. "I have observed," he wrote of the

Bar Association, "that it was only in exceptional cases that men of my faith were appointed on committees of the organization." [66]

Many young Jews sought and found professional careers in public school teaching, but here, again, obstacles were present. A survey of teacher agencies in the Midwest in 1925 showed that 95 per cent of their calls were for "Protestants only," and Jewish teachers, in general, were not welcomed in small towns.[67] In the large cities, such as New York, which had instituted a system of appointment by competitive examination, Jewish teachers were more successful, but there were still some complaints of prejudice. In 1923, Marshall threatened to bring charges against a member of the Board of Examiners in New York who allegedly had shown anti-Semitic tendencies, and as late as 1928 only one of the thirty-six District Superintendents in New York was Jewish.

Anti-Semitism affected the chances of Jews seeking positions on the faculties of American colleges and universities. One young Jewish scholar informed Marshall that it was "almost impossible for a young Jewish Ph.D. to get an opportunity to become an instructor in a university." [68]

The religious handicap of Jews seeking employment or professional careers during the 1920's was considerable, but not insuperable. Economic success could still be achieved in those fields of business manufacturing which remained Jewish specialities. Even in the areas where Jews encountered resistance, such as medicine, anti-Semitism retarded upward mobility but did not prevent it.

Marshall tried to counter anti-Jewish economic discrimination largely through letters of protest and rational argument, and this technique may have had some slight impact. Generally, however, Marshall regarded prejudice by private companies and institutions as something that could not be remedied through pressure. In any event, economic discrimination, although it limited Jewish choice and thereby inflicted damage, could be and was overcome by most Jews during the prosperity of the 1920's.

Religious Discrimination

Horace Kallen, writing in 1923 in the *Nation* on "The Roots of Anti-Semitism," theorized that contemporary anti-Jewish attitudes in America could be traced back ultimately to Christian theology in which Jews were held to be the enemies of God and of mankind, a rejected people who were the villains in the drama of salvation. Marshall, although he was not as philosophical, regarded the religious angle of anti-Semitism as still potentially dangerous. Perhaps remembering his school days in Syracuse and the difficulties encountered by Jewish students around Good Friday, he always considered the crucifixion story as something which might lead in the future, as it had in the past, to "massacres and pogroms." [69]

In 1927, Cecil B. De Mille completed a motion picture on the life of Jesus, titled *King of Kings,* and had begun to distribute it when protests began to pour in to Marshall and other Jewish leaders that the film stimulated hatred against Jews. Marshall, who confessed that he had not seen more than five or six pictures in his life, and whose eyesight was poor, arranged with William Fox, the noted producer, for a private showing of the film to a small group of leading Jews.[70] Joined by Felix Warburg, Cyrus L. Sulzberger, Max J. Kohler, and Rabbis H. G. Enelow, Samuel Schulman, and David de Sola Pool, Marshall saw it and then conferred with his associates on appropriate action. The group unanimously concluded that the film was highly objectionable in that it portrayed Jews as bloodthirsty and cruel, allegedly arousing anti-Jewish feeling in the average movie-goer. Marshall was particularly concerned about the film's effect if shown in foreign countries where anti-Semitism was already rife, such as Germany, Poland, Rumania, and Hungary. A decision was reached that the picture would not be approved under any circumstances, but that pressure should be applied for certain modifications and a promise that it would not be distributed to specified areas of Europe.

In the meantime, the B'nai B'rith entered the scene, working with Will Hays, President of the Motion Picture Producers and Distributors Association, for changes in the film. Marshall now joined these negotiations and before long Hays and De Mille bowed to their demands. Rabbi Pool submitted suggested modifications and De Mille announced he would prepare a foreword to the film which would "exculpate the Jews of guilt for the death of Jesus." Assurances were also given that the film would not be distributed in certain European countries.[71]

Feeling in the Jewish community had been strong on the danger of *King of Kings*. Rabbi Stephen Wise called it "vicious, defiling, and wanton"; the New York Board of Jewish Ministers had adopted a resolution against its public showing and local groups were prepared to undertake action against it. Both Marshall, acting for the American Jewish Committee, and the B'nai B'rith, however, cautioned against attempts at suppression. In addition, Marshall was worried that the use of Jewish pressure to change the film might receive public attention, for Will Hays had told him that representatives of a large body of Christian ministers had been urging him not to make any modifications. When the affair was over, Marshall sadly admitted that the film aroused anti-Semitic passions, "but probably not much more than is occasioned by the reading of the New Testament or the teachings in Sunday schools or the traditions that are passed on from generation to generation." [72]

About a year after the *King of Kings* episode, the Jewish community was similarly troubled by the so-called Freiburg Passion Play, presented in New York by the well-known Jewish theatrical entrepreneur, Morris Gest. The production, which Gest had picked up after a somewhat successful Midwestern tour, was actually one of the latest, least known, and most unimpressive of the German passion plays. It had, however, the usual handsome, Nordic Jesus and the repulsive Judas and mob. Gest, working in cooperation with his father-in-law, David Belasco, proudly announced that the play would open in New York at the 6,000-seat Hippodrome.

Marshall immediately addressed a strong protest to Gest and Belasco, charging that the presentation would be an "act of hostility to the Jews of this country" and would cause "great mental agony and deep humiliation." [73] Despite Marshall's letters, telegrams, and telephone messages, and pressure which Marshall exerted through Adolph S. Ochs and others, Gest defiantly insisted there was nothing offensive in the play and that he would allow the critics and the public to judge it. Even a threat from the District Attorney, with Marshall's approval, that police action might be taken to close the play under a city ordinance forbidding the representation of the Deity on the stage, failed to take effect. Father Francis P. Duffy, the Federal Council of Churches of Christ, and Rev. John Haynes Holmes likewise protested without result.

The passion play went on as scheduled, but it was soon apparent that audiences were staying away. Those who did go to see it, including the critics, found it exceedingly dull and crude, and perhaps more objectionable to Christians than to Jews.[74] Marshall again appealed to Gest to cancel the play, but the latter, still insistent, announced that he was inviting 1,000 Protestant, Catholic, and Jewish clergymen to see it for themselves. Nevertheless, the Freiburg Passion Play soon closed in New York, a complete financial as well as artistic failure. Marshall, who feared its effects might be worse than *King of Kings,* was satisfied. The aspect of the affair which troubled him most, however, was that Jews should have been "the purveyors of a drama which was likely to stir up hatred against those of their own faith." [75]

Marshall dealt also with prejudice in the guise of attempted conversion. In 1927, he was much alarmed over the activities of Radio Station WHAP in New York, owned by Mrs. Augusta E. Stetson, a schismatic Christian Scientist.

Her announcers and lecturers specialized in anti-Jewish and anti-Catholic remarks:

> I plead with you, modern Children of Israel, to come out from the cruel bondage into which you have been betrayed by false leadership, by ruthless scholasticism and rabbinical superstition. I address myself to the Christ Jew, as opposed to the Judas Jew. . . .[76]

Marshall protested directly to Mrs. Stetson, condemning her station's attacks on Jews and Catholics. At the same time, he asked the Christian Science Church for assistance and cooperated with Catholic leaders in dealing with Mrs. Stetson. Through Lewis L. Strauss, he informed Herbert Hoover of the situation. Largely through these efforts, the federal government refused to grant the station a broadcasting license.

The most shocking incident of the twenties which might be considered religious or traditional anti-Semitism was the ritual murder accusation involving the Jewish community of Massena, New York, in 1928. On Saturday, September 22nd of that year, two days before Yom Kippur, Barbara Griffith, a four year old girl, disappeared from her home in Massena.[77] When she failed to reappear that night, search parties were sent into the woods. The following day, with the girl still missing, excitement in the town was intense. At 12:30, Corporal H. M. McCann of the New York State Police telephoned the local rabbi, Berel Brennglass, and asked him to report to the police station. Before telephoning the rabbi, the trooper had been in consultation with Mayor W. Gilbert Hawes and had gone with a civilian assistant to visit a Jewish resident who was known among non-Jews. This man was asked whether, in the old country, Jews used human blood in holiday services. He replied that he did not know about the old country, but American Jews certainly had no such custom.

When Rabbi Brennglass called at the police station, a crowd of three or four hundred angry townspeople had gathered outside. On pre-arrangement with Mayor Hawes, Trooper McCann interrogated the rabbi: "Is tomorrow a big holiday, a fast day? Can you give any information as to whether your people in the old country offer human sacrifices?" Sensing danger, the rabbi acquitted himself well and was released. In the meantime, the Jewish community of nineteen families was thoroughly alarmed and did not know whether it would be able to hold the Kol Nidre service scheduled for that night. Fortunately, at 4:30 that afternoon, the missing child was found, having been lost in the woods overnight. She was completely unharmed, but rumors persisted that the Jews had let her go only because the rabbi had been questioned. The day after Yom Kippur, Mayor Hawes, Corporal McCann, and a State Police Lieutenant conferred with the Jewish leaders of Massena and the Mayor confessed that he had been responsible for instigating the wild charge. Apologies were tendered, but the synagogue officials refused to accept them.[78]

By this time, news of the episode had reached Marshall in New York City. He was thoroughly upset at this first incident of its kind in the United States. On October 1, he wrote, as President of the American Jewish Committee, to Mayor Hawes of Massena, demanding an immediate and public written apology, approved by himself, together with a letter of resignation. If this were not done, Marshall threatened, legal action for the Mayor's removal from office would be taken. He also wrote to the Superintendent of State Police, asking that he require Corporal McCann to send an open letter of apology, and that he be either reprimanded or dismissed. "What has occurred," Marshall wrote,

> does not merely affect the Jews of Massena, but the entire Jewish population of this country and the world is directly concerned. . . . The very thought that public officials in this day and age can seriously entertain the idea that adherents of one of the great religions of the world practice human sacrifice, is an abomination and betokens unfitness for public office.[79]

Marshall deliberately chose to pursue a very vigorous course "so that such outrageous occurrences cannot occur in this country." [80] In this desire, Marshall was not alone. Stephen Wise, acting for the American Jewish Congress, had already demanded apologies; Governor Al Smith denounced the Mayor; the Commander of the Jewish War Veterans threatened to institute suit; newspapers expressed editorial horror; and the Permanent Commission on Better Understanding Between Christians and Jews in America appealed to all citizens to prevent the spread of the blood libel.[81]

At this point, a certain amount of confusion appeared, due to lack of coordination between Marshall and the American Jewish Committee, and Wise and the American Jewish Congress. On October 4, Mayor Hawes and Trooper McCann issued a public apology to Rabbi Wise and sent a copy to Marshall. McCann was also summoned to Albany for a hearing by the Superintendent of State Police and, in the presence of Wise and the president of the Massena congregation, he was reprimanded severely and suspended. Marshall announced publicly that he accepted the Mayor's apology and was satisfied with the treatment accorded Trooper McCann. Privately, however, he was incensed at the events that left him in a secondary position. It was also an election year, and Marshall felt that Wise and Smith, both Democrats, were using the Messena affair for political purposes. He therefore insisted that the apology sent to Wise was not adequate and he asked Mayor Hawes to sign another prepared by himself; Hawes refused. Marshall also complained to Superintendent John Warner of the State Police about the hasty hearing held on Corporal McCann, that he had not been invited to. He protested angrily the action of the Massena congregational leader who went to Albany on his own, without consulting Marshall, and expressed dissatisfaction to Rabbi Brennglass for having accepted an inadequate apology without his approval.

Marshall's pique at not having dominated the proceedings was partly the result of personal vanity and partly because of the political implications he saw in the case. He felt that his own approach in this crucial affair was best, and that it had been compromised through lack of cooperation. In the heat of the moment, Marshall termed the Massena episode "the most serious offense ever perpetrated in this country upon the Jewish people, infinitely worse than anything that Henry Ford ever did." [82] The importation into America, even unsuccessfully, of the ancient, ritual murder myth which had caused so much anguish to European Jews, was indeed explosive. Fortunately, however, despite Marshall's qualms, the American people were not prepared to accept such lies, and even those who originated it in Massena were somewhat shamefaced about it. The unanimous and immediate rejection of the Massena accusation by American governmental authorities and public opinion undoubtedly contributed to quashing it permanently in the United States.

Church-State Relations

Another area involving Jewish rights which concerned Marshall was the church-state relationship. Marshall adamantly opposed, for example, the inquiry by census authorities into racial background or religious belief. The American Jewish Committee consistently fought repeated attempts to institute this procedure, thereby earning the scorn of certain Jewish organizations which accused it of being assimilationist. Marshall, who believed that the world had gone mad on "nationalism and ethnological and anthropological subdivisions of the human family," saw such efforts at government supervised classification as a threat to the separation of church and state.[83] Similarly, he opposed a plan suggested by the Cleveland Board of Education to conduct a census of school children in Jewish, Negro, and other "racial" groups. "We have had too much of this pseudo-scientific nonsense," he remarked. "I regard such an inquiry as un-American and impertinent." [84]

Marshall worked consistently for legislation which would exempt Jews from commercial restrictions of state and local Sunday laws. Year after year, he supported bills in Albany and elsewhere which would have allowed Jewish storekeepers to open their shops on Sundays if they observed the Sabbath on Saturday. This was in accord with his basic conviction that the United States could not be considered a Christian country. He was unsuccessful, however, in accomplishing any tangible legislative results in this field, owing to the weight of tradition and the opposition of Christian clergy, labor organizations, trade associations, and "what to some might be surprising but to me is not, by some of our Jewish brethren." [85]

A teetotaler himself, Marshall always advocated compliance with the Eighteenth Amendment, although he regarded it as an infringement on the private life of the citizen. Prohibition raised questions for Jews, however, because of the apparent ritual need for wine. The government recognized this requirement, but access to wine for religious purposes sometimes led to abuses which were quickly publicized by anti-Semites. Marshall and many other Jews felt that the regulations on wine placed Jews in the somewhat embarrassing position of demanding exceptional treatment by the government. He therefore strongly advocated the substitution of grape juice for wine, a procedure which had the approval of rabbinical authorities. Most Jews, however, did not share his reservations and continued to prefer wine.

A church-state issue that continued to disturb many American Jews was the widespread practice of daily reading from the Bible in public schools. Marshall knew from personal experience the difficulties this raised and that teachers sometimes read passages offensive to Jewish children, but he refused to adopt a doctrinaire approach on this, feeling that on the whole it would be beneficial if children became acquainted with the Bible. The solution, he believed, would be for Protestant, Catholic, and Jewish representatives to agree on a list of unobjectionable readings. Marshall was also very much in favor of the system of released time for religious instruction which was then being advocated. As long as it was not carried out in public buildings, he felt, Jews should not object to it, for religious training was a vital necessity for the survival of the Jews.

Although the Anti-Defamation League of B'nai B'rith waged a relentless campaign against the reading of *The Merchant of Venice* in the public schools and had succeeded in removing it from the curriculum in many cities, Marshall was inclined to be more tolerant. As a student in Syracuse High School, he had written an elaborate essay on the play and subsequently claimed to have seen the role of Shylock acted by Booth, Barrett, Keene, Mansfield, Irving, and Adler. He was convinced that Shylock was the only human and sympathetic character in the play, and that, in any case, it was better that it be read in the schools where proper guidance was presumably available. Most Jews did not agree with him on this matter, however, enabling such organs as the *Dearborn Independent* self-righteously to accuse the Jews of doing away with Shakespeare.[86]

Marshall was his most characteristic when he indignantly rebuked public officials for displaying anti-Semitic prejudice. In 1922, a judge in Iowa, while rendering a decision in litigation involving both Christian and Jewish defendants, made derogatory allusions to Jewish commercial practices. Marshall jumped into the fray and engaged the judge in lengthy correspondence; gave legal counsel to a Des Moines newspaper editor who had been cited for contempt by the judge for criticizing his intemperate remarks; informed Benjamin Cardozo, Felix Frankfurter and other prominent jurists; and threatened to make the whole affair public. The judge freely confessed to Marshall that he had both an inherited and an acquired anti-Semitic attitude, and that if Marshall knew the facts concerning fly-by-night Jewish stock salesmen, he would seek to forget his origin. This, to Marshall, was insufferable:

Have you manifested a desire to forget your origin because the principal actors in the fraud that you have denounced were Christians? I can assure you that, so long as life remains in my body, I shall remember my origin, and that, so long as I am physically able to do so, I shall not cease to admonish all Jews to emulate the virtues of the hundred generations of their ancestry who preferred the martyr's death to a life conditioned upon the abandonment of the ethical, moral and religious principles inculcated by their prophets, their poets, their sages and their teachers, and which constitute the foundation of all existing law, order, and civilization in Europe and America.[87]

epilog

The emancipation of the majority of world Jewry from the civil and political disabilities they had existed under for countless generations was not accomplished until the end of the nineteenth and, in some cases, well into the twentieth century. In the United States, political emancipation was almost complete from the very start of its national existence. Governmental and official anti-Semitism which persisted in certain areas of the Western world was practically unknown in America.

The opportunities afforded by an expanding economy made the United States uniquely attractive to European Jews who were propelled from their homes by economic necessity and political or religious insecurity. In the New World, hundreds of thousands of Jewish immigrants found that the law knew no discrimination between Jew and gentile. They also learned that the anti-Semitic prejudices inculcated for more than two millennia in the minds of non-Jews had not disappeared, but had assumed more private and subtle forms. Nevertheless, American Jews were able to make extraordinary material and cultural progress.

Their exceptional mobility, drawing strength from traditional middle-class values, led to their rapid transformation from immigrant proletarians into educated white-collar employees, businessmen, and professionals.

The first three decades of this century were when this transition was in its most crucial state. They were also years in which the nation was undergoing a readjustment from the simple, basically rural, homogeneous society of the nineteenth century to the more complex, industrialized, urbanized, and ethnically varied society of the twentieth. The isolation of the earlier period was giving way to the entrance of the United States into world power politics during a time of highly disturbed international relations. The conjunction of serious internal issues and the upward push of Jewish immigrants created conditions in which the submerged, but uneradicated, anti-Semitism threatened to come to the surface.

For the most part, anti-Jewish feelings were veiled, usually part of a much broader, xenophobic nationalism, as in the crusade for immigration restriction. The propagation of direct, ideological anti-Semitism during the post-war era, exemplified by the Protocols of Zion and the *Dearborn Independent,* showed a more dangerous trend which might have affected the civil and political status of American Jews. Social discrimination, under a variety of guises, also operated directly on Jews with somewhat mounting intensity during the 1920's, limiting their mobility.

The American-Jewish community, although it never regarded its position as immediately and fundamentally threatened, was aware of the problems it faced in the United States. Social disabilities and embryonic political anti-Semitism were most keenly felt by the deracinated, American-born, second generation and by those who, to all appearances, already had deep roots in America. But all Jews, consciously or subconsciously bearing within themselves the psychological uneasiness of their past, were to some degree sensitive to anti-Semitism. The head of the American Jewish Committee, Louis Marshall, concerned himself to a great extent with the defense of Jewish rights in America, and it was as spokesman for the Jews that his reputation largely rested.

Marshall's Leadership

Louis Marshall fought valiantly and devotedly in defense of Jews against the hostile encroachments of anti-Semitism. His success, however, was limited by his leadership, his basic assumptions and tactics, and the character of his opponents and temper of his day.

The kind of Jewish leadership exemplified by Marshall was symbolic of the self-designated elite whose claim to prominence was based on economic, social, and political influence. Although they ordinarily used this influence for what they considered the benefit of all Jews, a growing proportion of their constituency gradually came to regard it as inconsistent with the democratic way of American life. Benevolent autocracy—feasible and satisfactory when the community was small, cohesive, and homogeneous—could not survive when that community became greatly enlarged, highly complex, and heterogeneous. The Jewish community was being transformed during Marshall's era by the growth of new national organizations and independent movements, eventually leading to more decentralized, anonymous, and impersonal leadership.

In the defense of Jewish rights, Marshall's credo was that "this was America," that Jews unquestionably constituted an integral part of the nation, and that they were entitled to privileges equal to those of all other citizens. He was hostile, therefore, to all ideologies or tendencies within Jewish life, such as Zionism or snobbery by uptown Jews toward immigrants, that questioned the complete and undivided Americanism of Jews or which promoted self-segregation. For the same reason, he opposed actions and ideas emanating from non-Jewish sources, such as the immigration quota system and educational discrimination, both of which attempted to negate equality. He realized, also, that full Jewish rights could not be permanently secured as long as the rights of other minority groups were insecure; with this in mind, he engaged in a wide range of civil-liberties actions relating to Catholics, Negroes, Japanese, Indians, socialists, and aliens.

The Jewish community dealt, during this period, only with symptoms of existing prejudice and only when this prejudice rose to public view, creating embarrassing emergencies. Representing primarily a relatively self-satisfied, comfortable class of enlightened, Americanized Jews, Marshall assumed that occasional unpleasant episodes could be handled as they arose more or less *ad hoc*. The battle against anti-Semitism was thus conducted negatively by numerous counter-measures temporarily dealing with narrow issues, rather than by comprehensive strategy for a general offensive against anti-Semitism itself.

Largely, this approach was determined by a strong feeling of confidence in America. The annual reports of the American Jewish Committee during the 1920's usually contained prefatory remarks that anti-Semitic agitation had collapsed, or that religious bigotry was diminishing, or that respectable Americans gave no aid or comfort to prejudice. Defense tactics were consistent with this confident spirit, for they stressed moderation and cautious watchfulness. Marshall was continually warning against exaggerating the danger of anti-Semitism:

> We must avoid . . . continually crying "Wolf! Wolf!" when there is no wolf. Should the time ever arrive when a wolf really exists, our cries would be as useless as were those of the boy in the fable. There is nothing more unfortunate than to acquire the persecution complex.[1]

> I have no hesitation in saying that the constant dinning away at the subject of anti-Semitism, the discussion of these delicate problems at

public meetings, the multiplication of surveys, reports, interviews and publications of every kind, are doing much more harm than good.[2]

Except during the Russian treaty affair, Marshall avoided mass meetings, public demonstrations, and what he regarded as agitation. Along with other Jewish leaders of his class and milieu, he favored such traditional Jewish approaches to defense activities as intercession, appeals to influential personages, rational argument, and the quiet application of pressure. Publicity was sought only when it almost certainly would not be detrimental to Jews or further stimulate the anti-Semites.

Marshall refused to be drawn into the defense of Jews when he believed it would dissipate his effectiveness, or when an incident was minor. In most cases, Marshall also opposed direct and prolonged public controversy with anti-Semitic propagandists: "It is not consonant with our dignity to take up the gauntlet and enter into a controversy with those who utter conscious falsehoods for selfish purposes. . . ."[3]

While he generally professed indifference or contempt to anti-Semitic intolerance, Marshall struck back when he saw it breaking out in virulent form. Every incident could not be dealt with, but "such subjects as are of vital importance to all Jews everywhere in the world" had to be acted upon. Marshall's major efforts in defense of Jewish rights shared common characteristics. They were either cases in which governmental authority was in some way being used for prejudicial action or propaganda against Jews, or in which highly regarded or potentially powerful institutions and individuals were engaged in prejudiced activities which might eventually influence public policy toward Jews.

Marshall did sometimes remonstrate on issues of discrimination involving private or personal anti-Semitism, but he did not feel himself on sure ground and did not embark on major campaigns. On public or semi-public matters, or those which threatened to become such, Marshall firmly believed he was defending not only Jews but his conception of a democratic and constitutional system in America. One of his prime techniques, and one he used sincerely, was the reiteration that chauvinistic, bigoted movements or activities, such as the Ku Klux Klan, were American rather than Jewish problems.

Marshall reserved the right to pursue defensive action when, in his judgment, the circumstances required intervention; however, that did not mean he was silent on all except particularly grave matters. On the contrary, even seemingly insignificant anti-Jewishness drew from him letters of remonstrance, protest, condemnation and instruction, but it was usually because some larger issue or principle was involved.

No large scale educational campaign against anti-Semitism was attempted during the period of Marshall's leadership. When he was approached by a Jewish social scientist with a proposal for a thorough, scientific investigation of "the fundamental concepts and the underlying psychological motives involved in racial discrimination, with special reference to anti-Jewish feeling," Marshall replied that he did not believe he could interest any of his friends in financing such a study.[4] Nevertheless, he was not entirely inaccurate when he claimed that he and the American Jewish Committee had tried "in a hundred different ways to educate the public mind."[5] In countless public utterances, in hundreds of letters, in dozens of appearances before governmental bodies, Marshall used moral fervor, legal arguments, and oratorical eloquence to counter anti-Semitic canards or implications. Statistics were diligently collected to demonstrate that Jews served honorably in the armed forces and that they constituted a smaller proportion of the inmates of prisons or of poorhouses than their population warranted. Manifestos, such as that on *The "Protocols," Bolshevism, and the Jews,* in 1920, also were for educational purposes. Apologetic works, including those of Isaac Hourwich on the immigration question and Herman Bernstein on the Protocols, were initiated and subsidized by the American Jewish Committee;

while books on the Jewish faith, patriotism, and contributions to American civilization, especially if written by non-Jews, were warmly endorsed and supported. Some beneficial effects may have been achieved through these activities, but it is impossible to gauge their precise impact.

More significant in the fight against anti-Semitism was that Marshall was a Jewish leader in democratic America when the Jewish population more than tripled in size. This provided him with a weapon which went beyond the traditional arsenal of Jewish leaders in previous periods and in unemancipated lands. Jews represented a considerable portion of the American electorate and their votes were vital in certain areas for the political success of the contending parties. Identified with the Republican Party at a time of its national ascendancy, Marshall, although he did not deliberately manipulate a Jewish vote, nevertheless used Jewish voting power as leverage in dealing with governmental authorities. The existence of large numbers of Jews endowed with the right to vote in itself diminished the chances of successful anti-Semitic movements and provided Marshall with an important source of strength.

One of the striking features of Marshall's campaign in defense of Jewish rights was his strong feeling that Jews themselves, through misbehavior and the use of unwise tactics, were endangering their own security and encouraging anti-Semitism. Continually recurring in Marshall's private correspondence was the theme that his moderate approach to problems of discrimination was jeopardized by indiscretions, intemperateness, or rivalry by fellow Jews. Marshall's attitude was not based purely on personal vanity, although this cannot be excluded, but rather on his fundamental beliefs that the Jewish position in America was sound, that great public controversies were ordinarily unnecessary, and that Jews could deal more effectively with anti-Semitism by their own example than by attacks on their enemies. In part, also, this feeling was the consequence of the rise of competing Jewish organizations.

"The Jew," Marshall stated, "must live so that suspicion cannot touch him." [6] While publicly using his influence to urge the press to stop identifying criminals as Jews, Marshall privately confessed that it might be beneficial to the Jews "to know that if any one of them does an act which is contrary to the public welfare attention will be drawn to the fact that he is a Jew. In a sense, therefore, it puts every Jew on his best behavior." [7] To dispute every false statement concerning Jews was folly, Marshall asserted; of much greater importance was that

> . . . the Jews themselves shall be impressed with the fact that every one of them owes a duty to his fellow-Jews, as well as to the world, to cultivate our ancient virtues, to respect the law. . . . Every Jewish bootlegger does more harm to the Jews as a body than . . . all the Fords could possibly inflict with their falsehoods, their libels and their slanders. . . . Let us not indulge in trying to throw bouquets at ourselves. It would be much more wholesome if we tried to recognize our real faults and then proceed to correct them.[8]

The real remedy for Jewish moral laxity, Marshall suggested, was a thorough Jewish religious education. This would not only tend to eliminate the objectionable characteristics used as excuses by anti-Semites, but would provide the necessary moral fibre enabling Jews to endure the attacks of bigots.

Barring the unlikely fortune of attaining the utopian state in which Jews would shed their vices and Christians their prejudices, Marshall rested his ultimate trust in "the unfailing sense of fairness and of decency of the American people as a whole. . . ." [9] Momentarily confused by barrages of anti-Semitic propaganda, the American people would eventually assert its sense of toleration and fair play. A significant trend appeared during the 1920's apparently confirming this faith of Marshall's. This was the goodwill movement, which—starting in the beginning of the decade with such groups as the Amos Society, the Better Understanding Society, the American Committee on the Rights of Religious Minorities, Goodwill Committees of the Federal Council of

Churches, and the Central Conference of American Rabbis—
was metamorphosed into the Permanent Commission on
Better Understanding and, by 1928, into the National Conference of Christians and Jews.[10]

One might have expected that Marshall would have been
greatly pleased at this development, and he did indeed participate in it. A symbolic event took place in 1926, when the
American Christian Fund for Jewish Relief held a great
meeting at the Cathedral of St. John the Divine, during
which Marshall occupied the pulpit along with General John
J. Pershing, Bishop William T. Manning, Dr. S. Parkes Cad-
man, and General John F. O'Ryan. But Marshall was not in
the forefront of the goodwill movement. He suspected that
"so far as the Churches are concerned they are principally interested in good-will as a mechanism for the attainment of
their conversionist ends." [11] The "love-feast" had to be
watched very carefully, and in 1929 Marshall engaged in a
dramatic correspondence with one of the Protestant founders
of the movement, Rev. Dr. Alfred W. Anthony, insisting that
conversionary attempts should not be propagated under the
cloak of goodwill. Regardless of reservations, however, Marshall did grant that the goodwill movement was doing excellent work. During a decade when Klansmen flouted Christian
principles in the name of a Protestant America, it was
heartening to see the foundation of a goodwill movement
emanating largely from liberal Protestant circles.

In the twenties, however, the goodwill movement was still
in its infancy and overshadowed by developing hostility. Native American anti-Semitism was being complicated by the
introduction of European themes, and the national psyche
was undergoing severe emotional strains. The tactics of discreet intercession, official representations, and scholarly apol-
ogia could not disarm the irrational fears and hatred of anti-
Semites and were not effective against deep-rooted mass
movements. Marshall's work, therefore, was directed primarily at stressing the principle of Jewish equality and preventing prejudice from affecting the nation's laws or the behavior

of public officials and important institutions. In this area, with the exception of the immigration laws, his achievements were considerable.

American Anti-Semitism

Seen from the vantage point of post-World War II Western civilization, American anti-Semitism of the 1920's seems a relatively minor, temporally limited, and ultimately ineffective movement. Contrasted with German anti-Semitism during the same years, from which came the terrible holocaust of the 1930's and 1940's, the American brand seems pallid indeed.* There was only one permanent legislative result of the post-war agitation: the final reversal of the historic American immigration policy, but even this was not directed exclusively or primarily at Jews.

To American Jews of the 1920's, confident though their leaders were, anti-Semitism and the defense of Jewish rights in the United States could not be dismissed as inconsequential. The country was passing through a period when intense nationalism, racism, and nativism created uncomfortable conditions for all minorities, and it was little comfort to know that anti-Jewish manifestations were part of, or related to, the larger national problem. The Protocols of the Elders of Zion, the attacks of Henry Ford's *Dearborn Independent,* the critiques of "Russian Jews," and the raising of bars in higher education may not have undermined the Jewish position in America, but they left enduring psychological legacies.

* Marshall, although he recognized the extreme gravity of Hitler's anti-Semitism, could never quite believe his threats to destroy the Jews. See Marshall to Abraham I. Weinberg, March 19, 1923; to Norman Anthony, ed. *Judge,* September 15, 1925, MP-AJA.

To many Jews, the attacks and insults were blows to their self-esteem and sense of participation in America. Some reacted indignantly, as did the man who wrote to Marshall, "I am the son of a veteran of the Civil War and love my country. It is about time a halt be called and rally all the Jews of America and show our colors." [12] For most, the greatest impact of anti-Semitism, as it has always been, was an intensification of in-group loyalty and a wariness verging, in some cases, on rejection of the outside world. Marshall's own insistence on the importance of Jewish education and his growing rapproachement with Zionism perhaps reflected this mood. The bitterness of one young Jewish intellectual, Maurice Samuel, demonstrated the passion the "mild" anti-Semitism of the 1920's could lead to:

And I know that soon enough these crimson sluices will be opened again, and we shall bleed from a thousand wounds as we have bled before. In the Ukraine, or in Russia, in Poland or in Germany—and who knows when the same will not come to pass in England, in America, in France? . . . . Is not the blood libel alive today? And its companion viper, "the Elders of Zion?" Will poison work forever in the blood and never break out? Did not hundreds of thousands of Englishmen, Frenchmen, Germans, Americans read these legends without protesting, without seeking to punish the libelers? . . . . "Kill the Jews, the Christ-killers," does indeed ring strange these days. But does "a damn good dose of lead for the Jewish Bolsheviks," sound very remote? . . . . Whatever we do we are damned—and I would rather be damned standing up than lying down.

Although most Jews were not materially damaged, the anti-Semitic agitation of the twenties left emotional scars of varying depths. At the same time, it amplified and intensified the anti-Jewish stereotypes of non-Jewish Americans. With depression and war in succeeding decades, the danger increased that this substratum could be manipulated more directly by powerful mass movements. Fortunately, this did not materialize and, following World War II, there was, instead, a decline in overt anti-Semitism. Nevertheless, the barriers of social discrimination, whose seeds had sprouted during Marshall's lifetime, did not crumble. Jews became culturally indistinguishable from other Americans, but, in the opinion of a noted sociologist more than two decades after Marshall's death, "the line that divides them from the others remains sharper than that separating any other white group of immigrants." [13]

Whatever success Marshall achieved in defending the Jews depended on the soundness of America and the resulting strength or weakness of opposing forces, rather than on Jewish activities or lack of them. It was the commitment of the American system to guarantees of freedom for all religious groups; the inability of intolerant organizations to unite on common, achievable political objectives; and the return of national economic prosperity, together with America's political stability, that checked the danger of anti-Semitism in the 1920's. Marshall's sometimes shaken, but always abiding, faith in the American people, his vigor in the defense of the constitutional liberties of all minorities, and his passionate patriotism affirmed his conviction that the health of America determined the fortunes of its Jewish citizens.

notes

The following abbreviations are used:

AH *(American Hebrew);*
AJA *(American Jewish Archives);*
AJC *(American Jewish Committee);*
AJYB *(American Jewish Year Books);*
DI *(Dearborn Independent);*
JSS *(Jewish Social Studies);*
JT *(Jewish Tribune);*
NYT *(New York Times);*
PAJHS *(Publications of the American Jewish Historical Society).*

Chapter one

1.   The statistical data of tables 1 through 5, and all other demographic information in this chapter derive from these sources: Jacob Lestchinsky, "Economic and Social Development of American Jewry," *The Jewish People: Past and Present* (New York, 1955), IV, 56; Harry S. Linfield, *The Jews in the United States* (New York, 1929); Uriah Zvi Engelman, "Jewish Statistics in the U.S. Census of Religious Bodies (1850–1936)," *JSS,* IX (April, 1947),

129–62; Louis Finkelstein (ed.), *The Jews: Their History, Culture, and Religion* (3rd ed.; New York, 1960), II, 1554–55; Mark Wischnitzer, *To Dwell in Safety: the Story of Jewish Migration Since 1800* (Philadelphia, 1948), p. 289; *AJYB* (1921), p. 294; Rudolf Glanz, "The Immigration of German Jews up to 1880," *YIVO Annual of Jewish Social Science,* II–III (1948), 87–89; Nathan Glazer, "Social Characteristics of American Jews, 1654–1954," *AJYB,* LVI (1955), 10; John S. Billings, "Vital Statistics of the Jews in the United States," *Census Bulletin* (December 30, 1890), p. 4; Samuel Joseph, *Jewish Immigration to the United States from 1881 to 1910* (New York, 1914), pp. 95, 117; U.S., Congress, Senate, Immigration Commission, *Reports,* No. 747, 61st Cong., 3rd Sess., 1910, I, 97–113; Alexander M. Dushkin, *Jewish Communal Register of New York City, 1917–1918* (New York, 1918), pp. 87–89; S. D. Oppenheim, *The Jewish Population of the United States* (Philadelphia, 1918), pp. 31–32; Oscar and Mary F. Handlin, "A Century of Jewish Immigration to the United States," *AJYB,* L (1948), 24; Charles S. Bernheimer (ed.), *The Russian Jew in the United States* (Philadelphia, 1905), p. 43; Moses Rischin, *The Promised City: New York's Jews, 1870-1914* (Cambridge, 1962); Charles Reznikoff (ed.), *Louis Marshall: Champion of Liberty* (Philadelphia, 1957).

2.   Quoted by Zosa Szajkowski, "The Attitude of American Jews to East European Jewish Immigration (1881–1893)," *PAJHS,* XL (March, 1951), 232. See also Irving Aaron Mandel, "Attitude of the American Jewish Community toward East–European Immigration," *AJA,* III (June, 1950), 33–34; Glanz, *loc. cit.,* p. 96; C. Bezalel Sherman, *The Jew Within American Society* (Detroit, 1961), pp. 57–83.

3.   Will Herberg, *Protestant–Catholic–Jew* (Garden City, N.Y., 1955), p. 193.

4.   See Oscar and Mary F. Handlin, "The Acquisition of Political and Social Rights by the Jews in the United States," *AJYB,* LVI (1955), 70; John Higham, *Social Discrimination Against Jews in America, 1830–1930* (New York, 1957), p. 9; Jacob J. Weinstein, "Anti–Semitism," *The American Jew,* ed. Oscar I. Janowsky (New York, 1942), p. 185; Howard M. Sachar, *The Course of Modern Jewish History* (Cleveland, 1958), p. 179; Glazer, *loc. cit.,* p. 9. Higham regards Grant's order as the "principal nativistic incident of the war years"; see John Higham, *Strangers in the Land* (New Brunswick, N.J., 1955), p. 13.

5.   Louis Marshall to James W. Wadsworth, April 9, 1909, in Marshall Papers (American Jewish Archives, Cincinnati, Ohio). Cited hereafter as MP-AJA; Oscar and Mary F. Handlin, *Danger in Discord* (New York, 1948), pp. 24–29; Charles S. Bernheimer, "Prejudice Against the Jews in the United States," *Independent,* LXV (1908), 1106.

6.   Higham, *Strangers,* p. 26.

7.   E. J. Kuh, "The Social Disability of the Jew," *Atlantic Monthly,* CI (April, 1908), 436; John Higham, *Anti–Semitism in the Gilded Age* (New York, 1957), p. 10.

8.   For a dissenting view on Donnelly, see Norman Pollack, "The Myth of Populist Anti–Semitism," *American Historical Review,* LXVIII (October,

1962), 76–80. See also Martin Ridge, *Ignatius Donnelly; the Portrait of a Politician* (Chicago, 1962); Walter T. K. Nugent, *The Tolerant Populists: Kansas Populism and Nativism* (Chicago, 1963).

9.   See Joseph D. Herzog, "The Emergence of the Anti-Jewish Stereotype in the United States" (Thesis, Hebrew Union College, 1953), *et passim;* Oscar Handlin, "American Views of the Jew at the Opening of the 20th Century," *PAJHS,* XL (June, 1951), 323–44; Benjamin R. Epstein and Arnold Forster, *Some of My Best Friends* (New York, 1962), pp. 5–7.

10.   David Starr Jordan, *Unseen Empire* (Boston, 1912), pp. 9–24; Burton J. Hendrick, "The Jewish Invasion of America," *McClure's,* XL (March, 1913), 125–65.

11.   Kuh, *loc. cit.,* p. 433.
12.   *Ibid.,* p. 434.

Chapter two

1.   For the story of the events leading to the founding of the AJC and the issues involved in its early years, see Marshall to Adolf Kraus, December 26, 1905; to Cyrus Adler, December 30, 1905; to Rabbi Joseph Stolz, January 12, 1906; to Henry S. Stix, January 16, 1907; to Joseph B. Wolfe, June 28, 1921, MP-AJA. See also AJC, *Ninth Annual Report, AJYB* (1917), 324 ff.; Nathan Schachner, *The Price of Liberty* (New York, 1948), chaps. 1–3, *et passim;* Peter Wiernik, *History of the Jews in America* (New York, 1912), pp. 366–72.

2.   Quoted in Schachner, *op. cit.,* p. 28.

3.   See Marshall to Central Union Trust Company, May 16, 1924, MP-AJA. For general biographical information on Marshall, consult Cyrus Adler, *Louis Marshall: a Biographical Sketch* (New York, 1931); Max J. Kohler, "Louis Marshall," *Dictionary of American Biography,* VI (New York, 1933), 326–27.

4.   James O. Young, "Marshall Looks Back Over 70 Years," *NYT Magazine,* December 12, 1926, p. 9.

5.   From a radio address by Marshall quoted in *NYT,* March 7, 1928, p. 27.
6.   Marshall to Joseph V. McKee, September 26, 1925, MP-AJA.
7.   Marshall to Judge George C. Holt, May 11, 1923, MP-AJA.
8.   Marshall to Rev. Dr. Joseph Silverman, March 12, 1910, MP-AJA.
9.   Marshall to Irving H. Fisher, August 14, 1922, MP-AJA. Marshall stated that both Orthodoxy and Reform "promote and advance the cause of religion, of morality, of good citizenship and of Judaism."

10.   Marshall to Samuel Shinbach, December 16, 1927, MP-AJA.
11.   Marshall to ed., *American Israelite,* August 23, 1926, MP-AJA.
12.   Quoted in Oscar Janowsky, *The Jews and Minority Rights, 1898–1919* (New York, 1933), p. 304.

13. Marshall to Judah L. Magnes, June 7, 1923, MP-AJA.

14. Louis Marshall, "Is Ours a Christian Government?," *The Menorah* (January, 1896), pp. 1–9.

15. Marshall to William D. Guthrie, April 7, 1924, MP-AJA.

16. *Ibid.*

17. *NYT,* March 9, 1925, p. 7.

18. Cyrus Adler, *Jacob H. Schiff: His Life and Letters* (Garden City, N. Y., 1928), II, 295–96.

19. Marshall to Joseph Stolz, January 12, 1906, MP-AJA.

20. U.S., Congress, Senate, Committee on Immigration, *Hearings, on Emergency Immigration Legislation,* 66th Cong., 3rd. Sess., 1921, p. 110.

21. Marshall to Rabbi Israel H. Leventhal, May 9, 1923; to Saul J. Cohen, January 31, 1920, MP-AJA.

22. Marshall to William Fox, December 2, 1927, MP-AJA.

23. Marshall to Rabbi Isaac Landman, September 10, 1921, MP-AJA.

24. Marshall to Edwin H. Jonson, December 23, 1924, MP-AJA.

25. Marshall to Charles Jacobson, November 3, 1920, MP-AJA.

26. See AJC, *Nineteenth Annual Report, AJYB,* XXVIII (1926), 468.

27. Marshall to Jacob Landau, March 10, 1927, MP-AJA.

28. James Weldon Johnson to Marshall, August 24, 1924; W. E. B. DuBois to Marshall, August 26, 1924; Marshall to DuBois, August 27, 1924, MP-AJA.

29. Marshall to Solomon Ulmer, January 29, 1927, MP-AJA.

30. Marshall to Henry Astor, June 7, 1923, MP-APA.

31. Marshall to Jacob Landau, March 10, 1927, MP-AJA.

32. Marshall to Julius Henry Cohen, April 10, 1926, MP-AJA.

33. Marshall to Harry Schneiderman, May 24, 1921, MP-AJA.

34. Marshall to Edwin Kaufman, May 8, 1920, MP-AJA.

35. Marshall to A. Leo Weil, December 21, 1918, MP-AJA.

36. Marshall to Isaac W. Frank, June 3 1921, MP-AJA.

37. Marshall to Jacob H. Schiff, April 8, 1918, MP-AJA.

38. Reznikoff, *op. cit.,* II, 715–16; Marshall to Secretary of State Robert Lansing, April 15, 1918, MP-AJA; Moses Rischin, "The American Jewish Committee and Zionism," *Herzl Year Book,* V (1963), 65–81.

39. *NYT,* October 29, 1923, p. 10. The word "national," with its Zionist implications, disturbed some American Jews. One wrote to Marshall that it was detrimental to Jewish interests to find in the telephone directory a listing of organizations such as the Hebrew National Food Products Corp., Hebrew National Noodle Company, Hebrew National Sausage Factory, and Hebrew National Orphan Home. See E. G. Kohnstamm to Marshall, January 11, 1929, MP-AJA; see also Naomi W. Cohen, "The Reaction of Reform Judaism in America to Political Zionism, 1897–1922," *PAJHS,* XL (June, 1951), 361–94.

40. Cyrus Adler to Jacob H. Schiff, July 15, 1920, MP-AJA.

41. Quoted by Schachner, *op. cit.,* p. 79.

42. Louis Marshall, "The Loyalty of the American Jew," *AJYB* (1926), pp. 469ff.

43. On Marshall's cooperation with the Zionists, see Samuel Halperin, *The Political World of American Zionism* (Detroit, 1961), pp. 75, 117, 192–93.

44. United Jewish Appeal, *The Rebuilding of Palestine* (New York, 1927), p. 6.

45. Chaim Weizmann, *Trial and Error* (New York, 1949), pp. 309, 311–12.
46. Marshall to Lindon W. Bates, Jr., October 22, 1908, MP-AJA.
47. Marshall to Albert Rosen, April 8, 1921, MP-AJA.
48. Marshall to Louis Friedman, December 29, 1919, MP-AJA.
49. Benjamin Stolz to Marshall, July 19, 1923, MP-AJA.
50. "If there is anybody in this country who has more consistently opposed the hyphen . . . than I have, it would interest me greatly to know who it is" (Marshall to ed., *Boston Evening Transcript*, May 23, 1925. MP-AJA).

51. Marshall to Sen. James A. Reed, December 12, 1914, MP-AJA.

52. On the Educational Alliance, see Paul Abelson, "The Education of the Immigrant by the Educational Alliance," *JSS*, XLIV (1906), 163–72; Morris I. Berger, "The Settlement, the Immigrant and the Public School," (unpublished Ph.D. dissertation, Teachers College, Columbia University, 1956), pp. 45–79.

53. Marshall to Judge Samuel Greenbaum, January 27, 1919, MP-AJA; see his letters to Greenbaum, March 23, 1917; February 3, 1919, MP-AJA.

54. Louis M. Cole to Marshall, May 3, 1922; Marshall to Cole, May 12, 1922, MP-AJA; New York State Bar Association, *Proceedings of Forty-Seventh Annual Meeting* (January, 1924), p. 302. When the non-Yiddish speaking Sephardic Jews began to appear in New York City in substantial numbers, Marshall suggested that they be directed instead to South America where they would find less of a language block to integration. See Marshall to Henry Morgenthau, Ambassador to Turkey, June 1, 1914, MP-AJA.

55. New York State Constitutional Convention, 1915, *Record*, III (Albany, 1915), 2917–19 Marshall's suggestion was defeated. See also Marshall to Thaddeus M. Sweet, March 17, 1917, MP-AJA.

56. Marshall to Cyrus L. Sulzberger, June 14, 1902; to Herman Bernstein, October 16, 1919, MP-AJA; Lucy S. Dawidowicz, "Louis Marshall's Yiddish Newspaper, *The Jewish World:* A Study in Contrasts," *JSS*, XXV (April, 1963), 102–32.

57. Marshall to Dr. Solomon Schechter, February 19, 1915, MP-AJA.

58. Marshall to State Sen. N. A. Elsberg, January 14, 1902; to Rev. Max D. Klein, June 17, 1911; to Julius Rosenwald, January 2, 1913, MP-AJA. For a discussion of the sociological aspects, see Nathan Glazer, *American Judaism* (Chicago, 1957), pp. 73–74; J. Milton Yinger, "Social Forces involved in Group Identification or Withdrawal," *Daedalus* (Spring, 1961), pp. 247–62; Marshall

Sklare, *Conservative Judaism: An American Religious Movement* (Glencoe, Ill., 1955).

59.   Marshall to John Paley, June 28, 1907, MP-AJA.
60.   Marshall to Cyrus L. Sulzberger, August 1, 1916, MP-AJA.
61.   Marshall to Isaac W. Frank, June 3, 1921, MP-AJA.
62.   See Werner Cohn, "The Politics of American Jews," *The Jews: Social Patterns of an American Group,* ed. Marshall Sklare (Glencoe, Ill., 1958), p. 622.

63.   Marshall to C. B. Slemp, Secretary to the President, September 2, 1924, MP-AJA.

64.   Marshall wrote to the President of the Board of Education and to Tammany leader Olvany on behalf of a Jewish candidate for District Superintendent of Schools; Marshall to George J. Ryan, Pres., Board of Education, December 9, 1926; to George W. Olvany, March 1, 1928, MP-AJA.

65.   Marshall to Simon Wolf, February 4, 1922, MP-AJA. Oscar Straus, Judge Abram Elkus, and Henry Morgenthau had served previously as Ambassadors to Turkey.

66.   Marshall to Benjamin Marcus, March 8, 1912, MP-AJA.

67.   Cohen, *op. cit.,* p. 525; Simon Wolf, *The Presidents I Have Known from 1860 to 1918* (2nd ed.; Washington, 1918), pp. 437–39.

68.   Marshall to ed., *Der Tog,* November 1, 1916, MP-AJA. This letter was not published in *Der Tog.*

69.   AJC, *Sixteenth Annual Report, AJYB,* XXVI (1924), 637.

70.   *Ibid.,* p. 639; AJC, *Executive Committee Minutes* (November 17, 1923); *NYT,* October 26, 1923, p. 36; Marshall to Jacob Landau, October 23, 1923, MP-AJA.

71.   *NYT,* October 29, 1923, p. 10.

72.   Marshall to Simon Wolf, October 23, 1920; to Rep. James W. Wadsworth, Jr., February 28, 1925, MP-AJA.

73.   Marshall to J. H. Stolper, January 20, 1917, MP-AJA. See Harry Schneiderman to Marshall, December 16, 1927, MP-AJA.

74.   See note 72.

75.   Form letter, dated October 23, 1919, MP-AJA. Mrs. Annie Nathan Meyer returned her copy to Marshall with the notation, "I do not see what is gained by one partner praising another. I certainly do not vote to sustain Tammany's hold on the judiciary. . . ."

76.   Marshall to Pres. Calvin Coolidge, May 5, 1925, MP-AJA.

77.   Marshall to Samuel S. Koenig, Pres., New York County Republican Committee, June 5, 1920, MP-AJA; *NYT*, June 3, 1920, p. 16.

78.   *NYT*, August 6, 1923, p. 2.

79.   William E. Leuchtenburg, *The Perils of Prosperity, 1914–32* (Chicago, 1958), p. 134.

80.   Marshall to S. Stanwood Menken, Pres., National Security League, September 30, October 10, 1924, MP-AJA. Marshall wrote Menken:

> Do you think that the world will be bettered by having one part of the community charge the other with treason, blood-guilt and lack of patriotism. . . ? It is such an attitude of mind . . . which stimulates radicalism and makes the judicious grieve. Why this irresponsible fury? Why this excitement? Why this inquisitorial method? Why this smug better than thou policy?

For Marshall's attack on LaFollette's Supreme Court views, see *NYT*, September 28, 1924, Sec. 8, p. 3.

81.   *NYT*, October 9, 1928, p. 6; *Boston Herald*, November 1, 1928.

82.   Stephen S. Wise, *Challenging Years* (New York, 1949), pp. 113–14; *NYT*, October 22, 1928, p. 5.

83.   John Q. Tilson to Marshall, October 20, 1928, MP-AJA.

84.   Marshall to ed., *The Nation*, October 17, 1928; to Chancellor Charles W. Flint, Syracuse University, September 6, 1928; to Louis M. Nussbaum, October 27, 1928; Ethel H. Barron to Marshall, October 28, 1928, MP-AJA.

85.   *NYT*, October 24, 1928, p. 18; November 1, 1928, p. 10; October 29, 1928, p. 12.

86.   *NYT*, October 19, 1928, p. 29.

87.   For statistics, see Lawrence H. Fuchs, *The Political Behavior of American Jews* (Glencoe, Ill., 1956), pp. 50–51, 67–69.

88.   James W. Wise, *Jews Are Like That!* (New York, 1928), p. 190.

89.   Marshall to Judge Horace Stern, September 11, 1925, MP-AJA. Abram L. Sachar has observed that Marshall was "an almost exact antithesis, mentally and temperamentally" of Stephen Wise. "Where Wise was accused of theatricality, Marshall was criticized for autocracy, for dominating every cause and every institution that he served." (Abram L. Sachar, *Sufferance is the Badge: The Jew in the Contemporary World* [New York, 1939], p. 519).

90.   Weizmann, *op. cit.*, p. 309.
91.   *JT*, LXXXIX (December 10, 1926), 7.
92.   *Jewish Communal Register of New York City, 1917–1918*, p. 1383.
93.   *JT*, LXXXIX (December 10, 1926), 9.

Chapter three

1. Reznikoff, *op cit.*, pp. 12–14; Fremont Rider, *Melvil Dewey* (Chicago, 1944), p. 106; Bernard G. Richards, "The Melvil Dewey Affair," *Congress Weekly*, XXI (April 20, 1954), 12–13.

2. Marshall to Mrs. Bertha Rosenberg, February 16, 1905, MP-AJA.

3. Marshall to Kaufman Mandell, February 23, 1905; to Dr. N. I. Stone, November 24, 1923, MP-AJA.

4. Marshall to Rev. Dr. I. K. Funk, February 11, 1905, MP-AJA.
5. AJC, *Executive Committee Minutes*, November 9, 1912
6. Marshall to State Sen. Martin Saxe, May 22, June 3, 1907, MP-AJA. New York's Civil Rights Law of 1895 was largely unenforced and, in Marshall's opinion, inadequate. His proposal added a ban on discriminatory advertisements.

7. *American Israelite*, August 12, 1913; Marshall to Lawrence F. Abbott, Pres., *The Outlook*, June 12, June 17, 1913, MP-AJA.

8. For the background on the Russian passport affair and specific instances of Russia's discriminatory application of the treaty, consult Cyrus Adler and Aaron Margalith, *With Firmness in the Right: American Diplomatic Action Affecting Jews, 1840–1945* (New York, 1946), pp. 171–281; Carl G. Winter, "The Influence of the Russo-American Treaty of 1832 on the Rights of American Jewish Citizens," *PAJHS*, XLI (December, 1951), 165–89; Cohen, *op. cit.*, pp. 335–43; Thomas A. Bailey, *America Faces Russia* (Ithaca, 1950), Chap. 18; Naomi W. Cohen, "The Abrogation of the Russo-American Treaty of 1832," *JSS*, XXV (January, 1963), 3–41.

9. Marshall to James M. Beck, February 24, 1911, MP-AJA.
10. Marshall to Dr. Herbert Friedenwald, February 4, 1908, MP-AJA.
11. Marshall to Jacob H. Schiff, December 24, 1910, MP-AJA.
12. Louis Marshall, *Russia and the American Passport* (Address to the Delegates at the Twenty-second Council, Union of American Hebrew Congregations, January 19, 1911).

13. Marshall to Rep. Herbert Parsons, January 28, 1911; to Jacob H. Schiff, February 9, 1911, MP-AJA.

14. Marshall felt that Secretary of State Philander Knox was the evil genius whose arguments had swayed the President. See Marshall to Simon Wolf, November 23, 1912, MP-AJA.

15. Marshall to Simon Wolf, August 16, 1911, MP-AJA; see also Marshall to Oscar Straus, October 17, October 18, 1911; to the ed. of *The Outlook*, October 13, 1911; to Jacob H. Schiff, October 17, 1911; to Simon Wolf, October 24, 1911, MP-AJA.

16. Marshall to Benjamin Stolz, December 22, 1911, MP-AJA.

17. Marshall to George L. Beer, December 5, 1912; to Henry Green, February 2, 1912, MP-AJA.

18. *NYT,* March 20, 1915, p. 4; Marshall to the ed. of the *Times,* August 24, 1916, MP-AJA. This letter was published only in part by the *Times.*

19. *New York Evening Journal,* June 28, 1916; Marshall to Adolph S. Ochs, September 1, 1916, MP-AJA.

20. On the restrictionist movement, see Higham, *Strangers, et passim;* William S. Bernard (ed.), *American Immigration Policy: A Reappraisal* (New York, 1950), pp. 1–21.

21. Oscar Handlin, *Immigration as a Factor in American History* (Englewood Cliffs, N.J., 1959), p. 167.

22. Charles Howland (ed.), *Survey of American Foreign Relations* (New York, 1929), p. 425. This work contains an unusually good summary of immigration data. The statistics cited do not reflect the re-emigration rate.

23. Edward A. Ross, *The Old World in the New* (New York, 1914), pp. 195–281.

24. *Ibid.,* pp. 285, 287, 293.

25. Frank J. Warne, *The Immigrant Invasion* (New York, 1913), pp. 177–78, 316.

26. Ross, *op. cit.,* pp. 146–48, 165. In the earlier years of the twentieth century, Ross, sharing a general relaxation of nativist tensions, expressed greater optimism concerning America's assimilative powers. See Higham, *Strangers,* pp. 109–10.

27. Madison Grant, *The Passing of the Great Race* (New York, 1916), pp. 16, 81.

28. Quoted in Solomon, *op. cit.,* p. 174.

29. An 1882 speech, quoted in S. M. Dubnow, *History of the Jews in Russia and Poland* (Philadelphia, 1918), III, 297.

30. U.S., Congress, Senate, Immigration Commission, *Reports,* No. 747, 61st Cong., 3rd Sess. 1910, I–II. For an analysis of this report, see Oscar Handlin, *Race and Nationality in American Life* (New York, 1957).

31. U.S., Immigration Commission, *op. cit.,* I, 48.

32. U.S., *Statutes at Large,* XXXIX, Part 1, 1917, p. 877. The only languages specifically named in the law were Hebrew and Yiddish.

33. Marshall to Rep. John L. Burnett, May 21, 1912, MP-AJA.
34. Cyrus Adler, *I Have Considered the Days* (Philadelphia, 1941), p. 297.

35. Marshall to William Barnes, Jr., February 1, 1915, MP-AJA.

36. Marshall to Edward Lauterbach April 23, 1912, MP-AJA

37. Wolf, *op. cit.,* pp. 328–33.

38. Marshall to Herbert Friedenwald, December 23, 1913, MP-AJA.

39. C. Vann Woodward, *Tom Watson, Agrarian Rebel* (New York, 1938), p. 435.

40. C. P. Connolly, *The Truth About the Frank Case* (New York, 1915), p. 14.

41. *NYT,* May 26, 1915, p. 12; Connolly, *op. cit.,* p. 4. Connolly reported the case for *Collier's.*

42. Marshall to Judge Irving Lehman, September 9, 1913, MP-AJA.

43. The case was *Frank* v. *Mangum,* 237 U.S. 309; see *NYT,* February 26, 1915, p. 7; April 20, 1915, p. 1; Marshall to Herbert J. Haas, April 21, 1915; to Henry W. Taft, June 23, 1924 MP-AJA.

44. The *Atlanta Journal* later saw outside interference as vilification— see " 'Vilifying' a State," *Nation,* CI (August 26, 1915), 251–52. On Watson's role, see Woodward, *op. cit.,* pp. 437–43. John Higham believes that Watson followed public opinion rather than shaped it (Higham, *Strangers,* p. 370 n).

45. Woodward, *op. cit.,* p. 439.

46. Quoted from *The Jeffersonian, ibid.,* pp. 438–39; Connolly, *op. cit.,* p. 42.

47. Marshall to Gov. John M. Slaton, June 21, 1915, MP-AJA. Marshall had great confidence in Slaton and felt that the commutation might have been followed by a complete pardon. See Marshall to Felix Vorenberg, October 5, 1923, MP-AJA, and Marshall's letter in *NYT,* September 18, 1915, p. 8.

48. *NYT,* June 24, 1915, p. 5.

49. *NYT,* August 17, 1915, pp. 1, 4.

50. Woodward, *op. cit.,* p. 443.

51. *NYT,* August 18, 1915, pp. 1, 3, 10; August 21, 1915, p. 4.

52. Quoted in Woodward, *op. cit.,* pp. 443, 445.

53. *NYT,* September 12, 1916, p. 3.

54. *NYT,* December 31, 1914, p. 6; for other comments by Jewish leaders, see *NYT,* December 28, 1914, p. 4.

55. Quoted in Higham, *Strangers,* p. 186.

Chapter four

1. See Paul L. Murphy, "Sources and Nature of Intolerance in the 1920's," *Journal of American History,* LI (June, 1964), 60–76; E. Digby Baltzell, *The Protestant Establishment: Aristocracy and Caste in America* (New York, 1964), Chap. 9.

2.   Francis Russell, "The Coming of the Jews," *Antioch Review,* XV (March, 1955), 23.

3.   Hugh A. Studdert Kennedy, "Am I a Jew?" *The Forum* LXXVI (December, 1926), 915.

4.   Russell, p. 34.

5.   S. Miles Bouton, "The Persecution of Jews in Europe: The Problem of Anti-Semitism, IV," *The Forum,* LXXV (June, 1926), 827.

6.   Ralph P. Boas, "Jew-Baiting in America," *Atlantic Monthly,* CXXVII (May, 1921), 663.

7.   Philip Marshall Brown, "Zionism and Anti-Semitism," *North American Review* CCX (November, 1919), 662.

8.   Don C. Seitz, "Jews, Catholics, and Protestants," *Outlook,* CXLI (November 25, 1925), 478.

9.   John Jay Chapman to Marshall, December 13, 1920, MP-AJA. On Chapman and Jews, see Carey McWilliams, *A Mask for Privilege: Anti-Semitism in America* (Boston, 1949), pp. 73–76.

10.   Boas, *loc. cit.,* p. 828.
11.   Hilaire Belloc, *The Jews* (London, 1922), 10–14.
12.   Marshall to Adolph S. Ochs, August 28, 1916, MP-AJA.
13.   *NYT,* March 27, 1917, p. 2; March 31, 1917, p. 10; April 6, 1917, p. 8; November 12, 1917, p. 11; AJC, *Eleventh Annual Report, AJYB* (1918), pp. 391–92.

14.   Marshall to Judah L. Magnes, June 1, 1917; to Prof. Richard Gottheil, August 6, 1917, MP-AJA.

15.   Marshall to Jacob Maisel, December 16, 1919, MP-AJA. One hundred per cent Americanism led to proposals after the war that Jewish congregations admit only American citizens to full membership. Marshall opposed this: "We must avoid the charge of . . . being more Bourbon than the Bourbons" (Marshall to B. Littman, January 30, 1920, MJ-AJA).

16.   Marshall to Gov. W. L. Harding, July 9, 1918, MP-AJA.

17.   Marshall to Gov. Norbeck, February 20, 1919; to Harry Schneiderman, February 17, 1919; to Rabbi Julius Hess, February 17, 1919, MP-AJA. The same bill would have prohibited the teaching of foreign languages in secondary schools.

18.   *NYT,* April 7, 1918, Sec. 1, p. 4; November 11, 1918, p. 24; February 24, 1919, p. 6.

19. Marshall to Rev. Dr. Isaac Landman, February 17, 1919; to Simon Wolf, March 1, 1920, MP-AJA.

20. *NYT*, April 17, 1918, p. 13.

21. *NYT*, October 17, 1917, p. 1; Marshall to Newton D. Baker, October 17, 1917, MP-AJA.

22. Marshall to Lee Shubert, March 13, 15, 1918, MP-AJA.

23. Marshall to John D. Ryan, Dir. of Aircraft Construction, July 24, 1918, MP-AJA.

24. Marshall to Philander P. Claxton, U.S. Commissioner of Education, October 1, 1918, MP-AJA.

25. Marshall to George Blumenthal, July 1, 1917; to Henry P. Davison, May 11, 1918; to Cornelius N. Bliss, May 13, 1918; to Joseph M. Hartfield, May 22, 1918, MP-AJA; *NYT*, June 30, 1917, p. 10.

26. Marshall to Henry P. Davison, May 28, 1920, MP-AJA; to Leo Wise, November 4, 1919, MP-AJA.

27. See Robert K. Murray, *Red Scare: A Study in National Hysteria, 1919–1920* (Minneapolis, 1955); Frederick Lewis Allen, *Only Yesterday* (New York, 1957).

28. Higham, *Strangers,* p. 280.

29. U.S., Congress, Senate, Judiciary Committee, *Hearings on Bolshevik Propaganda,* 65th Cong., 3rd Sess., 1919.

30. *Ibid.,* p. 112.
31. *Ibid.,* p. 116.
32. *Ibid.,* p. 115.
33. *Ibid.,* p. 141.
34. Sen. Lee S. Overman to Marshall, February 21, 1919, MP-AJA.
35. U.S., Congress, Senate, Judiciary Committee, *op. cit.,* pp. 206–7, 269–70, 320.

36. *The Protocols and World Revolution* (Boston, 1920), pp. 76–79.

37. James A. Whitemore to Harry Cutler, May 26, 1920; June 3, 1920; Cutler to Whitemore, June 2, 1920; June 7, 1920, MP-AJA.

38. A. J. Sack to Marshall, June 10, 1922, MP-AJA; *New York American,* June 10, 1922.

39. *AH*, CVI (February 6, 1920), 343. On Churchill's use of the Protocols, see Theodor H. Gaster's comments in "Elders of Zion, Protocols of," *Universal Jewish Encyclopedia*, IV (New York, 1941), 58.

40. Marshall to Richard V. Lindabury, October 24, 1919, MP-AJA.
41. Marshall to Simon Wolf, February 15, 1919, MP-AJA.

42. Marshall to ed., *The Jerseyman,* Morristown, N.J., February 10, 1919, MP-AJA.

43. Marshall to M. Raschkind, February 25, 1919, MP-AJA.

44. Isaac Don Levine, "Russian Jews Against Bolshevik Rule," *B'nai B'rith News,* XII (March, 1920), 1–2; S. Poliakoff, "The Men About Lenine," *AH,* CVI (February 13, 1920), 383; *ibid.,* CVII (August 27, 1920).

45. Marshall to Simon Wolf, January 6, 1920, MP-AJA.
46. Marshall to Jacob Massel, December 16, 1919, MP-AJA.
47. Marshall to Assemblyman Simon Adler, March 31, 1920, MP-AJA.
48. Marshall to city ed., *Syracuse Journal,* January 13, 1920, MP-AJA.
49. Marshall to Rev. Dr. Samuel Schulman, January 30, 1920, MP-AJA.
50. *NYT,* April 5, 1920, p. 6.
51. Marshall to A. E. Stevenson, Associate Counsel, Joint Legislative Committee to Investigate Seditious Activities, April 20, 1920, MP-AJA; *NYT,* May 15, 1920, p. 1.

52. Marshall to Leo Wise, ed., *American Israelite,* April 12, 1920, MP-AJA.

53. The best surveys of the origins and content of the Protocols are: Herman Bernstein, *The History of a Lie* (New York, 1921); *idem., The Truth About "The Protocols of Zion"* (New York, 1935); "Elders of Zion, Protocols of," *Universal Jewish Encyclopedia,* IV (New York, 1941), 46–60; John S. Curtiss, *An Appraisal of the Protocols of Zion* (New York, 1942); Mark Vishniak, "New Studies on the 'Elders of Zion,' " *YIVO Annual of Jewish Social Science,* II–III (1948), 140–45. The Curtiss book, issued under the auspices of a committee of distinguished American historians, including Carl Becker, Sidney B. Fay, Dixon R. Fox, Carlton J. H. Hayes, William Langer, Allan Nevins, Geroid T. Robinson, and Bernadotte E. Schmitt, concluded that the Protocols "beyond doubt . . . are rank and pernicious forgeries" (pp. vi–vii).

54. See the edition called, *The Protocols of the Wise Men of Zion* (New York, 1920).

55. See "Is There a World-Wide Jewish Peril?" *Current Opinion,* LXIX (December, 1920), 840.

56. Lucien Wolf to Cyrus Adler, July 15, 1920, MP-AJA.

57. *The Jewish Peril: Protocols of the Learned Elders of Zion* (2nd ed.; London, 1920), note facing p. 1.

58. Marshall to Cyrus Adler, December 30, 1919; Lucien Wolf to Cyrus Adler, July 15, 1920; Marshall to A. C. Ratshesky, September 10, 1920; Herman Bernstein to Marshall, December 19, 1920, MP-AJA.

59. On Brasol, see AJC, *Fourteenth Annual Report, AJYB* (1921), p. 314; Norman Hapgood, "The Inside Story of Henry Ford's Jew-Mania," *Hearst's International,* XLI (June, 1922), p. 18; Adler, *I Have Considered . . . , op. cit.,* p. 329; Marshall to Cyrus Adler, July 1, 1920; to Harry Schneiderman,

September 16, 1920; Casimir Pilenas to Marshall, December 31, 1923, MP-AJA; Isaac Don Levine, "Comrade Boris Brasol-Bolshevik," *JT*, LXXXIX (October 22, 1926), 1, 8.

60. See Herman Bernstein's report to Marshall, February 4, 1921, MP-AJA.
61. *The Cause of World Unrest* (New York, 1920).
62. *Ibid.*, pp. iii–v, xxiii, 208. See the review by Harry Schneiderman in *Survey* (November 27, 1920), p. 322.

63. Marshall to Maj. G. H. Putnam, October 13, 1920, MP-AJA.
64. Marshall to Maj. G. H. Putnam, October 28, 1920, MP-AJA.
65. *AJC, Sixteenth Annual Report, AJYB*, XXV (1923), 54–55; Hapgood, *loc. cit.* (September, 1922), p. 48.

66. *The Protocols of the Wise Men of Zion* (New York, 1920), frontispiece.
67. Marshall to Harris Weinstock, October 11, 1920, MP-AJA.
68. Marshall to Cyrus Adler, April 26, 1921; to John Jay Chapman, December 9, 1920, MP-AJA; *Philadelphia Public Ledger,* October 27, October 28, 1919.

69. Boris Brasol, *The World at the Cross Roads* (Boston: Small, Maynard and Co., 1921).

70. Lucien Wolf, *The Myth of the Jewish Menace in World Affairs*. . . . (New York, 1921); William D. Hard, *The Great Jewish Conspiracy* (New York, 1920); C. A. Windle, *The Tyranny of Intolerance* (Chicago, 1921).

71. Hard, p. 45.

72. On the Bernstein-Marshall collaboration, see Marshall to Rabbi Aaron Teitelbaum, December 4, 1920; to Lester Markel, March 5, 1921; to A. C. Ratshesky, March 5, 1921; to M. Vinaver, May 16, 1921, MP-AJA.

73. See Princess Catherine Radziwill, "The History of the Protocols," MP-AJA (typescript). Princess Catherine Radziwill to Felix Warburg, January 21, 1921; Marshall to John Spargo, February 7, 1921; Marshall to Mrs. Rebekah Kohut, March 16, 1921, MP-AJA; *NYT*, March 4, 1921, p. 13.

74. An English translation of the du Chayla article appeared in AJC, *Sixteenth Annual Report, op. cit.,* pp. 360–69; see also Marshall to M. Vinaver, May 16, 1921, MP-AJA.

75. Marshall to James N. Rosenberg, August 31, 1921; to Adolph S. Ochs, August 31, 1921, MP-AJA; *NYT*, September 4, 1921, Sec. 7, p. 1; Sec. 2, p.2.

Chapter five

1. *DI*, May 22, 1920, pp. 1–3.
2. *DI*, July 10, 1920, pp. 8–9.
3. Henry Ford, *My Life and Work* (Garden City, N.Y., 1923), pp. 250–51.

4. *DI,* January 10, 1925, p. 8; May 29, 1920, pp. 2–3; May 21, 1921, pp. 8–9; December 10, 1921, pp. 8–9.

5. *DI,* December 25, 1920, pp. 8–9.
6. See Margaret L. Coit, *Mr. Baruch* (Boston, 1957), pp. 359–63.
7. *DI,* November 26, 1921, pp. 8–9.
8. *DI,* November 12, 1921, pp. 8–9.

9. *The International Jew,* pub. by the *DI* in series of four booklets; No. 2, p. 29.

10. *DI,* September 25, 1920, pp. 8–9; August 28, 1920, pp. 8–9; October 2, 1920, pp. 8–9.

11. *Jewish Daily Bulletin,* July 29, 1925.

12. *DI,* November 13, 1920, pp. 8–9; see also *DI,* September 24, 1921, pp. 8–9; October 1, 1921, pp. 8–9; *NYT,* March 1, 1921, p. 12.

13. *DI,* November 26, 1921, pp. 8–9.
14. *DI,* January 7, 1922, pp. 1, 9; January 14, 1922, pp. 1, 8.
15. Allan Nevins and Frank Ernest Hill, *Ford: Expansion and Challenge, 1915–1933* (New York, 1957), p. 311.

16. Leuchtenburg, *op. cit.,* p. 187.
17. *DI,* March 5, 1921, pp. 8–9.
18. Jonathan Norton Leonard, *The Tragedy of Henry Ford* (New York, 1932), p. 197.

19. Nevins and Hill, *op. cit.,* p. 312; Marshall to Abram I. Elkus, August 24, 1920; Marshall to John Spargo, December 31, 1920, MP-AJA. The large loan of 1919 was procured through a Boston firm. See William C. Richards, *The Last Billionaire: Henry Ford* (New York, 1948), p. 89.

20. *NYT,* December 5, 1927, p. 23.

21. E. G. Pipp, "Ford's Recantation Analyzed," *AH,* CXXI (July 15, 1927), 49.

22. Harry Bennett, *We Never Called Him Henry* (New York, 1951), p. 47.

23. Quoted from an interview with Ford, in Judson Churchill Welliver, "Henry Ford, Dreamer and Worker," *Review of Reviews,* LXIV (November, 1921), 492.

24. Henry Ford, "If I Were President," *Collier's,* LXXII (August 4, 1923), 6. Ford saw the power of the Jews everywhere. In commenting on the progress of his factory in Ireland, he said, "The only trouble in Ireland is caused by the politicians and the Jews" (*AH,* CVII [September 17, 1920], 533).

25. *NYT,* December 5, 1921, p. 33.
26. Welliver, *loc. cit.,* p. 492.
27. *New York Evening Journal,* February 23, 1921, p. 20.

28. Ford, *op. cit.,* pp. 251–52.
29. Keith Sward, *The Legend of Henry Ford* (New York, 1948), p. 147.
30. Allan L. Benson, *The New Henry Ford* (New York, 1923), pp. 355–56; see also Ford, *loc. cit.,* p. 6; Welliver, *loc. cit.,* p. 481.

31. Richards, *op. cit.,* p. 90.

32. David A. Brown to Marshall, September 14, 1920; Marshall to Cyrus Adler, September 24, 1920, MP-AJA.

33. Robert Littell, "Henry Ford and His Secret," *The Outlook* (London), LII (December 1, 1922), 407–8.

34. Charles Merz, *And Then Came Ford* (New York, 1929), p. 189.
35. James M. Miller to Marshall, December 3, 1923, MP-AJA.
36. *Pipp's Weekly,* April 1, 1922, p. 7; July 9, 1921, p. 1; *Jewish Daily News,* August 17, 1926, p. 4.

37. *NYT,* June 10, 1921, p. 3.
38. *AH,* CVII (July 16, 1920), 235.
39. *Pipp's Weekly,* July 2, 1921, pp. 1, 3; see also Bennett, *op. cit.,* p. 48; Marshall to David A. Brown, September 17, 1920, MP-AJA. Marshall remarked of Cameron, "He is said to be a clergyman. That makes his offense against humanity so much more horrible. . . ."

40. *DI,* September 11, 1920, p. 1.

41. C. C. Sharpe, Dearborn and Enrollment Division, Ford Motor Company, to Gentlemen, MP-AJA.

42. Marshall to Henry Perlman, May 11, 1921; to Jacob Epstein, June 3, 1921, MP-AJA.

Chapter six

1. *Philadelphia Ledger,* January 18, 1921; *Albany Times-Union,* October 22, 1920; *Hartford Courant,* March 22, 1922; *Rochester Post,* January 10, 1922.

2. Herbert Adams Gibbons, "The Jewish Problem," *Century Magazine,* CII (September, 1921), 786–87.

3. Marshall to Chancellor James R. Day, January 19, 1922; to T. Aaron Levy, January 11, 1922, MP-AJA.

4. Examples of politicians' opinions can be seen in *NYT,* December 14, 1920, p. 16; April 28, 1921, p. 25; William G. McAdoo to Marshall, December 14, 1920; Marshall to Julius Levy, December 29, 1920, MP-AJA. Sinclair Lewis condemned Ford for his ignorance of Jewish history. See *NYT,* February 21, 1921, p. 11.

5.   William Howard Taft, *Anti-Semitism in the United States* (Chicago, 1921). This is the text of Taft's Chicago speech; see also, *NYT*, December 24, 1920; November 19, 1920, p. 15; Leon L. Lewis to Marshall, January 18, 1921, MP-AJA.

6.   *Salt Lake Tribune*, April 5, 1921.
7.   *New York American*, March 14, 1921; *NYT*, December 29, 1924, p. 17.
8.   Rev. A. E. Potter to Marshall, March 17, 1921, MP-AJA.
9.   Marshall to Rev. Potter, April 8, 1921, MP-AJA.
10.   Marshall to Rev. Charles S. Macfarland, January 8, 1921; to Rabbi Joel Blau, November 24, 1922, MP-AJA.

11.   Marshall to Chancellor James R. Day, December 4, 1920, MP-AJA.

12.   Warren G. Harding to John Spargo, January 4, 1921; George B Christian, Jr., to Marshall, January 12, 1921; John Spargo to Marshall, December 30, 1920; January 3, 1921; Marshall to Spargo, December 31, 1921, MP-AJA.

13.   *NYT*, January 17, 1921, p. 11.

14.   Marshall to Rabbi Isaac Landman, November 6, 1920, MP-AJA. Additional evidence of Jewish alarm can be seen in the letters to the editor, *AH*, CVII (July 2, 1920), and the series of articles on "Henry Ford's Jewmaniacy," *ibid.*, CVII (August 20, 27; September 3, 1920); also, in Abram I. Elkus to Marshall, July 6, 1920, MP-AJA.

15.   Louis D. Gross, *Fallacies of Henry Ford* (Brooklyn, n.d.), p. 3.

16.   Elisha M. Friedman, "The Challenge of Anti-Semitism," *Menorah Journal*, VII (February, 1922), 20.

17.   Cyrus Adler to Marshall, September 1, 1920, MP-AJA.

18.   *AJYB* (1922), pp. 316–17; Marshall to Julius Rosenwald, June 3, 1920; to Harris Weinstock, October 28, 1920, MP-AJA.

19.   *AJYB* (1922), pp. 316–17. The spelling, "antizamitism," was deliberate.

20.   Marshall to Dearborn Publishing Company, June 5, 1920; to Julius Rosenwald, June 5, 1920, MP-AJA.

21.   Marshall's version of the dispute is given in letters to David A. Brown, August 13, 1920; to Rabbi Joseph Krauskopf, October 29, 1920, MP-AJA.

22.   Marshall to David A. Brown, August 13, 1920, MP-AJA.

23.   Rabbi Leo M. Franklin to Marshall, November 6, 1920; Marshall to Simon Fleischmann, November 19, 1920, MP-AJA.

24.   Marshall to Rabbi Leo M. Franklin, July 31, 1927; Harry Schneiderman to Marshall, July 29, 1927, MP-AJA.

25.   Marshall to Adolf Kraus, November 3, 1920, MP-AJA.

26.   Simon Fleischmann to Marshall, November 17, 27, 1920, MP-AJA. Adolf Kraus suggested that the parts of the statement dealing with Jewish opposition to Bolshevism be toned down in the fear they might jeopardize the position of Russian Jews. See Kraus to Marshall, November 23, 1920, MP-AJA.

27.   Marshall to Morris Weinberg, December 8, 1920; to Henry Sachs, December 8, 1920, MP-AJA.

28.   See Julius Levy to Marshall, December 1, 1920; A. C. Ratshesky to Marshall, December 1, 1920; Harris Weinstock to Marshall, December 1, 1920, MP-AJA. Marshall was dissatisfied with the response of the Yiddish press, which did not give the address sufficient prominence, in his opinion. See Marshall to Morris Weinberg, December 8, 1920, MP-AJA.

29.   Reported to Marshall by A. D. Lasker, in letter of December 4, 1920, MP-AJA; reprinted in *AH*, CVIII (December 31, 1920), 226.

30.   Joseph A. Deatherage to Marshall, January 18, 1921, MP-AJA.
31.   Marshall to Simon Fleischmann, August 25, 1921, MP-AJA.
32.   Lester Markel to Marshall, March 5, 1921; Paul A. Sinsheimer to Marshall, December 4, 1920, MP-AJA.

33.   Harris Weinstock to Marshall, December 2, 1920, MP-AJA.
34.   *NYT*, February 6, 1921, p. 9.
35.   *New York Sun*, November 18, 1920; Julius Levy to Marshall, December 1, 1920, MP-AJA.

36.   Adolf Kraus to Marshall, December 3, 6, 1920; Marshall to Kraus, December 4, 1920, MP-AJA. Kraus also opposed Landman's scheme.

37.   *AH*, CVIII (November 19, 1920), 20; Isaac Landman to Marshall, November 15, 1920, MP-AJA.

38.   Marshall to Henry Perlman, May 11, 1921, MP-AJA.
39.   Marshall to Gov. Nathan L. Miller, February 21, 1921, MP-AJA.
40.   *NYT*, February 2, 1921, p. 17; February 3, 1921, p. 3.
41.   *NYT*, July 9, 1923, p. 17.
42.   *JT*, January 21, 1927, p. 7.
43.   *Pittsburgh Jewish Criterion*, August 10, 1923; see *AH*, CVIII (March 4, 1921), 447.

44.   *New York World*, February 21, 1921.
45.   Marshall to Benjamin Stolz, December 14, 1923, MP-AJA.
46.   *New York World*, February 21, 1921; *NYT*, December 5, 1921, p. 33.
47.   *AH*, CVII (July 23, 1920), 251.
48.   Marshall to Sieg Natenberg, November 9, 1925, MP-AJA.
49.   Cyrus Adler to Jacob Schiff, July 15, 1920, MP-AJA; *Baltimore Jewish Times*, February 10, 1922.

50.   Marshall to Cyrus Adler, April 26, 1921, MP-AJA.
51.   Marshall to Benjamin L. Grey, March 16, 1921, MP-AJA.
52.   Marshall to Lewis Drucker, April 27, 1921, MP-AJA.

53. *Pipp's Weekly*, August 20, 1921, p. 4.
54. John Spargo, *The Jew and American Ideals* (New York, 1921).
55. Marshall to John Spargo, March 8, 1921, MP-AJA.
56. Marshall to Pres. Warren G. Harding, July 25, 1921, MP-AJA. For the background of this episode, see Marshall to Cyrus Adler, July 27, 1921, MP-AJA.

57. Marshall to Albert D. Lasker, July 28, 1921; Lasker to Marshall, August 6, 1921; Marshall to Lasker, September 22, 1921, MP-AJA.

58. Marshall to Albert D. Lasker, September 7, 1923, MP-AJA.
59. *NYT*, January 6, 1922, p. 9; January 17, 1922, p. 6.
60. Benson, *op. cit.*, p. 357.
61. Marshall to Rabbi Isaac Landman, January 11, 1922, MP-AJA.
62. *NYT*, October 29, 1922, p. 5.
63. *DI*, December 29, 1923, p. 9; May 3, 1924, p. 3; November 8, 1924, p. 2.
64. James N. Rosenberg urged Marshall, Warburg, and Lehman to bring suit against Ford. See Rosenberg to Marshall, October 17, 1924, MP-AJA.

65. Marshall to ed., *NYT*, October 15, 1924, MP-AJA. The letter was printed on the *Times's* editorial page and received acclaim among Jews. See David M. Bressler to Marshall, October 17, 1924, MP-AJA.

66. *DI*, November 8, 1924, p. 8; see Marshall's reaction in a letter to Jacob Landau, November 11, 1924, MP-AJA.

67. Marshall to Charles D. Hilles, September 12, 1924, MP-AJA.

68. Marshall to Pres. Calvin Coolidge, March 18, 1925, MP-AJA. In 1922, Marshall had written to Senator William E. Borah on the connection between Ford and Russian émigré counter-revolutionists. See Marshall to Sen. Borah, April 14, 1922; April 15, 1922, MP-AJA.

69. See *NYT*, May 13, 1924, p. 5; June 3, 1924, p. 10, for accounts of Jewish mass meetings on Ford in New York City.

Chapter seven

1. See William Adams Simonds, *Henry Ford: His Life, His Work* (Indianapolis, 1943), p. 210, for information on Robert Morgan.

2. *DI*, April 19, 1924, pp. 4–5.
3. *DI*, April 26, 1924, p. 4.
4. On Sapiro's background and activities, see Grace H. Larsen and Henry E. Erdman, "Aaron Sapiro: Genius of Farm Co-operative Promotion," *Mississippi Valley Historical Review*, XLIX (September, 1962), 242–68.

5. *NYT*, January 7, 1925, p. 9; April 23, 1925, p. 6; *Jewish Daily Bulletin*, April 24, 1925.

6.   Marshall to F. A. Fisher, March 21, 1927; to G. Lowenstein, March 29, 1927, MP-AJA.

7.   *NYT*, March 23, 1927, p. 1; March 26, 1927, p. 4.
8.   *NYT*, March 19, 1927, p. 1.
9.   *NYT*, June 10, 1921, p. 3.
10.   Nevins and Hill, *op. cit.*, pp. 319–20; Bennett, *op. cit.*, p. 53.
11.   *NYT*, May 23, 1927, p. 23; May 28, 1927, p. 14.
12.   On the mistrial, see *NYT*, April 20, 1927, p. 1; April 21, 1927, p. 1; April 22, 1927, p. 1; Sward, *op. cit.*, pp. 55–56.

13.   *NYT*, November 5, 1927, p. 19. Bennett reported a slightly different conversation between himself and Ford: "It's pretty bad, Mr. Ford."—"I don't care how bad it is, you sign it and settle the thing up" (Bennett, *op. cit.*, p. 56). Nevins writes, "Just who wrote the text of his long retraction, which was issued through his [Ford's] friend Arthur Brisbane, we do not know" (Nevins and Hill, *op. cit.*, p. 320). Marshall's authorship was not publicly divulged at the time.

14.   For the complete text of the apology, see Henry Ford, *Statement by Henry Ford* (New York, 1927); *NYT*, July 8, 1927, p. 1; *Forward*, July 8, 1927, pp. 1, 4; July 9, 1927, pp. 1, 7, 16.

15.   For the full text, see Marshall to Henry Ford, July 5, 1927, MP-AJA.
16.   Marshall to Julius Rosenwald, July 22, 1927, MP-AJA.
17.   *NYT*, July 8, 1927, p. 1.
18.   See *Jewish Daily Bulletin*, July 11, 1927, for a review of press opinion.

19.   *JT*, July 15, 1927, p. 18. Thomas's attribution of the recantation to the consumer boycott was exaggerated. The decline in Ford sales was due more to dissatisfaction with the Model T.

20.   Marshall to Julius Rosenwald, July 22, 1927, MP-AJA; see the statement by Herman Bernstein, *NYT*, November 7, 1927, p. 21. The Ford apology was reported in the German press; *Forward*, July 11, 1927.

21.   Marshall to Melville Levy, August 26, 1927, MP-AJA.

22.   *NYT*, October 10, 1927, p. 26; *JT*, July 15, 1927, p. 13; *Jewish Daily Bulletin*, July 10, 1927. Rabbi Leo Franklin still implied that Ford was on the verge of signing a retraction back in 1920 on his urging, when Marshall's aggravating telegram dissuaded him (Rabbi Franklin to Marshall, August 4, 1927, MP-AJA).

23.   Marshall to Julius Rosenwald, July 22, 1927, MP-AJA.
24.   *AH*, CXXI (July 15, 1927), 1.
25.   Marshall to Henry Sliosberg, August 18, 1927; David Bressler to Marshall, July 27, 1927, MP-AJA.

26.   *JT*, November 18, 1927, p. 1; *NYT*, November 8, 1927, p. 29; November 21, 1927, p. 15.

27.   *JT*, November 25, 1927, p. 6.
28.   *Philadelphia Jewish Times*, January 20, 1928.

29.   *JT*, December 2, 1927, p. 1.
30.   Marshall to Herman Bernstein, February 21, 1928, MP-AJA.
31.   Sward, *op. cit.*, p. 157.
32.   On the Fritsch affair, see Marshall's letters to Arthur Brisbane, July 19, 1927; to Joseph A. Palma, August 17, October 14, 1927; to Earl J. Davis, August 25, September 6, 1927; to Martin C. Ansorge, September 20, 22, 1927; to Henry Ford, October 14, December 21, 1927; January 10, 23, February 21, April 3, May 12, 1928—MP-AJA.

33.   See the thirtieth printing of Henry Ford, *Der internazionale Jude* (Leipzig, 1933), issued by Hammer-Verlag in August, 1933, with a self-congratulatory foreword by the publisher.

34.   Marshall to The Britons, September 17, 1927; Sec., The Britons, to Marshall, October 11, 1927, MP-AJA.

35.   *The Jewish Question: A Selection of the Articles (1920–22) Published by Mr. Ford's Paper, The Dearborn Independent.* . . . (London, n.d.), pp. 7–15.

36.   Nevins and Hill, *op. cit.*, p. 321; Sward, *op. cit.*, p. 159.
37.   On Ford's later anti-Semitic activities, see Sward, *op. cit.*, pp. 450–56.
38   Marshall to Rabbi Emanuel Schreiber, August 18, 1927, MP-AJA.
39.   *The International Jew I: The Jew in Character and Business* (Atlanta, 1941). This was published by the Knights of the Ku Klux Klan.

40.   Göran Göransson, *Henry Ford om Judarna* (Stockholm, 1954).

Chapter eight

1.   .For older analyses of the Klan and its mentality, see John M. Mecklin, *The Ku Klux Klan: A Study of the American Mind* (New York, 1924); Frank Tannenbaum, *Darker Phases of the South* (New York, 1924); Kallen, *op. cit.*, pp. 9–43. For recent treatments, see Higham, *Strangers*, pp. 285–99; Arnold Rice, *The Ku Klux Klan in American Politics* (Washington, 1962); David M. Chalmers, *Hooded Americanism* (Garden City, N.Y., 1965).

2.   Leuchtenburg, *op. cit.*, pp. 210–11; Rice, *op. cit.*, pp. 12–13. Leuchtenburg estimates maximum Klan membership as closer to 5,000,000.

3.   Emerson H. Loucks, *The Ku Klux Klan in Pennsylvania* (New York, 1936), pp. 162–63. On the opposition of the Klan to Catholics, see Chapters 7, 8, 9.

4.   Henry P. Fry, *The Modern Ku Klux Klan* (Boston, 1922), p. 120; Fry to Marshall, January 2, 1923, MP-AJA.

5.   Statement of Imperial Wizard H. W. Evans, *NYT*, August 31, 1924, p. 6.

6. *New York World,* January 2, 1923.

7. U.S., Congress, House, Committee on Rules, *Hearings, Ku Klux Klan,* 67th Cong., 1st Sess., 1921, p. 75.

8. *NYT,* October 25, 1923, p. 1.

9. Dr. Evans, quoted in Lee J. Levinger, *The Causes of Anti-Semitism in the United States* (Philadelphia, 1925), pp. 79–80.

10. Dr. Evans, *Jewish Daily Bulletin,* December 7, 1925.
11. Dr. Evans, *NYT,* December 8, 1922, p. 19.
12. Charles Jacobson to Marshall, March 20, 1923, MP-AJA.
13. Rev. Oscar Haywood, national lecturer for the Klan, *NYT,* November 27, 1922, p. 2.

14. Marshall to Amos L. Beatty, Pres., The Texas Company, January 13, 1925; to Theodore Mack, January 19, 1925, MP-AJA.

15. Daniel Alexander to Marshall, May 16, 1923, **MP-AJA.**
16. U.S., Congress, *Hearings, Ku Klux Klan, op. cit.,* p. 19.
17. *NYT,* March 1, 1923, p. 19.
18. Marshall to M. E. Lubin, December 21, 1922, MP-AJA.
19. Marshall to C. B. Slemp, Secretary to the President, September 2, 1924; to Leonard Mason, September 12, 1924, MP-AJA.

20. *New York World,* October 28, 1923.

21. Marshall to Henry Wollman, October 9, 1924; to Judge Aaron J. Levy, November 24, 1922; to Henry P. Fry, November 27, 1922; to Don Marquis, June 2, 1924, MP-AJA.

22. See Henry P. Fry to Marshall, November 25, 1922; December 29, 1922; January 2, 1923; Marshall to Felix Warburg, November 27, 1922; to Paul M. Warburg, May 3, 1924, MP-AJA.

23. Stephen Wise to Marshall, December 5, 1922, MP-AJA.

24. Judge Aaron J. Levy, Grand Master of Order B'rith Abraham, *NYT,* November 23, 1922, p. 23; November 30, 1922, p. 21.

25. *NYT,* December 14, 1922, p. 24.
26. Marshall to Jesse Winburn, October 21, 23, 1922, MP-AJA.
27. William D. Guthrie, *JT,* LXXXIX (December 10, 1926), 9.
28. See Marshall to Cyrus Adler, March 12, 1925, MP-AJA; *American Israelite,* June 11, 1925; *Jewish Daily Bulletin,* March 25, 1925. Lawyers for the Protestant Episcopal Church also participated in this appeal; the case was *Pierce* v. *The Society of Sisters of the Holy Name,* 268 U.S. 510 (1925).

29. Marshall to Rev. John J. Burke, June 6, 1925, MP-AJA.
30. *NYT,* January 24, 1923, p. 6.
31. For statistics on the volume of immigration, see Roy F. Garis, *Immigration Restriction* (New York, 1927), pp. 206, 209; *AJYB,* XLIII (1941), 683; Higham, *Strangers,* p. 308.

32. *Ibid.,* p. 301.
33. Annie M. Allen to Marshall, January 2, 1923, MP-AJA.
34. Rev. A. E. Potter to Marshall, March 17, 1921, MP-AJA.
35. Fry, *op. cit.,* p. 256.
36. Marshall to Benjamin Stolz, March 5, 1926, MP-AJA.
37. Burton J. Hendrick, "The Jews in America," *World's Work,* XLV (1922–23), 144–61, 266–86, 366–77, 591–601.

38. Hendrick to Louis Rosenzweig, February 27, 1923, MP-AJA.
39. Hendrick, *loc. cit.,* p. 377.
40. *Ibid.,* p. 601.
41. *Ibid.,* p. 144.
42. *System,* January, 1923, p. 246.
43. Hendrick, *op. cit.,* prefatory note.
44. Herman Bernstein to Marshall, June 20, 1923, MP-AJA.
45. Marshall to Frank N. Doubleday, February 8, 21, 1923, MP-AJA.
46. Marshall to Doubleday, June 23, 1923, MP-AJA.
47. The June 23, 1923 letter to Doubleday was published in Arthur Brisbane's editorial column in the *New York Evening Journal,* June 29, 1923.

48. "Another Jewish Menace," *The Freeman,* VII (July 18, 1923), 436–37; see also *Nation,* CXVII (October 24, 1923), 468, for a review by Johan J. Smertenko; *AH,* CXII (February 23, 1923), 478 (reviewed by Max J. Kohler); *JT,* June 29, 1923, p. 1 (reviewed by Maurice Fishberg).

49. *Journal of Social Forces,* II (March, 1924), 451 (review by Clifford Kirkpatrick, Brown University).

50. Kenneth L. Roberts, *Why Europe Leaves Home* (Indianapolis, 1922).
51. *Ibid.,* p. 6.
52. *Ibid.,* p. 15.
53. *Ibid.,* p. 49.
54. *Ibid.,* pp. 96–97.
55. *Ibid.,* p. 117–18.
56. *Ibid.,* p. 98.
57. Boris Bogen to Marshall, March 17, 1922, MP-AJA.
58. Gino Speranza, "The Immigration Peril," *World's Work,* XLVII (November, 1923), 57–65; (December, 1923), 147–60; (January, 1924), 256–70; (February, 1924), 379–409; (March, 1924), 479–90; (April, 1924), 643–48; XLVIII (May, 1924), 62–68. *World's Work* had previously published the Hendrick articles.

59. *World's Work,* XLVII, 64.
60. *Ibid.,* p. 63.
61. *Ibid.,* p. 405.
62. *Ibid.,* p. 407.
63. *Ibid.,* p. 409.
64. *Ibid.,* XLVIII, 68.
65. Marshall to Harry Schneiderman, October 27, 1923, MP-AJA.
66. Reuben Frank, "Visas, Immigration, and Official Anti-Semitism," *Nation,* CXII (June 22, 1921), 870–72.

67.   U.S., Congress, Senate, Committee on Immigration, *Hearings, Emergency Immigration Legislation*, 66th Cong., 3rd Sess., 1921, pp. 11–12.

68.   Marshall to Solicitor-General James M. Beck, January 11, 1923, MP-AJA.

69.   Marshall to Albert Shiels, Vice-Pres., Inter-Racial Council, August 4, 1920, MP-AJA.

70.   Marshall to Sen. David A. Reed, April 10, 1926, MP-AJA.
71.   Marshall to Rep. Isaac Siegel, January 9, 1919, MP-AJA.
72.   For Marshall's testimony, see U.S., Congress, *Hearings, Emergency Immigration Legislature, op. cit.*, pp. 100–16.

73.   *Ibid.*, p. 107.
74.   *Ibid.*, pp. 110–11.
75.   *Ibid.*, p. 213.
76.   *Ibid.*, p. 678, statement of Francis H. Kinnicutt.
77.   Marshall to Pres. Harding, May 17, 1921, MP-AJA.
78.   Marshall to Israel Zangwill, June 24, 1921, MP-AJA.
79.   U.S., Congress, Senate, Committee on Immigration, *Hearings, Selective Immigration Legislation*, 68th Cong., 1st Sess., 1924, pp. 120–35.

80.   *Ibid.*, p. 127. See the supporting testimony given by Marshall's son-in-law, Jacob Billikopf (*ibid.*, p. 265).

81.   Marshall to Leopold Plaut, March 21, 1924, MP-AJA.

82.   U.S., Congress, Senate, *Hearings, Selective Immigration Legislation, op. cit.*, p. 124.

83.   Marshall to Pres. Coolidge, May 22, 1924, MP-AJA.
84.   Marshall to Rep. Samuel Dickstein, May 27, 1924, MP-AJA.
85.   *NYT*, April 14, 1924, p. 4.
86.   Marshall to Cyrus Adler, February 26, 1925, MP-AJA.
87.   Marshall to Israel Zangwill, June 24, 1921, MP-AJA.
88.   Marshall to Felix Warburg, January 22, 1921, MP-AJA.
89.   Marshall to Abram Spelke, January 23, 1924, MP-AJA.
90.   Marshall to Rabbi Sh. Karlinsky, December 19, 1924; to Simon Wolf, February 14, 1922, MP-AJA.

91.   Marshall to Solomon Sufrin, February 5, 1925, MP-AJA; see also Marshall to Percy Fridenberg, April 23, 1925; *Jewish Daily Bulletin*, February 10, 1925.

92.   Marshall to Lucien Wolf, August 22, 1922, MP-AJA.
93.   Cyrus Adler to Lucien Wolf, August 22, 1922, MP-AJA.
94.   Based on statistics in Wischnitzer, *op. cit.*, p. 289.

Chapter nine

1.   Heywood Broun and George Britt, *Christians Only* (New York, 1931), p. 20.

2.   Henry Pratt Fairchild, *Immigration* (rev. ed.; New York, 1933), p. 362.
3.   Marshall to Louis P. Goldberg, May 11, 1920, MP-AJA.
4.   Marshall to Nathan D. Shapiro, October 28, 1926, MP-AJA.
5.   Broun, *op. cit.*, pp. 250–51; Red Lion Inn to Otto S. Mayer, September 17, 1923; Marshall to Roy Rogers, July 22, 1927, MP-AJA; advertisement in *Syracuse Journal*, July 13, 1927.

6.   "The Jew and the Club," *Atlantic Monthly*, CXXXIV (October, 1924), 453.

7.   Marshall to Isidor Lewi, April 12, 1921, MP-AJA.
8.   Marshall to Henry B. Wilson, November 7, 1907, MP-AJA.
9.   Marshall to William C. Breed, January 6, 1922, MP-AJA.
10.   Marshall to Frank J. Oliver, Jr., August 24, 27, 1926; to George D. Pratt, August 25, 1926; to Frank S. Hackett, October 16, 1926, MP-AJA.

11.   Marshall to Hackett, February 18, 1928, MP-AJA.
12.   Marshall to Robert Marshall, January 19, 1928, MP-AJA.
13.   Seitz, *loc. cit.*, p. 479.
14.   Russell, *loc. cit.*, p. 34. On the movement from the immigrant ghettos to areas of second settlement, see Louis Wirth, *The Ghetto* (Chicago, 1928), pp. 241–61.

15.   Broun, *op. cit.*, p. 259. The Astor site became the home of the new building of Temple Emanu-El.

16.   Marshall to Julius Bendheim, November 1, 1923, MP-AJA.
17.   AJC, *Executive Committee Minutes*, October 5, 1924.
18.   Marshall to Howard E. Coffin, April 13, 1929, MP-AJA; AJC, *Executive Committee Minutes*, April 14, 1929; June 16, 1929.

19.   Marshall to A. J. Gordon, April 20, 1929, MP-AJA.
20.   *Ibid.*
21.   Jess Perlman to Marshall, August 4, 1926, MP-AJA; *NYT, New York World,* July 27, 1926.

22.   Russell, *loc. cit.*, p. 31.
23.   *Ibid.*, p. 33.
24.   *AJYB* (1921), p. 399.
25.   Aaron E. Stein, Sec. Council on American Jewish Student Affairs, to Marshall, January 12, 1928, MP-AJA.

26.   William Lieberman, Counsel, Kehillah of New York City, to Marshall, August 20, 1919; see also Lieberman to Marshall, October 3, 1919, MP-AJA.

27.   Prof. A. S. Isaacs to Cyrus Adler, September 28, 1919, MP-AJA.
28.   Marshall to William Lieberman, October 18, 1919, MP-AJA.
29.   Virginia C. Gildersleeve, "Class and Creed at Barnard," *Nation*, CXV (December 6, 1922), 607.

30.   *NYT*, June 1, 1922, p. 6; *JT*, XXXIX (June 9, 1922), 2.

31.   William T. Ham, "Harvard Student Opinion on the Jewish Question," *Nation*, CXV (September 6, 1922), 225–27.

32. *American Israelite*, LXVIII (June 29, 1922), 4.

33. *NYT*, September 19, 1922, p. 3.

34. "What Was Your Father's Name?" *Nation*, CXV (October 4, 1922), 322; see also "May Jews Go to College?" *Ibid.*, CXIV (June 14, 1922), 708.

35. *NYT*, January 27, 1923, p. 7.

36. *NYT*, January 15, 1923, p. 17; *JT*, XXXIX (June 9, 1922), 2.

37. Statements of Rabbi Louis L. Mann, *NYT*, July 4, 1922, p. 8; Rabbi James G. Heller, *American Israelite*, November 9, 1922, p. 1. See also Heller, "Americanizing Our Universities," *AH*, CXI (November 10, 1926), 686.

38. *American Israelite*, July 6, 1922, p. 4.

39. Louis I. Newman, *A Jewish University in America?* (New York, 1923), p. 11.

40. Horace M. Kallen, "The Roots of Anti-Semitism," *Nation*, CXVI (February 28, 1923), 242.

41. For the Lowell-Benesch correspondence, see *NYT*, June 17, 1922, p. 1; *AH*, CXI (June 23, 1922), 162.

42. *American Israelite*, November 9, 1922, p. 4.

43. *NYT*, January 15, 1923, p. 17; *AH*, CXII (January 26, 1923), 391.

44. *AH*, CXI (June 23, 1922), 151; *JT*, June 23, 1922, p. 4.

45. Marshall to A. C. Ratshesky, Pres., U. S. Trust Co., Boston, June 17, 1922, MP-AJA.

46. Marshall to Abraham Cahan, January 8, 1923, MP-AJA; *Forward*, December 9, 1922.

47. *NYT*, June 6, 1922, p. 2; *AH*, CXI (June 9, 1922), 114.

48. *Ibid.*, CXI (June 23, 1922), 176; *NYT*, June 23, 1922, p. 1; June 24, 1922, p. 15.

49. *Ibid.*; *JT*, June 30, 1922, p. 9.

50. Marshall to Cyrus Adler, August 23, 1922, MP-AJA.

51. *NYT*, April 10, 1923, p. 1; "Admission to Harvard University," *School and Society*, XVIII (April 21, 1923), 441–44.

52. *Harvard Crimson*, March 26, 1926, pp. 1, 2.

53. Marshall to Judge Frank H. Hiscock, December 6, November 19, 1927, MP-AJA.

54. Marshall to Frederick R. Mann, February 16, 1928, MP-AJA.

55. Marshall to Louis E. Kirstein, February 5, 1927; to Samuel Shinbach, December 16, 1927, MP-AJA.

56. Marshall to Archie Smith, December 4, 1928, MP-AJA.

57. Marshall to Dr. W. H. P. Faunce, February 21, 1928, MP-AJA.

58. Marshall to Rabbi Solomon Gandz, December 3, 1928; to Julius Rosenwald, August 6, 1929, MP-AJA.

59. Marshall to J. D. Weingarten, February 20, 1919, MP-AJA.
60. Marshall to Nomer Gray, October 11, 1923, MP-AJA.
61. Nomer Gray, High School of Commerce, to E. M. Neary, October 5, 1923, MP-AJA. Neary was Marshall's legal secretary.

62. Quoted by Broun, *op cit.,* p. 125.
63. *Ibid.,* p. 145.
64. On the Kings County case, see *NYT*, July 2, 1927; *JT*, June 24, 1927, p. 17; July 1, 1927, p. 34.

65. George Gordon Battle, "Jew and Non-Jew in the Legal Profession," *AH* (September 22, 1922), p. 449.

66. Marshall to William D. Guthrie, April 9, 1926, MP-AJA.

67. McWilliams, *op cit.,* p. 37; Samuel Tenenbaum. "The Problem of the Jew as Teacher," *JT,* October 14, 1927, p. 1.

68. John Slawson to Marshall, June 10, 1924, MP-AJA.
69. Marshall to W. Morgan Shuster, January 23, 1928, MP-AJA.
70. Marshall to William Fox, December 2, 23, 1927, MP-AJA.
71. On the negotiations, see Marshall to Rev. George Reed Andrews, January 4, 1928; to Rev. Dr. H. Pereira Mendes, October 13, 1928, MP-AJA; AJC, *Executive Committee Minutes,* February 12, 1928; *B'nai B'rith Magazine,* XLII (January, 1928), 84, *NYT,* December 28, 1927, p. 27; January 6, 1928, p. 16.

72. Marshall to Alfred M. Cohen, President, I. O. B'nai B'rith, January 28, 1928, MP-AJA.

73. Marshall to Morris Gest, April 2, April 18, May 1, 1929; to David Belasco, April 5, 1929, MP-AJA.

74. See review by Brooks Atkinson, *NYT,* April 30, 1929, p. 32.
75. Marshall to Rev. Dr. John Haynes Holmes, May 13, 1929, MP-AJA.

76. *Justice* (New York, 1926), p. 8, reprint of radio address by Vida Milholland, Radio Station WHAP, October 20, 1926.

77. For a dramatic account of these events, see Jacob Landau to Marshall, October 1, 1928, MP-AJA.

78. Jacob Shulkin, Pres., Congregation Adath Israel, Massena, N.Y., to Marshall, September 28, 1928, MP-AJA.

79. Marshall to Maj. John A. Warner, Supt. Division of State Police, October 1, 1928, MP-AJA.

80. Marshall to Jacob Billikopf, October 2, 1928, MP-AJA.

81. *NYT,* October 6, 1928, p. 21; October 6, 1928, p. 21; October 7, 1928, p. 31; Marshall to Henry Perlman, October 9, 1928; Rep. Samuel Dickstein to Marshall, October 3, 1928, MP-AJA.

82. Marshall to Jacob Shulkin, October 6, 1928, MP-AJA.

83. Marshall to Felix Warburg, October 26, 1926, MP-AJA.

84. Marshall to Charles I. Cooper, April 1, 1925, MP-AJA.

85. Marshall to Lotta Levensohn, October 28, 1916; to Assemblyman Samuel Dickstein, January 24, 1920; to C. S. Longacre, Sec. Religious Liberty League, December 4, 1928; to Morris D. Waldman, April 2, 1929—MP-AJA.

86. Marshall to H. Friedberg, March 16, 1911, MP-AJA; *DI*, March 19, 1921, pp. 8–9.

87. Marshall to Judge James C. Hume, September 4, 1922, MP-AJA.

EPILOG

1. Marshall to David Adler, December 16, 1924, MP-AJA.

2. Marshall to Jacob Landau, March 10, 1927, MP-AJA.

3. *NYT*, January 24, 1923, p. 6.

4. John Slawson to Marshall, June 10, 1924; Marshall to Slawson, June 26, 1924, MP-AJA. See also Ben Selekman, "Research and Leadership," *Menorah Journal* (April-May, 1926), pp. 117–26.

5. Marshall to Messrs. Blumenthal Brothers, May 16, 1928, MP-AJA.

6. *NYT*, December 27, 1920, p. 8.

7. Marshall to Walter J. Lippman, ed., *New York World*, May 5, 1926; to Saul Schackne, July 2, 1929, MP-AJA.

8. Marshall to Sieg Natenberg, November 9, 1925, MP-AJA. See also Marshall to Morris M. Wolff, December 30, 1927, MP-AJA. For evidence of Marshall's concern over the possible dangers of the Leopold-Loeb case, see Marshall to Jacob M. Loeb, June 24, September 12, 1924, MP-AJA.

9. *NYT*, January 24, 1923, p. 6.

10. For a description of the origins of the goodwill movement, see Claris Edwin Silcox and Galen M. Fisher, *Catholics, Jews, and Protestants* (New York, 1934), pp. 312–37.

11. Marshall to Rev. Dr. H. G. Enelow, June 20, 1929, MP-AJA.

12. Edwin Kaufman to Marshall, April 26, 1925, MP-AJA.

13. Nathan Glazer, "What Sociology Knows about American Jews," *Commentary*, IX (March, 1950), 279. Glazer's conclusion is based on studies of intermarriage.

bibliography

Manuscript and Archival Sources

The basic source for this book was the collection of Louis Marshall's correspondence and miscellaneous papers at the American Jewish Archives, Cincinnati, Ohio. This collection consists of approximately 75 letterbooks, containing Marshall's outgoing correspondence, and over 100 boxes of incoming correspondence, copies of addresses and essays, newspaper and magazine clippings, and miscellaneous reports and documents submitted to Marshall. There are also copies of letters written by associates of Marshall, such as Cyrus Adler. The collection is uncatalogued but is arranged in rough chronological order. It was searched especially diligently for 1914–1929.

A helpful selection from Marshall's correspondence and essays has been edited by Charles Reznikoff: *Louis Marshall: Champion of Liberty* (2 vols.; Philadelphia, 1957); it includes a small fraction of the total correspondence, together with a biographical introduction by Oscar Handlin. Photostatic copies of the letters printed in these volumes are available in the Library of the AJC, New York, while the originals are in the American Jewish Archives, Cincinnati.

The minute books of the American Jewish Committee's Executive Committee, located in the AJC's archives in New York, were consulted for 1912–1929.

An interview on March 14, 1962 with James Marshall, Louis Marshall's son, supplied valuable background information.

Reports and Public Documents

The *Annual Reports* of the AJC for 1908–1929 provided information on the organization and the problem of anti-Semitism. They are available separately at the Committee's archives, and can be found also in the corresponding years of the *American Jewish Year Book*. The volumes of the *AJYB*, consulted for 1900–1962, contain useful statistics and important essays.

New York State. *Report of the Commission on Immigration of the State of New York*. Albany, 1909.

New York State Constitutional Convention, 1915. *Record*. Albany, 1916.

U. S. House of Representatives, Committee on Foreign Affairs. *Hearings on Termination of the Treaty of 1832 between the United States and Russia, December 11, 1911*. 62nd Cong., 2nd Sess., 1911.

U. S. House of Representatives, Committee on Rules. *Hearings on the Ku Klux Klan*. 67th Cong., 1st Sess., 1921.

U. S. Immigration Commission. *Reports*, vols. I–II. Washington, 1910.

U. S. Senate, Foreign Relations Committee. *Hearings on Treaty of 1832 with Russia, December 13, 1911*. 62nd Cong., 2nd Sess., 1911.

U. S. Senate, Judiciary Committee. *Hearings on Bolshevik Propaganda, February 11–March 10, 1919*. 65th Cong., 3rd Sess., 1919.

U. S. Senate, Committee on Immigration. *Hearings on Emergency Immigration Legislation*. 66th Cong., 3rd Sess., 1921.

U. S. Senate, Committee on Immigration. *Hearings on Selective Immigration Legislation*. 68th Cong., 1st Sess., 1924.

U. S. *Statutes at Large*. Vol. XXXIX, Part 1, 1917.

Books and Pamphlets

Adams, Samuel Hopkins. *Incredible Era*. Cambridge, 1939.

Adler, Cyrus. *I have Considered the Days*. Philadelphia, 1941.

————. *Jacob H. Schiff: His Life and Letters*. 2 vols. Garden City, N.Y., 1928.

————. *Louis Marshall: A Biographical Sketch.* New York, 1931.

Adler, Cyrus and Aaron Margalith. *With Firmness in the Right: American Diplomatic Action Affecting Jews, 1840–1945.* New York, 1946.

Adler, Felix. *The Revival of Anti-Semitism.* New York, 1921.

Allen, Frederick Lewis. *Only Yesterday.* New York, 1957.

American Jewish Committee. *The "Protocols," Bolshevism, and the Jews: an Address to their Fellow-Citizens by American Jewish Organizations.* New York, 1921.

Anthony, Alfred Williams. *The Jewish Problem: an Essay in Understanding and Goodwill.* New York, 1924.

Bailey, Thomas A. *America Faces Russia.* Ithaca, 1950.

Baltzell, E. Digby. *The Protestant Establishment: Aristocracy and Caste in America.* New York, 1964.

Belloc, Hilaire. *The Jews.* London, 1922.

Bennett, Harry. *We Never Called Him Henry.* New York, 1951.

Benson, Allan L. *The New Henry Ford.* New York, 1923.

Bentwich, Norman. *For Zion's Sake: a Biography of Judah L. Magnes.* Philadelphia, 1954.

Bernard, William S. (ed.). *American Immigration Policy: a Reappraisal.* New York, 1950.

Bernheimer, Charles S. (ed.). *The Russian Jew in the United States.* Philadelphia, 1905.

Bernstein, Herman. *The History of a Lie.* New York, 1921.

————. *The Truth about "The Protocols of Zion."* New York, 1935.

Bill, Annie C. *The Jew and Henry Ford.* Washington, n.d.

Bloch, Josef Samuel. *Israel und die Völker nach jüdischer Lehre.* Berlin, 1922.

Brasol, Boris. *The World at the Cross Roads.* Boston, 1921.

Broun, Heywood and George Britt. *Christians Only.* New York, 1931.

Burlingame, Roger. *Henry Ford.* New York, 1954.

Caldwell, Cy. *Henry Ford.* London, 1955.

The Cause of World Unrest. London; New York, 1920.

Chalmers, David M. *Hooded Americanism.* Garden City, N.Y., 1965.

Coben, Stanley. *A. Mitchell Palmer: Politician.* New York, 1963.

Coit, Margaret L. *Mr. Baruch.* Boston, 1957.

Connolly, C. P. *The Truth about the Frank Case.* New York, 1915.

Cowen, Philip. *Memories of an American Jew.* New York, 1932.

Curtiss, John S. *An Appraisal of the Protocols of Zion.* New York, 1942.

Davis, Maurice R. *World Immigration.* New York, 1936.

Davis, Moshe. "The Human Record: Cyrus Adler at the Peace Conference, 1919," *Essays in American Jewish History.* Cincinnati, 1958, pp. 457–91.

Dawidowicz, Lucy S. "Louis Marshall and the *Jewish Daily Forward:* An Episode in Wartime Censorship," *For Max Weinreich on his Seventieth Birthday.* The Hague, 1964, pp. 31–43.

Divine, Robert A. *American Immigration Policy, 1924–1952.* New Haven, 1957.

Dubnow, S. M. *History of the Jews in Russia and Poland.* 3 vols. Philadelphia, 1916–1918.

Epstein, Benjamin R. and Arnold Forster. *Some of My Best Friends.* New York, 1962.

Fairchild, Henry Pratt. *Immigration,* revised ed. New York, 1933.

———. *The Melting Pot Mistake.* Boston, 1926.

Fineberg, Solomon Andhil. *Overcoming Anti-Semitism.* New York, 1943.

Ford, Henry. *Der internazionale Jude.* Leipzig, 1933.

———. *My Life and Work.* Garden City, N.Y., 1923.

Fry, Henry P. *The Modern Ku Klux Klan.* Boston, 1922.

Fuchs, Lawrence H. *The Political Behavior of American Jews.* Glencoe, Ill., 1956

Garis, Roy L. *Immigration Restriction.* New York, 1927.

Gartner, Lloyd P. *The Jewish Immigrant in England, 1870–1914.* Detroit, 1960.

Glazer, Nathan. *American Judaism.* Chicago, 1957.

Göransson, Göran, *Henry Ford om Judarna.* Stockholm, 1954.

Grant, Madison. *The Passing of the Great Race*. New York, 1916.

Gross, Louis D. *Fallacies of Henry Ford*. Brooklyn, n.d.

Halperin, Samuel. *The Political World of American Zionism*. Detroit, 1961.

Handlin, Oscar and Mary F. *Adventure in Freedom*. New York, 1954.

——. *The American People in the Twentieth Century*. Cambridge, 1954.

——. *Danger in Discord*. New York, 1948.

——. *Immigration as a Factor in American History*. Englewood Cliffs, N.J., 1959.

——. *Race and Nationality in American Life*. New York, 1957.

——. *The Uprooted*. Boston, 1951.

Hard, William D. *The Great Jewish Conspiracy*. New York, 1920.

Hartmann, Edward George. *The Movement to Americanize the Immigrant*. New York, 1948.

Hendrick, Burton J. *The Jews in America*. New York, 1923.

Herberg, Will. *Protestant-Catholic-Jew*. Garden City, N.Y., 1955.

Higham, John. *Anti-Semitism in the Gilded Age*. New York, 1957. (Reprinted from *Mississippi Valley Historical Review*, March, 1957.)

——. *Social Discrimination Against Jews in America, 1830–1930*. New York, 1957. (Reprinted from *Publications of the American Jewish Historical Society*, September, 1957.)

——. *Strangers in the Land*. New Brunswick, N.J., 1955.

Hofstadter, Richard. *The Age of Reform*. New York, 1956.

Hourwich, Isaac A. *Immigration and Labor*. New York, 1912.

Howland, Charles P. (ed.). *Survey of American Foreign Relations*. New York, 1929.

The International Jew I: The Jew in Character and Business. Atlanta, 1941.

Janowsky, Oscar I. *The Jews and Minority Rights (1898–1919)*. New York, 1933.

—— (ed.). *The American Jew: a Reappraisal*. Philadelphia, 1964.

Jewish Communal Register of New York City, 1917–1918. New York, 1918.

The Jewish Peril. London, 1920.

The Jewish Peril: Protocols of the Learned Elders of Zion, 2nd ed. London, 1920.

Jones, Maldwyn A. *American Immigration.* Chicago, 1960.

Jordan, David Starr. *Unseen Empire.* Boston, 1912.

Joseph, Samuel. *Jewish Immigration to the United States from 1881 to 1910.* New York, 1914.

Justice. New York, 1926.

Kallen, Horace. *Culture and Democracy in the United States.* New York, 1924.

Lasker, Bruno (ed.). *Jewish Experiences in America.* New York, 1930.

Learsi, Rufus. *The Jews in America.* Cleveland, 1954.

Lenski, Gerhard. *The Religious Factor.* Garden City, N.Y., 1961.

Leonard, Jonathan Norton. *The Tragedy of Henry Ford.* New York, 1932.

Lestchinsky, Jacob. "Economic and Social Development of American Jewry," *The Jewish People: Past and Present.* New York, 1955, IV, 56–96.

———. "Jewish Migrations, 1840–1956," *The Jews: Their History, Culture, and Religion,* ed. Louis Finkelstein, 3rd ed. New York, 1960, II, 1536–96.

Leuchtenburg, William E. *The Perils of Prosperity, 1914–32.* Chicago. 1958.

Levinger, Lee J. *The Causes of Anti-Semitism in the United States.* Philadelphia, 1925.

Lewisohn, Ludwig. *Upstream.* New York, 1926.

Linfield, Harry S. *The Jews in the United States, 1927.* New York, 1929.

Loucks, Emerson H. *The Ku Klux Klan in Pennsylvania.* New York, 1936.

McCall, Samuel Walker. *The Patriotism of the American Jew.* New York, 1922.

McWilliams, Carey. *A Mask for Privilege: Anti-Semitism in America.* Boston, 1949.

Marcus, Jacob R. "Defenses Against Antisemitism," *Essays on Antisemitism,* ed. Koppel S. Pinson, revised ed. New York, 1946, pp. 49–58.

Mecklin, John M. *The Ku Klux Klan: A Study of the American Mind.* New York, 1924.

Merz, Charles. *And Then Came Ford.* New York, 1929.

Murray, Robert K. *Red Scare: A Study in National Hysteria, 1919–20.* Minneapolis, 1955.

Myers, Gustavus. *History of Bigotry in the United States.* New York, 1943.

Nevins, Allan and Frank Ernest Hill. *Ford: Expansion and Challenge, 1915–1933.* New York, 1957.

Newman, Louis I. *A Jewish University in America?* New York, 1923.

Nugent, Walter T. K. *The Tolerant Populists: Kansas Populism and Nativism.* Chicago, 1963.

Oppenheim, S. D. *The Jewish Population of the United States.* Philadelphia, 1918.

Perkins, Dexter. *Charles Evans Hughes and American Democratic Statesmanship.* Boston, 1956.

Plaut, W. Gunther. *The Jews in Minnesota.* New York, 1959.

The Protocols and World Revolution. Boston, 1920.

The Protocols of the Wise Men of Zion. New York, 1920.

Pusey, Merlo J. *Charles Evans Hughes.* 2 vols. New York, 1951.

Rice, Arnold S. *The Ku Klux Klan in American Politics.* Washington, 1962.

Richards, Bernard G. *Organizing American Jewry.* New York, n.d.

Richards, William C. *The Last Billionaire: Henry Ford.* New York, 1948.

Rider, Fremont. *Melvin Dewey.* Chicago, 1944.

Ridge, Martin. *Ignatius Donnelly: the Portrait of a Politician.* Chicago, 1962.

Rischin, Moses. *The Promised City: New York's Jews, 1870–1914*. Cambridge, 1962.

Roberts, Kenneth L. *Why Europe Leaves Home*. Indianapolis, 1922.

Ross, Edward A. *The Old World in the New*. New York, 1914.

Sachar, Abram L. *Sufferance is the Badge: The Jew in the Contemporary World*. New York, 1939.

Sachar, Howard M. *The Course of Modern Jewish History*. Cleveland, 1958.

Saloutos, Theodore and John D. Hicks. *Agricultural Discontent in the Middle West, 1900–1939*. Madison, 1951.

Sartre, Jean-Paul. *Anti-Semite and Jew*. New York, 1948.

Samuel, Maurice. *You Gentiles*. New York, 1924.

Samuels, Charles and Louise. *Night Fell on Georgia*. New York, 1956.

Schachner, Nathan. *The Price of Liberty*. New York, 1948.

Schriftgiesser, Karl. *This Was Normalcy*. Boston, 1948.

Sherman, C. Bezalel. *The Jew Within American Society*. Detroit, 1961.

Silcox, Claris Edwin and Galen M. Fisher. *Catholics, Jews, and Protestants*. New York, 1934.

Simonds, William Adams. *Henry Ford: His Life, His Work*. Indianapolis, 1943.

Sklare, Marshall. *Conservative Judaism: An American Religious Movement*. Glencoe, Ill., 1955.

Sklare, Marshall (ed.). *The Jews: Social Patterns of an American Group*. Glencoe, Ill., 1958.

Smith, William Carlson. *Americans in the Making: The Natural History of the Assimilation of Immigrants*. New York, 1939.

Solomon, Barbara Miller. *Ancestors and Immigrants*. Cambridge, 1956.

Spargo, John. *The Jew and American Ideals*. New York, 1921.

Stephenson, George. *A History of American Immigration, 1820–1924*. Boston, 1926.

Stoddard, Lothrop. *The Revolt Against Civilization*. New York, 1923.

———. *The Rising Tide of Color*. New York, 1923.

Strong, Donald S. *Organized Anti-Semitism in America: The Rise of Group Prejudice during the Decade 1930–40.* Washington, 1941.

Sward, Keith. *The Legend of Henry Ford.* New York, 1948.

Taft, William Howard. *Anti-Semitism in the United States.* Chicago, 1921.

Tannenbaum, Frank. *Darker Phases of the South.* New York, 1924.

The Truth about "The Protocols": a Literary Forgery; from the Times of August 16, 17 and 18, 1921. London, 1921.

United Jewish Appeal. *The Rebuilding of Palestine.* New York, 1927.

Warne, Frank J. *The Immigrant Invasion.* New York, 1913.

Weinstein, Jacob J. "Anti-Semitism," *The American Jew,* ed. Oscar I. Janowsky. New York, 1942, pp. 183–204.

Weizmann, Chaim. *Trial and Error.* New York, 1949.

White, William Allen. *A Puritan in Babylon.* New York, 1938.

Wiernik, Peter. *History of the Jews in America.* New York, 1912.

Windle, C. A. *The Tyranny of Intolerance.* Chicago, 1921.

Wirth, Louis. *The Ghetto.* Chicago, 1928.

Wischnitzer, Mark. *To Dwell in Safety: The Story of Jewish Migrations since 1800.* Philadelphia, 1948.

Wise, James Waterman. *Jews Are Like That!* New York, 1928.

Wise, Stephen S. *Challenging Years.* New York, 1949.

Wittke, Carl. *We Who Built America.* New York, 1939.

Wolf, Lucien. *The Myth of the Jewish Menace in World Affairs.* . . . New York, 1921.

Wolf, Simon. *The Presidents I Have Known from 1860 to 1918,* 2nd ed. Washington, 1918.

Woodward, C. Vann. *Tom Watson, Agrarian Rebel.* New York, 1938.

Yeomans, Henry Aaron. *Abbot Lawrence Lowell.* Cambridge, 1948.

Articles and Periodicals

Major periodicals, and the years consulted, were: *American Hebrew,* 1911, 1919–1928; *American Israelite,* 1913, 1922–1925; *Dearborn Independent,* 1919–1927; *Forward,* 1920–1922; *Jewish Daily Bulletin,* 1925; *Jewish Tribune,* 1922–1928; *New York Times,* 1905–1929; *Pipp's Weekly* 1921–1922; *Der Tog,* 1924–1926.

Abelson, Paul. "The Education of the Immigrant by the Educational Alliance," *Journal of Social Science,* XLIV (1906), 163–72.

"Admission to Harvard University," *School and Society,* XVII (April 21, 1923), 441–44.

"Amends to the Jews—What Then?" *Outlook,* CXLIV (July 20, 1927), 368–69.

"Another Jewish Menace," *The Freeman,* VII (July 18, 1923), 436–37.

"Anti-Semitism and the Frank Case," *Literary Digest,* L (January 16, 1915), 85–86.

Bent, Silas. "Three City-Bred Jews That the Farmers Trust," *Outlook,* CXXXIV (August 8, 1923), 553–56.

Bernheimer, Charles S. "Prejudice Against the Jews in the United States," *Independent,* LXV (1908), 1105–8.

Berthoff, Rowland T. "Southern Attitudes Toward Immigration, 1865–1914," *Journal of Southern History,* XVII (August, 1951), 328–60.

Billings, John S. "Vital Statistics of the Jews in the United States," *Census Bulletin* (December 30, 1890), pp. 3–23.

Bingham, Theodore A. "Foreign Criminals in New York," *North American Review,* CLXXXVIII (September, 1908), 383–94.

Boas, Ralph P. "Jew-Baiting in America," *Atlantic Monthly,* CXXVII (May, 1921), 658–65.

———. "Who Shall Go to College?" *ibid.,* CXXX (October, 1922), 441–48.

Bourne, Randolph S. "The Jew and Transnational America," *Menorah Journal,* II (December, 1916), 277–84.

Bouton, S. Miles. "The Persecution of Jews in Europe: the Problem of Anti-Semitism, IV," *The Forum,* LXXV (June, 1926), 820–28.

Browdy, Louis. "Morris Gest and the Passion Play," *Nation,* CXXVIII (June 12, 1929), 698–99.

Brown, Lewis P. "The Jew Is Not a Slacker," *North American Review,* CCVII (June, 1918), 857–62.

Brown, Philip Marshall. "Zionism and Anti-Semitism," *North American Review,* CCX (November, 1919), 656–62.

"The Case of David Halfant," *Jewish Social Service Quarterly,* IV (June, 1928), 349.

"A Census of Jewish University Students," *Menorah Journal,* II (October, 1916), 260–62.

Cohen, Naomi W. "The Abrogation of the Russo-American Treaty of 1832," *Jewish Social Studies,* XXV (January, 1963), 3–41.

———. "The Reaction of Reform Judaism in America to Political Zionism, 1897–1922," *Publications of the American Jewish Historical Society,* XL (June, 1951), 361–94.

Dawidowicz, Lucy S. "Louis Marshall's Yiddish Newspaper: *The Jewish World:* a Study in Contrasts," *Jewish Social Studies,* XXV (April, 1963), 102–32.

Dushkin, Alexander M. "The Jewish Population of New York," *Jewish Communal Register of New York City, 1917–1918.* New York, 1918, pp. 75–89.

"Elders of Zion, Protocols of," *Universal Jewish Encyclopedia,* IV (New York, 1941), 46–60.

Engleman, Uriah Zvi. "Jewish Statistics in the U.S. Census of Religious Bodies (1850–1936)," *Jewish Social Studies,* IX (April, 1947), 127–74.

Fink, Reuben. "Visas, Immigration, and Official Anti-Semitism," *Nation,* CXII (June 22, 1921), 870–72.

Ford Henry. "If I were President," *Collier's* LXXII (August 4, 1923), 5–6.

Fox, Samuel F. Darwin. "Judaism and Anti-Semitism: The Problem of Anti-Semitism, II–III," *The Forum,* LXXV (April, 1926), 503–9; (May, 1926), 684–90.

Friedman, Elisha M. "The Challenge of Anti-Semitism," *Menorah Journal,* VII (February, 1922), 15–22.

Gannett, Lewis S. "Is America Anti-Semitic?" *Nation,* CXVI (March 21, 1923), 330–32.

Gibbons, Herbert Adams. "The Jewish Problem," *Century Magazine,* CII (September, 1921), 785–92.

———. "Zionism and World Peace," *ibid.,* XCVII (January, 1919), 368–78.

Gildersleeve, Virginia C. "Class and Creed at Barnard," *Nation,* CXV (December 6, 1922), 607.

Glanz, Rudolf. "The Immigration of German Jews up to 1880," *YIVO Annual of Jewish Social Science,* II–III (1948), 81–99.

Glazer, Nathan. "What Sociology Knows about American Jews," *Commentary,* IX (March, 1950), 275–84.

Gorenstein, Arthur. "The Commissioner and the Community: The Beginnings of the New York City 'Kehillah' (1908–1909)," *YIVO Annual of Jewish Social Science,* XIII (1965), 187–212.

Grecht, Rebecca. "Anti-Semitism at Barnard," *Nation,* CXV (October 4, 1922), 327.

Hall, G. Stanley. "A Suggestion for a Jewish University," *Menorah Journal,* III (April, 1917), 98–101.

Ham, William T. "Harvard Student Opinion on the Jewish Question," *Nation,* CXV (September 6, 1922), 225–27.

Handlin, Oscar and Mary F. "American Views of the Jew at the Opening of the 20th Century," *Publications of the American Jewish Historical Society,* XL (June, 1951), 323–44.

———. "Historical Perspectives on the American Ethnic Group," *Daedalus,* (Spring, 1961), pp. 220–32.

Hapgood, Norman. "How Should Jews be Treated?" *Harper's Weekly,* LXXII (January 29, 1916), 104–6.

———. "The Inside Story of Henry Ford's Jew Mania," *Hearst's International,* XLI (June, 1922), 14–18; XLII (August, 1922), 44–48; (September, 1922), 45–48; (October, 1922), 36–39; (November, 1922), 70–73.

———. "Jews and College Life," *Harper's Weekly,* LXXII (January 15, 1916), 53–55.

———. "Schools, Colleges, and Jews," *ibid.* (January 22, 1916), 77–79.

Hendrick, Burton J. "The Jewish Invasion of America," *McClure's* XL (March, 1913), 125–65.

————. "The Jews in America," *World's Work,* XLV (1922–23), 144–61, 166–86, 366–77, 591–601.

"Henry Ford's Apology to the Jews," *Outlook,* CXLVI (July 20, 1927), 372–74.

"Is There a World-Wide Jewish Peril?" *Current Opinion,* LXIX (December, 1920), 840–43.

"The Jew and the Club," *Atlantic Monthly,* CXXXIV (October, 1924), 450–56.

"The Jewish Bloc in Mr. Ford's Presidential Path," *Literary Digest,* LXXVIII (August 25, 1923), 48–52.

"The Jews and the Colleges," *World's Work,* XLIV (1922), 351.

Kallen, Horace. "Democracy versus the Melting Pot," *Nation,* C (1915), 219–20.

————. "The Roots of Anti-Semitism," *ibid.,* CXVI (February 28, 1923), 240–42.

Kennedy, Hugh A. Studdert. "Am I a Jew?" *The Forum,* LXXVI (December, 1926), 912–16.

Kessler, Lawton *et al.* "American Jews and the Paris Peace Conference," *YIVO Annual of Jewish Social Science,* II–III (1948), 222–42.

Korff, S. A. "The Great Jewish Conspiracy," *Outlook,* CXXVII (February 2, 1921), 180–82.

Kuh, E. J. "The Social Disability of the Jew," *Atlantic Monthly,* CI (April, 1908), 433–39.

Larsen, Grace H. and Henry E. Erdman. "Aaron Sapiro: Genius of Farm Co-operative Promotion," *Mississippi Valley Historical Review,* XLIX (September, 1962), 242–68.

Lasker, Bruno, "Jewish Handicaps in the Employment Market," *Jewish Social Service Quarterly,* II (March, 1926), 170–85.

Levine, Isaac Don. "Russian Jews Against Bolshevik Rule," *B'nai B'rith News,* XII (March, 1920), 1–2.

Lewisohn, Ludwig. "The Jew Meditates," *Nation,* CXVIII (February 20, 1924), 200–201.

Lindeman, E. C. "Sapiro the Spectacular," *New Republic,* L (April 13, 1927), 216–18.

Littell, Robert. "Henry Ford and His Secret," *The Outlook* (London), LII (December 1, 1922), 407–8.

Mann, Arthur. "Gompers and the Irony of Racism," *Antioch Review,* XIII (June, 1953), 203–14.

Marshall, James, "Louis Marshall: A Man in Shirt Sleeves," *American Judaism,* VI (Rosh Ha-Shono, 1956), 12–13.

Marshall, Louis. "The American Jew of Today," *Harper's Weekly,* XLIX (December 2, 1905), 1742.

———. "Back to the Synagogue," *Union Bulletin,* XIII (March, 1923), 3–5.

———. "Is Ours a Christian Government?" *The Menorah,* XX (January, 1896), 1–19.

———. "The Jews and Immigration," *Harper's Weekly,* LXXIII (May 1916), 519.

———. "The Way Out," *Survey,* XXIII (January 1, 1910), 472–75.

"May Jews Go to College?" *Nation,* CXIV (June 14, 1922), 708.

Miller, Robert Moats. "A Note on the Relationship between the Protestant Churches and the Revived Ku Klux Klan," *Journal of Southern History,* XXII (August, 1956), 355–68.

"Mr. Ford and the Jews," *Independent,* CXVII (December 25, 1926), 723–24.

Moore, Samuel Taylor. "Consequences of the Klan," *Independent,* CXIII (December 20, 1924), 534–36.

Morgenstern, Julian. "Self-Protection or Self-Assertion," *B'nai B'rith News,* V (May, 1913), 4.

Murphy, Paul L. "Sources and Nature of Intolerance in the 1920s." *Journal of American History,* LI (June, 1964), 60–76.

"A Picture of Trotzky in Action," *Current Opinion,* LXIX (December, 1920), 844–48.

Pollack, Norman. "The Myth of Populist Anti-Semitism," *American Historical Review,* LXVIII (October, 1962), 76–80.

"Reaction and the Jew," *Nation,* CXI (November 3), 493.

Richards, Bernard G. "The American Jewish Congress," *Jewish Communal Register of New York City, 1917–1918.* New York: 1918, pp. 1385–1400.

————. "The Melvil Dewey Affair," *Congress Weekly*, XXI (April 20, 1954), 12–13.

Rischin, Moses. "The American Jewish Committee and Zionism, 1906–1922," *Herzl Year Book*, V (1963), 65–81.

Russell, Francis. "The Coming of the Jews," *Antioch Review*, XV (March, 1955), 19–38.

Sackler, Harry. "The Kehillah of New York," *Jewish Communal Register of New York City, 1917–1918*. New York, 1918, pp. 47–58.

Sapiro, Aaron. "An Experience with American Justice," *Free Synagogue Pulpit*, VIII (1927–28), 36.

Seitz, Don C. "Jews, Catholics, and Protestants," *Outlook*, CXLI (November 25, 1925), 478–79.

Selekman, Ben. "Research and Leadership," *Menorah Journal* (April–May, 1926), pp. 117–26.

Slosson, Edwin E. "The Anti-Semite Scare," *Independent*, CIV (December 25, 1920), 427–28.

Smertenko, Johan J. "The Passing of the Shtadlan," *Menorah Journal*. VI (June, 1920), 140–55.

Speranza, Gino. "The Immigration Peril," *World's Work*, XLVII (1923–1924), 57–65, 147–60, 256–70, 379–409, 479–90, 643–48; XLVIII (1924), 62–68.

Starr, Harry. "The Affair at Harvard," *Menorah Journal*, VIII (October. 1922), 263–76.

Stoddard, Lothrop. "The Pedigree of Judah: The Problem of Anti-Semitism, I," *The Forum*, LXXV (March, 1926), 321–33.

Szajkowski, Zosa. "The Attitude of American Jews to East European Jewish Immigration (1881–1893)," *Publications of the American Jewish Historical Society*, XL (March, 1951), 221–80.

"Trailing the New Anti-Semitism to its Russian Lair," *Current Opinion*. LXX (April, 1921), 501–04.

" 'Vilifying' a State," *Nation*, CI (August 26, 1915), 251–52.

Vishniak, Mark. "New Studies on the 'Elders of Zion,' " *YIVO Annual of Jewish Social Science*, II–III (1948), 140–45.

Weinberg, Gerhard L. "Hitler's Image of the United States," *American Historical Review*, LXIX (July, 1964), 1006–21.

Weitzenkorn, Louis. "A Jew among the Fords," *Nation*, CXII (May 4, 1921), 652–53.

Welliver, Judson Churchill. "Henry Ford. Dreamer and Worker," *Review of Reviews*, LXIV (November, 1921), 481–95.

"What Was Your Father's Name?" *Nation*, CXV (October 4, 1922), 321.

"Why Was Frank Lynched?" *The Forum*, LVI (December, 1916), 677–92.

"Wilson and Harding Defend Jews," *Independent*, CV (January 29, 1921), 118–19.

Winter, Carl G. "The Influence of the Russo-American Treaty of 1832 on the Rights of American Jewish Citizens," *Publications of the American Jewish Historical Society*, XLI (December, 1951), 165–89.

Wittke, Carl. "Immigration Policy Prior to World War I," *Annals of the American Academy of Political and Social Science*, CCLXII (March, 1949), 5–14.

Yinger, J. Milton. "Social Forces Involved in Group Identification or Withdrawal," *Daedalus* (Spring, 1961), 247–62.

Unpublished Material

Berger, Morris I. "The Settlement, the Immigrant, and the Public School." Unpublished Ph.D. dissertation, Teachers College, Columbia University, 1956.

Berman, Hyman. "The Era of the Protocol: a Chapter in the History of the International Ladies' Garment Workers Union." Unpublished Ph.D. dissertation, Columbia University, 1955.

Cameron, Dwight L. "Some Aspects of Race Prejudice in the United States." Unpublished Master's thesis, Columbia University, 1924.

Cohen, Naomi Wiener. "The Public Career of Oscar S. Straus." Unpublished Ph.D. dissertation, Columbia University, 1955.

Herzog, Joseph D. "The Emergence of the Anti-Jewish Sterotype in the United States." Unpublished ordination thesis, Hebrew Union College, 1953.

Rappoport, Joseph. "Jewish Immigrants and World War I: a Study of American Yiddish Press Reactions." Unpublished Ph.D. dissertation, Columbia University, 1951.

index

The manuscript was edited by Robert H. Tennenhouse. The book was designed by George Franks. The typefaces are Linotype Baskerville originally cut by John Baskerville about 1758 and Cheltenham Bold designed by Bertram Goodhue in 1896 for Mergenthaler Linotype in conjunction with American Typefounders.

The book is printed on S. D. Warren's Olde Style Antique white wove paper and bound in Columbia Mills' Riverside Chambray cloth over boards. Manufactured in the United States of America.

The author, Morton Rosenstock, is librarian and associate professor of Social Studies at Bronx Community College of the City University of New York. He holds a B.A. degree from Harvard University, and M.A., M.S., and Ph.D. degrees from Columbia University.

DATE DUE